Although signed for Strafford, car 164 was actually bound for 69th Street. The Strafford branch's Radnor stop is in the background. *Photo by Andrew Maginnis. Collection of Bob Foley.*

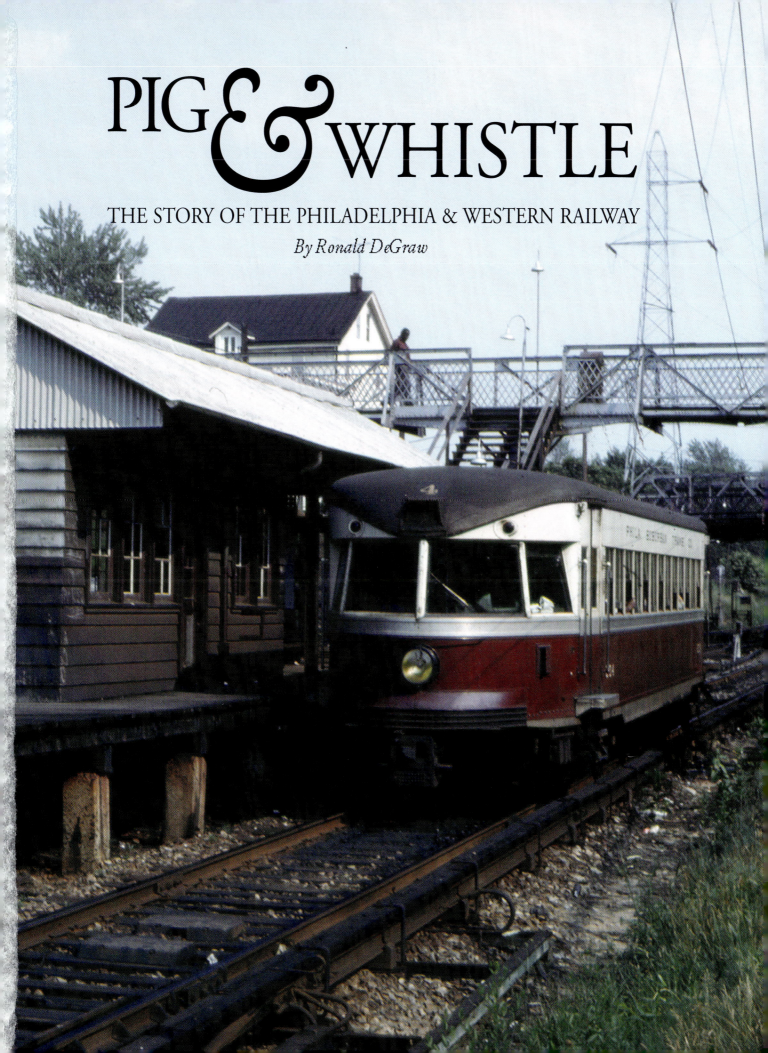

PIG & WHISTLE

THE STORY OF THE PHILADELPHIA & WESTERN RAILWAY

By Ronald DeGraw

THE STORY OF THE PHILADELPHIA & WESTERN RAILWAY
By Ronald DeGraw / Edited by G. Mac Sebree

Bulletin 140 of the Central Electric Railfans' Association

©2007 by the Central Electric Railfans' Association
An Illinois Not-for-Profit Corporation
P.O. Box 503, Chicago, Illinois 60690-0503, U.S.A

CERA DIRECTORS 2006

J. Terrell Colson	Dennis McClendon
Graham Garfield	Bruce G. Moffat
Daniel D. Joseph	Joseph Reuter
Walter R. Keevil	Jeffrey L. Wien

Paul F. Willer

All rights reserved. No part of this book may be commercially reproduced or utilized in any form, except for brief quotations, nor by any means electronic or mechanical, including photocopying and recording, nor by any informationalstorage/retrieval system, without permission in writing from the Central Electric Railfans' Association.

Pig & Whistle was designed by Curt Schultz Design. Procuation was coordinated by Bruce G. Moffat.

CERA Bulletins are technical, educational references prepared as historic projects by members of the Central Electric Railfans' Association, working without salary due to their interest in the subject. This bulletin is consistent with the stated purpose of the corporation: To foster the study of the history, equipment and operation of electric railways.

ISBN: 978-0-915348-40-4

Library of Congress
Control Number: 2007927737

Preceding page: Bullet #204 at Bryn Mawr. *Photo by Richard Lukin.*

Contents

Dedication 5

Acknowledgments 6

Preface 7

Chapter 1   **Visions of Grandeur (1902-1907)** 11
- Map: Gould's Eastward Expansion 13
- Map: P&W's Proposed Service to Parksburg . . 17
- The "Dinkies" 22
- The Phantom Cars 25

Chapter 2   **Settling In (1907-1910)** 29
- Map: Philadelphia & Western Railway–1909 . 40
- Service Patterns (1907-1910) 41
- Beechwood Powerhouse 42

Chapter 3   **Beechwood Park** 45
- Map: Beechwood Park–1907 47

Chapter 4   **Building for Survival (1911-1912)** 51
- Map: Strafford Terminal–1911 58
- Map: Philadelphia & Western Railway–1912 . . 65
- Map: Liberty Bell Route & Connecting Lines. . 69
- Service Patterns 1911-1912 73
- Stopping a Train 73
- LVT's Electric Empire 74

Chapter 5   **Prosperity and Competition (1913-1929)** 77
- Service Patterns 1913-1929 91
- Mitten's Revenge 92
- Power for the People 93
- The Ithan Tragedy 93

Chapter 6   **The First Buses** 97
- Map: Main Line Transfer's Bryn Mawr Loop . . 98

Chapter 7   **Dr. Conway to the Rescue (1930-1933)** 101
- Map: Norristown–1931 120
- Service Patterns 1930-1933 121
- Tickets, Please! 122
- P&W Leads in Streamlining 123

Chapter 8   **Bankruptcy and War (1934-1942)** **127**
       Map: 69th Street Terminal–1936 132
       Map: Competing Bus & Rail
       Lines (as of 1939) 133
       Service Patterns 1934-1942 140
       How Fast? 141

Chapter 9   **Buses Are Back** **145**
       Map: Main Line Transfer's Wayne Loop 148
       Map: Main Line Transfer
       System Map–1944 153

Chapter 10   **Moving the Freight** **157**
       Map: 72nd Street Yard Trackage &
       Related Facilities–1942 160

Chapter 11   **The Takeover (1943-1953)** **173**
       Service Patterns 1943-1953 187
       Running a Liberty Bell Car 188
       A Passenger's Perspective 191

Appendices   **193**
       Stations and Mileage 193
       The Maximum Schedule 194
       Corporate Organizational Chart 195
       Roster and Car Plans 196

Bibliography **217**
       Recommended Reading 222

"Bullet" car 2 (402) approaching the Garrett Hill station. *Photo by Richard Lukin.*

Dedication

I have literally had a lifetime of interest in the Philadelphia & Western because of my father. G. Harry DeGraw became a P&W motorman on October 1, 1945, right after the war ended. I was two years old at the time. He got his job through William D. Gable, who was my maternal grandfather's brother. Will Gable joined the P&W in 1910, three years after the railroad opened, as a signal maintainer. He rose to superintendent of the electrical department. He installed the railroad's new block signal system in the 1930s and he devised a method of changing the manual passenger semaphores at stations into automatic light signals. He retired involuntarily at age 69 in 1949, shortly after Red Arrow had taken over.

One of Will's brothers, Charles, operated P&W trains from 1908 until 1947. He was involved in a freak accident at Bridgeport siding. Early one morning a bullet car was being moved from overnight storage in the siding. The operator apparently wasn't paying attention and the car crashed into another on the main line at the switch, driven by Gable. The first car rolled partly down the embankment, but there were no injuries.

Two cousins of the Gable family, George and Frank Zimmerman, worked in the maintenance departments for nearly 40 years. Will Gable's son-in-law, Clark Fagan, also worked for the P&W for several years.

So you might say that working for the P&W was a family tradition. Dad enjoyed his work, and his enthusiasm rubbed off on me. When I was very young, my aunt, Alma Gable would often walk me to the nearby Beechwood-Brookline Station, where I was fascinated by tales of the old amusement park and powerhouse and used to play among the concrete ruins at Cobbs Creek.

Dad would stop his train at Brookline and I'd board and ride up front with him, thinking I was a real big shot. The bullet cars originally had a drop seat next the motorman. It was supposed to be used only in the rear of the car for passengers who wished to smoke, but I used the one up front and sat right behind the front windshield as we tore along the P&W at 80 miles an hour. It was much more exhilarating for a kid than today's computer games. By prearrangement, even the Liberty Bell Limited speedsters would come to a complete stop at little Brookline Station just so I could board. Part of the fun was knowing it was against the rules.

As I grew older I'd often take a Red Arrow trolley into 69th Street Terminal after school and meet Dad in the late afternoons. I'd ride with him until he quit for the day, about 6:30 or 7:00 P.M., then I'd go into the ramshackle trainmen's room at the terminal and watch while he spent a busy 20 minutes reconciling his thousands of dollars in cash and tickets onto a daily waybill, which had to be turned in to the dispatcher each night. Clerks checked each waybill overnight against the fare registers in the cars, and a motorman who was off by large amounts too often would be in trouble. A note was hung in the dispatcher's window each morning listing those employees whose fare collections did not agree with what the fare register indicated. The amounts could be as small as two cents. Most of the motormen's names appeared on the list at one time or another. Pennies were often exchanged with the dispatcher to balance the books.

Dad took me to visit a few other rail properties, and he did everything he could to stimulate my interest in electric railways. When we lived in Upper Darby, we weren't far from Red Arrow's Llanerch carbarn. I came to know not only all of the P&W motormen, but most of the shopmen in the P&W and the Red Arrow carbarns. I was able to wander at will through the fascinating shops, parts of which appeared never to have reached the 20th century.

It's surprising how many people a motorman gets to know. Almost invariably when our family would go out to dinner or shopping or the movies, at least one person would come up to Dad to exchange pleasantries. At 6'4", Dad was the tallest of the P&W motormen, and he was called "Big Harry."

After 23 years of service, "Big Harry" retired on a disability pension on December 1, 1968. He died on November 5, 1971, at the age of 59.

Dad was very pleased when I was able to join the Southeastern Pennsylvania Transportation Authority in January 1970, when it took over the Red Arrow and P&W operation. I became Director of Development for the Red Arrow Division of SEPTA, carrying on a family tradition that had begun in 1908 and would run until 1996. Seven members of my family logged more than 200 years of service with the P&W and its successor companies over nine decades.

Pig & Whistle is fondly dedicated to the memory of **G. Harry DeGraw.**

Ronald DeGraw
May 2005

Acknowledgments

It is impossible to compile a history of this magnitude without the generous and enthusiastic assistance of dozens of great friends. The research for this volume has taken four decades, and some of those friends are now deceased.

I shall always be grateful to David E. Crawford, who wrote a college paper on the Philadelphia & Western's history in 1953. I was able to read it while in high school because Dave rode the trains of my father, G. Harry DeGraw, who was a P&W motorman. I had always been interested in the P&W, but it was from Dave's paper that I first learned about its fascinating early history and saw some of the older photographs. A bound volume of Wendell Dillinger's college dissertation from the early 1950s on Red Arrow Lines, which reposed on the bookshelves of Red Arrow's president, provided important information for my first book, *The Red Arrow*, in 1972.

I am especially indebted to Andrew W. Maginnis, whose knowledge of local transportation minutiae seems to be unlimited and whose collection of electric railway data is unsurpassed, as is his willingness to lend material to struggling authors. Andy did the splendid car drawings for this book and assisted with much of the detailed car roster information. He has written several articles on P&W and the Lehigh Valley Transit Company. John F. Calnan produced the excellent computer generated maps for this volume. John P. Dezio was of great assistance in the scanning work required for the creation of the maps.

I am deeply grateful to Russell E. Jackson, J. William Vigrass and the late Harre W. Demoro for finding obscure but very useful documents that have helped make *Pig & Whistle* come more alive. Howard L. E. Price, a motorman on the P&W for more than three decades and a good friend, turned over his lifetime collection of items about the P&W and LVT. This source material has been invaluable.

There are many others I wish to thank who have been helpful in contributing information and photographs to this volume, some of whom have not lived to see it published. They are listed here in alphabetical order:

Richard Allman, Charles E. Bahm, Frederick E. Barber, David W. Biles, Edward H. Blossom, Mervin E. Borgnis, James P. Brazel, Eugene Cipriani, David H. Cope, Lee Cory, Harold E. Cox, O. R. Cummings, Robert Damon, E. Everett Edwards, Robert G. Foley, Aaron G. Fryer, Harry J. Garforth, Jr., Robert M. Goshorn, Edna M. Harris, John Hoschek, Robert Jackson, William C. Janssen, Donald R. Kaplan, James Kelly, David E. Kenney, Alan Martlew, William J. McKelvey, Jr., John H. Newhall, John R. Nieveen, Douglas E. Peters, Larry Plachno, George H. Pointon, Barton Proger, Gerhard Salomon, Bruce G. Saylor, Fred W. Schneider, III, William H. Slavin, John C. Smatlak, Donald D. Smith, John Gibb Smith, Thomas Roy Smith, Warren Speegle, Birdella Wagner and Andrew D. Young. The staff of the Hagley Museum and Library has always been very friendly and helpful, including Christopher Baer, Barbara Hall, Marjorie McNinch and Jon Williams.

I will forever be in debt to Merritt H. Taylor, Jr., Red Arrow's last president, whose trust and support enabled me to write my first history of Red Arrow Lines.

My wife Karin has been extremely helpful with research and proofreading, and extraordinarily tolerant and supportive. Her advice has helped to make this book more readable, and she has almost been turned into a railfan. My brother Richard offered some very useful suggestions to improve the manuscript.

The late Joseph T. Mack, the fourth general manager of the Southeastern Pennsylvania Transportation Authority, fulfilled a lifetime dream by enabling me to be Chief Operating Officer of the transit agency's Suburban Transit Division, which included Red Arrow, the P&W and the old Schuylkill Valley Lines.

The entire collection of the Philadelphia Suburban Transportation Company's records, tens of thousands of documents, has found an excellent home at the Hagley Museum and Library in Greenville, Delaware, where it is carefully indexed and available to serious students of electric railway history. Much of my personal material has joined Hagley's *Red Arrow Lines* collection.

Ronald DeGraw
May 2005

Preface

THE LITTLE P&W, with its odd nickname of Pig & Whistle, is perhaps more like a cat than a pig. It has assuredly gone through at least four of its nine lives already. It's remarkable, in fact, that the Philadelphia & Western Railway still exists.

It was built during the interurban boom in the first decade of this century, when people mistakenly looked upon electric railway stock certificates as gold plated. They soon learned better. The P&W was part of an industry that quickly grew to 17,000 route miles throughout the nation by 1917, and just as quickly settled down to a life of hardship and liquidation.

Most of those 17,000 miles of interurban system fell victim to the Great Depression, and all but two lines were gone by the 1960s. One of the survivors is the Chicago, South Shore & South Bend Railroad, a 90-mile route running from Chicago eastward. Some of its old interurban character remains, but it has really evolved into a railroad commuter line. The Philadelphia & Western's little 13.5-mile Norristown line is certainly no interurban any more, either, but it remains a viable electric commuter line that now carries more reverse-direction passengers in peak periods than it does traditional prevailing-direction passengers.

With an expenditure of $200 million over the last 20 years to modernize the P&W, its future is now guaranteed. But it was not always assured.

If Thomas Newhall had not had the foresight to build the 1912 extension to Norristown, the P&W would have probably struggled along unprofitably until it was hit by auto and bus competition in the 1920s. Then it would have collapsed. Its second reprieve came when the brilliant Thomas Conway entered the picture in 1930, carrying the line through bankruptcy and rebuilding to successfully battle the Great Depression and automobile competition. Its third life nearly ended in the late 1960s. Red Arrow was toying with "railbuses" and even placed an order for enough of them to replace the Media and Sharon Hill trolleys. One was tested on the P&W, and consideration was being given to converting the P&W into a high-speed bus route. The entry of the Southeastern Pennsylvania Transportation Authority into the picture in 1970 put an end to further such speculation.

Its fourth life was nearly used up in the mid-1980s. Several serious collisions had put a large part of the fleet out of service, and ridership was decreasing rapidly. At one point the rail line was closed entirely for a brief period and buses were substituted. This virtually destroyed the ridership. Serious thought was being given at SEPTA to abandoning the P&W as a rail line. Finally some temporary cars were obtained, a fleet of new cars was ordered and major capital programs were launched to revitalize the line.

It's now here to stay.

For such a small (some might even say insignificant) line, the P&W has a fascinating history. Its beginnings were far from humble. The men who originally created it dreamed of a coast-to-coast railroad, with the P&W as the eastern link into Philadelphia and New York City. This idea failed, but still the little P&W chugged along. Three decades after its conception it was operating the most revolutionary railway cars ever built, some of which ran for 59 years and more than five million miles.

A common practice in days gone by was to award railroads—particularly short lines—with nonsensical nicknames based on their initials. No one knows how or why this practice originated, but it caught on and many of the names stuck for the life of the railroad.

The Leavenworth, Kansas & Western became "Leave Kansas & Walk". The Missouri & Northern Arkansas was "May Never Arrive". The Fort Smith & Western became the "Footsore & Weary", and the Carolina & Northwestern was stuck with the moniker "Can't & Never Will". The Nevada, California & Oregon was "Narrow, Crooked & Ornery". The big Delaware, Lackawanna & Western was "Delay, Linger & Wait". After it merged with the Erie Railroad and faced severe financial problems, it became the "Erie-Lackamoney". The terms made no sense, but hundreds of railroads were stuck with these nicknames.

After it filed for bankruptcy in 1934, the Philadelphia & Western became the "Poor & Weary," which was perhaps somewhat appropriate.

In 1932, the trade publication *Transit Journal* included this dramatic drawing of the high-speed cars that would become synonymous with the P&W. *Collection of Ronald DeGraw.*

Car 35 was built by St. Louis Car Company in 1907 and served the P&W until the arrival of the high speed "bullet" cars in 1931. *Collection of Ronald DeGraw.*

There's no record of how the P&W got the whimsical name that stuck with it for the rest of its life: "Pig & Whistle". It's been called that since the 1930s, and longtime riders still recall the name. Mention Philadelphia & Western to an older Main Line resident and he'll usually respond: "Oh, you mean the old Pig & Whistle."

And so the "Pig & Whistle" it remains today, even half a century after the corporate name of Philadelphia & Western ceased to exist.

Join the venerable Pig & Whistle and marvel at its story.

"Strafford" car 166 pauses at Villanova station in June, 1953. *Photo by Andrew Maginnis. Collection of Bob Foley.*

Bullet cars represented the last word in aerodynamic design. *Collection of Ronald DeGraw.*

CHAPTER ONE
Visions of Grandeur
1902-1907

AFTER YEARS of frustration it was at last time for the first train to depart on the Philadelphia & Western Railway, and things were not going well. Company officials were on the platform at 69th Street Terminal just west of the Philadelphia city limits, preparing for a day of celebration for this little interurban electric line that would challenge the mightiest railroad in America.

To start with, the first train was delayed half an hour because of a derailment, there weren't enough new cars to operate the schedule and, worst of all, only one passenger was in sight. It was Wednesday, May 22, 1907, five tumultuous years after the line had been incorporated. The initial train was to leave its eastern terminus at 5:30 A.M., but just before train time another car nearby went off the track. The unlucky train finally left just before 6:00 A.M., but only Joseph McWilliams, who lived in the nearby town of Rosemont, showed up to buy a ticket.

Whistles from Market Street Elevated trains and from the P&W's own cars marked the departure of the first train to Strafford, 10.6 miles from 69th Street. Fortunately, additional passengers were waiting down the line and the car was full when it pulled into Strafford. At Rosemont, four young women with American flags boarded. They waved them from the windows, then gave them as souvenirs to Motorman Michael McAnany and Conductor John Walsh. The car was filled with standees on its return from Strafford, and P&W's Vice President and General Superintendent William H. Simms estimated that more than 1,500 passengers rode on the first day.

Above: The first cars were elegant in moss green paint with gold striping. They had high-back leather seats and green glass in the upper sashes and clerestories, and were built by St. Louis Car Company. While they were equipped with trap doors and steps, all of the line's platforms were built for high-level loading. Collection of Fred W. Schneider.
Left: The Whitehall Station on the old Philadelphia & Columbia Railroad was only a few feet from the spot where the P&W's Bryn Mawr Station was eventually built. This view is from 1860. The old hotel on the right was one of several in the Bryn Mawr area, which was a popular vacation spot for Philadelphians during the summer. Collection of Radnor Historical Society.

The St. Louis cars had "train doors" which permitted passage between cars. *P&W photo. Collection of Bob Foley.*

The North American, a leading Philadelphia newspaper, enthused the day after service began that the opening of the P&W marked "the beginning of a new era for Philadelphia… a small bit of railroad, indeed, but the pioneer… of lines which will bring deliverance to a city that has long been victim to the narrow, stupid and oppressive policies of its steam roads."

"This is not an ordinary trolley line with light rails, cheap construction and privilege upon a public highway," said the North American. "There is a private roadbed, fenced, ballasted, double-tracked, equal in every detail to the best steam road, and superior to any hereabouts in that it crosses not one carriage road at grade. There are no trolley poles or overhead wires. The cars are the best on any trolley road in Pennsylvania. There is swift movement; the fares are about half those asked upon the steam roads, and the country through which the line runs is equal in beauty to the loveliest suburban region in any land on earth."

And the editorial predicted that other lines like the P&W would be built around the Philadelphia region and would "end all talk about steam road monopoly."

GOULD'S BOLD VISION

According to the first timetable, trains would run every 15 minutes between 5:30 A.M. and 1:00 A.M. For the first week, however, trains ran only every half-hour until enough cars were ready and some minor construction on the line could be completed. The one way running time was scheduled at 29 minutes, but on Day One most trips took about 50 minutes.

The initial 22 dark green wooden cars were striped and lettered in gold and contained high-backed green leather seats, mahogany interiors and inlaid wood ceilings. Built by St. Louis Car Company with a top speed of only 45 miles an hour, they could be run in trains of up to four cars, although this seldom proved necessary. Officials said they were the finest interurban cars that money could buy.

Eleven of the 14 stations had ticket agents, including 69th Street Terminal, Beechwood Park, Haverford, Bryn Mawr, Rosemont, Garrett Hill, Villanova (spelled Villa Nova until 1929), Ithan, St. David's, Wayne and Strafford. The stations at Ardmore Junction, Ardmore Avenue and Radnor lacked ticket agents but did have small waiting shelters.

George J. Gould dreamed of fulfilling his father's concept of a coast-to-coast railroad. The P&W was to form the easternmost link. *Collection of Union Pacific Railroad.*

Though few realized it, the original concept for the P&W had been to create a competitor for the Pennsylvania Railroad, a most powerful institution. With its headquarters in Philadelphia, the PRR at the turn-of-the-century owned 4,800 passenger cars and 181,000 freight cars and operated nearly 900 million passenger miles each year.

Philadelphia & Western's basic idea dated back to 1868 when Jay Gould and James Fisk, Jr., wrested control of the Erie Railroad from Cornelius Vanderbilt. The Erie competed with Vanderbilt's New York Central & Hudson River Railroad for traffic across New York State, and Gould won the battle by aligning himself with the notorious William M. Tweed of Tammany Hall. The following year Gould and Fisk caused the national financial panic called "Black Friday" when they attempted to corner the gold market.

Gould quickly realized that control of railroads could add tens of millions of dollars to his personal coffers, and he began to imagine assembling a network of railroads that would cross the country. Gould was ousted from the Erie after only three years, but he had made a great deal of money. By the 1880s he controlled several important railroads, including the big Union Pacific. Gould was in it strictly for the money. As he prospered, his railroads suffered.

And he became one of the most hated men in America. Newspaper editor Joseph Pulitzer called him "one of the most sinister figures that have ever flitted bat-like across the vision of the American people." The New York Herald labeled him "the Skunk of Wall Street." Gould died at the age of 56 in 1892. His son George Jay Gould inherited the empire as well as his father's dream of a coast-to-coast railroad, not to mention his penchant for secrecy.

George Gould set out to expand his father's more than 15,000 route miles into the first truly transcontinental railroad in the United States. Spending recklessly, he stitched together the Western Maryland Railroad in 1902 to reach Baltimore, but the WM was unconnected to the rest of his network. So he spent another $45 million to push the Wabash Railroad into Pittsburgh in 1904, to thus compete with the Pennsylvania Railroad. The Pennsylvania fought hard to block the Wabash, but eventually lost to Gould. Andrew Carnegie, who controlled vast steel interests in Pittsburgh, encouraged the Wabash extension to help break the PRR's Pittsburgh monopoly. Finally, Gould spent another $35 million to connect the Wabash with the Western Maryland, which got him as far east in Pennsylvania as York.

The Gould Lines became an enormous amalgam of railroads running from York and Baltimore through Pittsburgh, Chicago, St. Louis and Kansas City to Ogden, Utah, with a great many additional routes west of the Mississippi River between Omaha and the Gulf of Mexico. Reaching Philadelphia and New York City

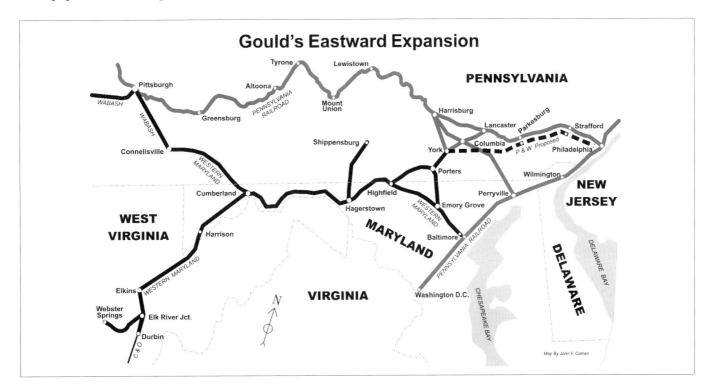

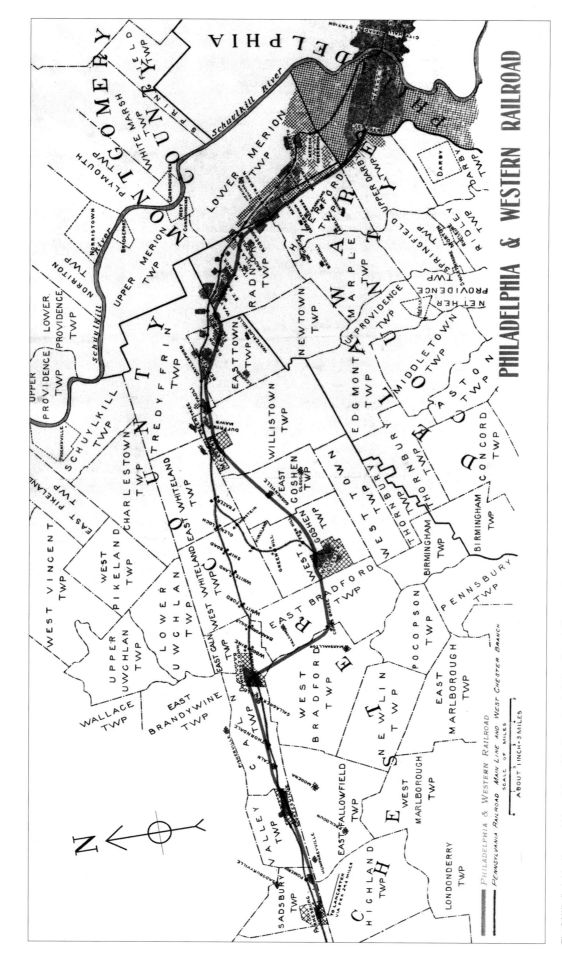

The P&W's first 44 miles would have followed the Pennsylvania Railroad's main line very closely, except that the P&W would have dipped south to serve West Chester. This map shows why the Pennsylvania was worried. *Collection of Ronald DeGraw.*

CHAPTER ONE

would have put him face-to-face with the powerful Pennsylvania Railroad, a challenge that appealed to Gould's vanity and avarice.

In the west, Gould formed the Western Pacific Railway in 1903 to bridge the gap between Utah and San Francisco. Had he succeeded in quickly constructing this extension and in combining his rail lines he would have controlled the biggest railroad system in the world. The Western Pacific, however, was thwarted by Edward H. Harriman, who controlled the Southern Pacific and the Union Pacific, and its opening was delayed until 1910.

THE EASTERN LINK

Our subject, the Philadelphia & Western Railway, was to have been Gould's eastern link to Philadelphia and New York City. The publicly announced proposal was to construct a 44-mile line from the western edge of Philadelphia to Parkesburg, a small town in Chester County. This would directly compete with the Pennsylvania Railroad through Philadelphia's Main Line area. The pretense was that the P&W would be independent, with no formal connection with the Gould Lines. But once the line reached Parkesburg, a link with the Gould lines at York would only be 40 miles away. At one point, the P&W even announced that one of its future extensions would run to York.

At Philadelphia, a connection may have been planned by Gould to use the Philadelphia & Reading Railway's trackage rights to reach Jersey City, just across the river from New York City. The Reading viewed the Pennsylvania Railroad as a chief competitor and would have undoubtedly been happy to link up with Gould.

The Pennsy immediately realized the significance of the P&W and fought to block its creation. This marked the second time that competition from Gould had threatened the Pennsylvania's monopoly across the Allegheny Mountains to Pittsburgh and beyond.

History shows that the PRR's main route west from Philadelphia had been an important transportation route almost from the time America was first settled. It began as an Indian trail and became one of the early highways in the nation. It became the first turnpike in America when the Philadelphia & Lancaster Turnpike Company was incorporated in 1792. This stone-ballasted, macadamized highway was a major corridor for the movement of produce and livestock to what was at the time the largest city in the country. The 70-mile toll road cost $464,000. It opened in 1795 and was an immediate success, but it was slow going. Stage coaches for passengers and covered wagons for freight (called Conestoga wagons), as well as drovers with flocks of sheep or herds of cattle, filled the highway. Dozens of taverns and inns dotted the highway, a few of which are still in existence.

RISE OF THE PENNSYLVANIA RAILROAD

By the 1820s canals were becoming popular in America, and the Commonwealth of Pennsylvania sought to improve east-west transportation. It created the Main Line of Public Works, a unique combination of railroads, boats on existing rivers and new canals, tunnels and inclined planes to cross the mountains. The Philadelphia and Columbia Railroad, serving the eastern 82 miles of this route, opened a portion of its line west from Philadelphia in 1832 and the balance in 1834. It was originally operated with horse-drawn rail cars, but the first train all the way to Columbia in 1829 was pulled by a steam locomotive, not long after the first practical steam engine had been developed in England. When it opened, it was the longest double-track railroad in the world. Locomotives and horse-drawn trains shared the tracks until 1844.

Pennsylvania's $10 million Main Line of Public Works ran nearly 400 miles to Pittsburgh, using a series of inclined planes, railroad tracks and canals for a journey that took five days and traversed 174 canal locks. But it was not an "all weather" route because the canals were inoperable for several months of the year

A typical portage on the Main Line of Public Works. The cars, which were shaped like boats, were hauled up the inclined planes by steam and ropes. They spent much of their time in the rivers that formed a great part a large portion of the trip between Philadelphia and Pittsburg. *From Pennsylvania Transportation History, by William H. Shank.*

due to winter's freezes, spring thaws, and summer droughts. It was slow and cumbersome, although at the time it was viewed as tremendous progress. Still, it only lasted for two decades.

The Pennsylvania Railroad, incorporated in 1846, completed a railroad from Pittsburgh to Harrisburg by 1854, effectively replacing much of the old portage and canal system. The PRR purchased the entire Main Line of Public Works in 1857, including the Philadelphia & Columbia Railroad, creating an all-rail route across the state that became an immediate success.

This did not amuse William H. Vanderbilt, who controlled the New York Central & Hudson River Railroad. This son of Cornelius Vanderbilt challenged the Pennsylvania's success in 1884 by creating the South Pennsylvania Railroad. Its purpose was to tap the lucrative coalfields and the Pittsburgh steel plants, breaking the PRR's Pittsburgh monopoly. So far as Vanderbilt was concerned, it was tit for tat because the PRR had constructed a line along the west bank of the Hudson River in direct competition with his New York Central, and he wanted revenge.

Carnegie and George Gould were active participants in the scheme. The South Pennsylvania began blasting through mountains and building bridges across Pennsylvania, spending millions of dollars constructing a line to closely parallel to the PRR between Pittsburgh and Harrisburg. To close the eastern gap, the South Pennsylvania was soon allied with the Philadelphia & Reading, whose tracks it would have used between Harrisburg and New York City.

Enter J. Pierpont Morgan, Wall Street's leading banker, who became annoyed because the South Pennsylvania battle was adversely affecting stock prices. Morgan mediated a solution that permitted the PRR to purchase the incompleted South Pennsylvania on the one hand, and the NYC&HR to lease the New York, West Shore & Buffalo Railroad along the Hudson River. The PRR's Keystone State monopoly was safe, but at a high price. The tunnels and roadbed constructed for "Vanderbilt's Folly" remained unused until the Pennsylvania Turnpike was built over much of the same right-of-way. Opened in 1940, it was the first modern turnpike in America and six of its seven tunnels had stood empty since having been constructed by the South Pennsylvania in 1884 and 1885.

THE MAIN LINE SUBURBS

The term "Main Line", from the old Main Line of Public Works, refers to the area of suburban Philadelphia from the city limits at Overbrook to Paoli. This was largely an upscale, chiefly residential area with a few small villages such as Ardmore, Bryn Mawr, Wayne and Paoli. The PRR encouraged its executives to live along the Main Line, which by the end of the 19th century had become one of the wealthiest suburbias in the nation.

But the Pennsy thought the Main Line needed more class. So the railroad simply changed the names of its stations, most taken from Welsh towns because this stretch had originally been a part of William Penn's "Welsh Barony", created shortly after Penn founded Pennsylvania in 1681. Athensville became Ardmore, Humphreysville became Bryn Mawr, Morgan's Corner was changed to Radnor, Louella became Wayne and Eagle became Strafford. Since the post offices were located in the train stations, residents of the towns had little choice but to go along.

Improvements were made; the PRR realigned many portions of the old Philadelphia & Columbia Railroad, smoothing out curves for higher speeds and shortening the route. The inclined plane at the edge of Philadelphia was eliminated. All this remained the main line of the Pennsylvania Railroad, and as traffic grew it was expanded to four tracks by 1900. In addition to dozens of long distance trains, the railroad by the turn of the century was operating many commuter trains. As this happened, the Main Line was rapidly developing as a popular place to live for Philadelphia's middle class as well as the location of hundreds of "country houses" for wealthy Philadelphians.

Alexander Cassatt was the PRR's president during the creation of the P&W, and he lived along the Main Line, with his residence in Haverford and his farm in Chesterbrook, near Berwyn. He was a Lower Merion Township commissioner from 1882 to 1898 and had been instrumental in improving the condition of Lancaster Pike. In 1880, with the backing of his railroad, Cassatt formed the Lancaster Avenue Improvement Association, which acquired 17 miles of the turnpike from Overbrook to Paoli. The group paved the highway and continued to operate it as a toll road until it was sold to the state in 1917 for $165,000. A second company-the Philadelphia, Bala and Bryn Mawr Turnpike Company-was also formed to control and improve Montgomery Avenue, the other major east-west road through Lower Merion.

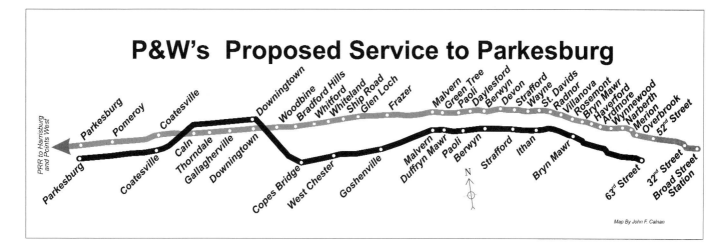

But the real reason for maintaining these two turnpike companies was to guarantee that Cassatt's railroad would not be bothered by any competition from the newfangled trolley companies, which sprang up all over America during the 1890s.

THE TROLLEY ARRIVES

Trolley lines traditionally ran alongside existing highways, or actually down the middle of roads through towns, avoiding expensive private rights-of-way. Incorporated during the 1890s were such companies as the Philadelphia & Merion Electric Railway, the Radnor Electric Passenger Railway, the Pennsylvania Traction, the Pembroke Railway, the Philadelphia & Rosemont Passenger Railway and other lines that would have had to use parts of either Lancaster Pike or Montgomery Avenue for their routes.

By controlling both of these highways within Lower Merion Township, the Pennsylvania Railroad thought it had successfully blocked any trolley competition.

It had not reckoned, however, with the wiliness of A. Merritt Taylor, president of the Philadelphia & West Chester Traction Company. Taylor in 1902 successfully opened a three-mile line to Ardmore, one of the principal towns in Lower Merion, from a junction with his West Chester interurban at Llanerch. Taylor formed the line originally under a steam railroad charter to allay suspicion, then actually operated it with trolleys. This infuriated the PRR, which took Taylor to court, but lost.

P&W THREATENS COMPETITION

There was also the new Philadelphia & Western Railway Company. Some 50 daily round-trip suburban commuter trains were operated along the Main Line by the PRR at the time the P&W was incorporated on May 21, 1902. Alarmed, the PRR quickly announced that it would run additional trains and would expand its four-track right-of-way to six tracks between Overbrook and Paoli.

A trolley counter-attack was to be launched. The Street Railway Journal in November 1903, reported that a group headed by PRR's Fourth Vice President Samuel Rea had been granted a charter for a new electric railway called the Overbrook, Bryn Mawr & Paoli Street Railroad. "Indications are growing that the Pennsylvania Railroad, either directly or through interests closely allied with it, proposes to go into the business of operating electric railways for the short haul traffic in and about Philadelphia," said the magazine.

Philadelphia & Western's plan was to establish a terminal at the western edge of the city at 63rd and Arch Streets, then run westward in a virtually parallel line with the PRR, serving Ardmore, Haverford, Bryn Mawr, Rosemont, Villanova, Radnor, St. Davids, Wayne, Strafford, Devon, Berwyn, Paoli and Malvern. The P&W would then dip southward to West Chester, then back north to serve Downingtown, Thorndale, Coatesville, Pomeroy and Parkesburg, which were also on the PRR.

While the southward dip into West Chester, the county seat, would have added mileage and running time to the P&W trains, it was a smart move because West Chester had a population of 9,500 and was served from both the north and south by two PRR branches that offered infrequent service. The PRR's Frazer branch from the north connected with the Main Line of Public Works and was opened in 1832 with horse drawn trains. The line from the south began in 1858, operating from West Chester through Media directly to Philadelphia.

VISIONS OF GRANDEUR

Most of the early stations were built so they could easily be moved back when the line was four-tracked, which never occurred. The overhead highway bridges were also built to accommodate four tracks. This car is heading toward 69th Street Terminal in 1907. The original Radnor Station had no waiting room or ticket agent. *Collection of Robert Goshorn.*

The P&W could have probably stolen away most of the PRR's West Chester passengers from both branches.

It may also have captured business from Taylor's Philadelphia & West Chester Traction Company, which had been running a 20-mile single-track interurban trolley line since 1899. The P&W's running time would have been faster than either the PRR trains or the trolleys. It would have also successfully competed for passengers on the West Chester-Downingtown-Coatesville trolley line operated by West Chester Street Railway and on the Coatesville-Parkesburg portion of the Conestoga Traction line.

The proposed P&W was not so well situated along the eastern portion of the Main Line as was the PRR's. The towns and villages literally surrounded the railroad stations. The P&W had to settle for an alignment just south of all of the towns, not really properly serving any of them. Not much activity was within walking distance of the P&W's stations on the eastern half of the proposed line. The town of Bryn Mawr was relatively close to the P&W station, and Villanova College was well served. This perhaps did not matter so much for a railroad grandly designed to run from the East Coast to the West Coast.

P&W took great pains to avoid locating any of its right-of-way in Lower Merion Township, where Cassatt held sway, and in fact it avoided Montgomery County entirely. The original 10.6-mile route ran completely within Delaware County, closely skirting the southern boundary of Lower Merion. But it was a close thing; at Penfield Station the Lower Merion boundary was only 1,000 feet away and at Bryn Mawr Station it was less than 100 feet.

Whatever its plans to provide an efficient commuter service for this area, in P&W's background stood the PRR's old nemesis, George Gould. A year before the company's 1902 incorporation surveys were conducted for the Wabash Railroad to find a suitable route through the area. The original survey books show that a favored route was from 54th Street and City Avenue in West Philadelphia westward to Parkesburg via Gladwyne, Gulph Mills and King of Prussia. This would have passed the old King of Prussia Inn, built in 1769. A branch line would have served West Chester. The alignment along the Main Line just south of the Pennsylvania Railroad was the one ultimately selected.

To allay suspicions, Gould named unknowns as the first presidents of P&W. Millard F. Thompson served from May, 1902, to March, 1905, and board meetings were held in Carlisle, about 70 miles west of Parkesburg. Most of the company's officers and directors resigned on March 6, 1905, and new ones were elected by prearrangement. Henry A. McCarthy was elected president, but served for only two months, and the meetings were moved to Philadelphia. William T. Van Brunt then took over. An associate of Gould, he was president of the St. Joseph and Grand Island Railroad, operating in Missouri, Kansas and Nebraska, and was also general superintendent of the St. Joseph Traction & Lighting Company. His election as head of the P&W increased the rumors swirling around the upstart railroad.

In July, 1905, P&W found it necessary to issue this statement: "None of the various railroads-the Pennsylvania, Wabash, Reading or Lehigh Valley-mentioned at various times as identified with the road are in any way interested, nor have they a dollar in the property. The only persons interested are George J. Kobusch, president of the St. Louis Car Company, and W. T. Van Brunt, and their financial friends." But this was not the truth.

Van Brunt, apparently attracting too much attention, stepped down as president after only three months, to be replaced by Kobusch, who headed one of the major streetcar builders in the country. He was a director of several interurban lines, including the St. Louis & Belleville Electric Railway Company, a trolley freight line that hoped to do major interchange business with the Wabash. The P&W's banker became the Mississippi Valley Trust Company, of St. Louis, which was closely allied with St. Louis Car. Mississippi Valley issued the P&W's first mortgage bonds. Not by coincidence, St. Louis was also the headquarters of Gould's Wabash Railroad.

LOCAL OPPOSITION

Not everyone was pleased about the budding P&W. A flyer was distributed to residents of Tredyffrin, Willistown and Easttown townships urging them to oppose construction. The Pennsylvania General Railroad Act of 1868 permitted railroads the right of eminent domain in acquiring property needed for rights-of-way. The flyer, signed by a number of prominent Main Liners, complained that the P&W would seriously injure the value of real estate, and stunt the building of new "country houses." Several property owners vainly attempted to block the P&W through court action. Two Radnor residents-Mary J. Chew and Martha M. Brown-fought the longest and hardest, continuing their court battles until 1914.

Of course the Pennsylvania Railroad also put up a challenge. About a mile west of 63rd and Arch Streets, proposed to be its eastern terminus, the P&W would cross PRR land that had been acquired for its proposed Darby Creek Low Grade Line. This was to have been a bypass of the PRR's main line for freight trains from Glen Loch to 56th Street. The PRR tried to block the P&W from crossing this property, just east of where City Avenue crosses the P&W at its West Overbrook Station, in September 1903, but did not succeed. PRR never built the Darby Creek Low Grade Line, but in 1923 a portion of the proposed bypass did become the Pennsylvania Railroad Golf Club!

In P&W's corner was the West Chester Daily Local News, which disclosed surveying teams at work to the east and west of town, and said local merchants and manufacturers would welcome competition to the lordly PRR. The newspaper reported in August 1902 that some right-of-way grading, including a cut 150 feet deep, was underway just west of Coatesville. The P&W actually graded 8,000 feet of double track line between Parkesburg and Coatesville in November 1902.

CONSTRUCTION AND FINANCIAL CHALLENGES

By mid-1904 it was reported that most of the right-of-way had been obtained. Ten acres for the proposed Parkesburg terminal at First Avenue and Church Street were bought for $3,000. "The Philadelphia & Western is heading this way rapidly," the West Chester newspaper announced in January, 1905, "as the work of building the road is going on weekday and Sunday without abatement…activity reigns all along the new line and there is every reason to believe that it will be in operation between Philadelphia and Wayne by July 1, as promised."

But it wouldn't be. Serious financial problems were interfering. The line was costing far more than had been anticipated, and Gould's once unlimited funding sources were diminishing.

Still, the P&W was always exploring possible route extensions. By May 1904 its engineers had surveyed a line from 63rd and Arch to the Delaware River at the southern part of the city, running north of Market Street to the Schuylkill River, then down the west bank of the Schuylkill to its confluence with the Delaware River. Such a route would have skirted the downtown area and run through the industrial region of South Philadelphia, although this plan was never publicized and never pursued.

The P&W was also now claiming that it would build branches to serve Lancaster, York, Norristown, Conshohocken, Chester and Wilmington, with the first section of the line serving as a trunk for all of the brances. In planning for this, the P&W had acquired a right-of-way to Strafford that was wide enough for four tracks. Only two were ever built, but all overhead bridges were built wide enough to accommodate two additional tracks. Actual grading was only done for two tracks. The wooden high-level stations, however, were placed on top of concrete footings so that when the time came they could easily be picked up and moved to make room for the two additional tracks.

ELECTRIC OR STEAM?

At one of the P&W's first board meetings, on October 13, 1902, it was decided to look at purchasing 12 locomotives, five baggage cars, 25 passenger cars and 18 freight cars. At another meeting on January 10, 1903, one of the directors suggested that the railroad should be run by electricity as well as steam, but nothing came of the idea at the time. Two months later the directors decided that trains should be run every 15 minutes using 20 eight-wheel passenger locomotives, four Consolidation-type freight locomotives, four six-wheel switch engines, 36 coaches, 10 combination baggage and mail cars, 20 box cars and 20 hopper cars. It was estimated that this would cost $912,000.

By early 1905 it had been finally decided to use electric cars for passenger service and steam locomotives for freight. The line was initially to have been powered by overhead wire, but by August 1905, the contract was changed to specify third-rail. Power generating stations were planned for Beechwood, Wayne, West Chester and Parkesburg. Several turntables for the steam locomotives were included in the first contract.

Twenty-two electric interurban passenger cars were ordered from St. Louis Car in July 1905. Alas, completion of the cars that September put the P&W in an embarrassing position. Construction of the line was far from complete, and the railroad was having serious financial problems and besides, the road wasn't ready to open, so P&W refused to accept the cars.

THE SOUTHEASTERN CONSTRUCTION COMPANY

P&W in early 1905 formed the Southeastern Construction Company as a subsidiary to build the first part of the line. The corporate secretary of Southeastern was Thomas Newhall, a socially prominent Philadelphian who lived along the proposed route and would soon play a key role in the P&W. Newhall's father-in-law ran J. L. Blackwell & Company, a banking and railroad promotion firm in Baltimore, headquarters of the Western Maryland Railroad. The Blackwell Company had incorporated the P&W, acting secretly for Gould.

Construction and "improvement" companies, often owned by the railroad's promoters, were a favorite means of siphoning off money. These companies performed construction work at greatly inflated prices in order to drain off funds from the railroad's investors and creditors. It was a method Gould (and others) had used many times. Payment to a construction company was often made in the railroad's stocks and bonds that were issued at a discount from their expected value. The construction company would then resell them to raise cash for construction. The discount was supposed to cover the risks of the resale, but it often hid substantial profits as well. While there is no evidence that Southeastern Construction Company operated in this manner, we know that within a few months after the company was created it owned 8,962 of the total 9,000 shares of P&W stock. Southeastern's laborers did not profit; they were paid 15 cents an hour.

By early 1906 it had been decided-reluctantly-to open the P&W in stages, the first part only as far as Strafford. Both local and express trains would be operated, every 10 minutes at first and eventually every five. The P&W claimed that the running time to Center City, including a transfer to the Market Street Elevated at 69th Street, would be the same as the PRR. Construction of the first 10-mile section cost $1.5 million. Right-of-way acquisition for the entire 44 miles had cost $2.5 million.

THE PHILADELPHIA TERMINAL

P&W's original eastern terminal was to be in the vicinity of 63rd and Arch, at the city's western boundary and a block north of Market Street. It was at 63rd and Market that the Market Street Elevated Passenger Railway, a subsidiary of Philadelphia Rapid Transit, was going to build its western terminus. Passengers from the P&W and from the Philadelphia & West Chester Traction Company's cars would transfer to the elevated trains for a fast ride to Center City. By 1905, plans for the consolidated terminal had been moved westward to a spot in Upper Darby Township which was being called 69th and Market Streets, although nothing existed there but fields. The track gauge of the elevated trains was 5'2¼", the same as most Pennsylvania trolley

Check No.	NAMES	Occupation	22	23	24	25	19	20	21	Total Time	Rate	Amount	Commissary	Rent	Total Deductions	Balance Due	REMARKS
	C. Anderson	Foreman	10	10	10	—	10		50	27½	1375					1375	Paid
	R. Anderson	"	10	10	10	—	10		50	30	1500					1500	Paid
	R. Condon	"	10	—	—	—	10	—	10	30	25	750				750	Paid
	B. G. Davis	Engineer	10	10	10	10	10		60	30	1800					1800	Paid
	G. Howard	Carpenter	10	10	10	—	10		50	37½	1875					1875	Paid
	E. L. Mathews	Supt.	10	10	10	10	10		60	60	3600					3600	Paid
	A. Marstello	Foreman	14	10	7	12	10		63	30	1890					1890	
	Wm. Madden	"	10	10	10	—	10		50	20	1000					1000	Paid
	F. Marchant	"	10	10	10	—	10		50	35	1750					1750	Paid
	B. Malone	"	10	10	10	—	10		50	30	1500					1500	Pd
	Merriman	B. Smith	10	10	—	10	10		50	30	1500					1500	Paid
	J. G. Rudolph	Foreman	10	10	10	10	10		60	41½	2500					2500	Paid
	C. Stieper	"	10	10	10	5	10		55	25	1375					1375	Paid
	C. F. Stieper	Ast. Fn.	10	10	10	—	10		50	15	750					750	Paid
	J. Small	"	10	10	10	10	10		60	16⅔	1000					1000	Paid
	B. Wilson	Carpenter	12	10	10	5	10		57	37½	2137					2137	Paid
	W. Wilson	"	10	10	10	5	10		55	30	1650					1650	Paid
	S. Mitchell	Foreman				5			5	30	150					150	Pd
700	Italian	Asst driller	10	10	10	10	10		60	17½	1050					1050	Pd
701	"	Laborer	10	10	10	—	10		50	15	750					750	Pd
702	"	Pipe layer	12	10	10	10	10		62	17½	1085					1085	Pd
703	"	Laborer								15							
704	"	"	10	10	10	—	10		50	15	750					750	Pd
705	"	Fireman	10	10	10	10	10		60	17½	1060					1060	Pd
706	"	Laborer	10	10	10	—	10		50	15	750					750	Pd
707	"	"								15							
708	"	"	10	10	10	—	10		50	15	750					750	Pd
709	"	"		—	8	10	—		18	15	270					270	Pd

A page of a pay sheet of 1905 from Southeastern Construction Company showing badge numbers and "Italian," rather than names of workers. Many Italian immigrants signed on as track workers. The hourly wage was 15 cents for laborers. *Collection of Ronald DeGraw.*

lines. The gauge of the P&W was the standard 4'8½" railroad gauge, which reassured the Pennsylvania Railroad that P&W trains would never be able to run directly into the city over the elevated line.

But Kobusch had a surprise for the PRR. He now proposed that the P&W would build its own subway and elevated line to downtown Philadelphia. P&W wanted to construct an elevated railway over Ludlow Street, an alley just south of Market Street, from 63rd Street to 33rd Street, then south to Chestnut Street. A new bridge would carry the trains over the Schuylkill River, then they would plunge into a subway under Chestnut Street and run almost to the Delaware River. From there they would go one block north to Market, then west on Market Street to Broad Street and down Broad to Chestnut, forming a huge loop in the commercial heart of the city.

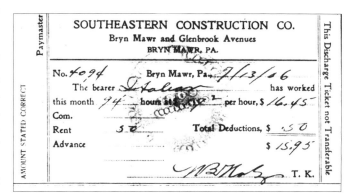

A pay voucher from Southeastern Construction Company in 1906 was made out simply to "Italian" for construction of the Strafford line. Many of the workers were immigrants from Italy, and even the company's record books did not show their real names, just their badge numbers. *Collection of Ronald DeGraw.*

VISIONS OF GRANDEUR

THE "DINKIES"

The first powered vehicles on the Philadelphia & Western were not electric interurbans. Two tiny steam engines arrived in October, 1905, to aid in the construction of the line, and they were already 24 years old.

Electrically powered rail vehicles had not been perfected when New York City's elevated railways were constructed, and even after the first successful trolley line was opened in 1888 it remained impossible to operate several cars together in a train with central control. Thus elevated railways depended on little 0-4-0T Forney-type steam locomotives until Frank J. Sprague invented the multiple-unit control system in 1898. The New York elevateds then replaced inefficient steam engines with electric cars, and many of the engines were sold to industrial or construction railroads.

Southeastern Construction Company, P&W's subsidiary, acquired two of them. Nos. 286 and 288 had been built in 1881 by Baldwin for the Sixth Avenue Elevated Railway. This line was absorbed by the Manhattan Railway in 1891, and the Manhattan was controlled by George Gould. The little steam engines were called "dinkies" by the P&W and had no numbers. They aided in building the Strafford extension in 1911 and the Norristown branch in 1912, then remained out of service behind the carbarn until they were sold in 1920 for $1,300.

Both locomotives appeared on the completed railroad from time to time. Here is one at Haverford Station in 1908. *Collection of Ronald DeGraw.*

Two little Forney locomotives were purchased to aid in construction of the P&W. They were sold in 1920. *Collection of Bob Foley.*

Both "dinkies" were involved in a wreck during construction of the Norristown branch in 1912 near Conshohocken Road Station. *Collection of Ronald DeGraw.*

Philadelphia Rapid Transit officials were aghast at the proposal. They had been given the franchise to build a subway-elevated from Broad and Market Streets west to 69th Street. The line was well underway, and construction had begun on the big joint terminal building at 69th and Market. The PRT line would suffer tremendously if P&W also was permitted to build to downtown, and it was under criticism for being behind schedule in building its subway-elevated, but millions of dollars had already been put into it.

Half of the front page of the North American the next day was devoted to announcing: "Competing Railroad Offers to Build Elevated and Subway, on 35-year Franchise, Paying City Share of the Receipts." A map eight columns wide was included. If Kobusch was looking for a bombshell, he had found it. Within a day 12,000 shares of PRT stock had changed hands and its value had fallen 10 percent.

There was much intrigue behind the P&W's bold new plan, and P&W's generous terms were designed to tempt the city to accept. The city would get two percent of the line's gross earnings initially. The amount would increase by one percent annually to a maximum of five percent. After 35 years, the entire subway-elevated would be turned over to the city free of charge. Then, the P&W would lease the line from the city for 40 years at an annual rental of $400,000 plus five percent of gross receipts. It was estimated that the arrangement would produce at least $25 million for the city over the 75-year period, and many businessmen and several newspapers urged the city to accept the offer. Mayor Weaver called it "a splendid proposal" and said he was "most heartily in favor of it."

The elevated line would cost about $15 million to build, and Kobusch said, if successful, it would be feasible eventually to extend it to Camden by tunneling under the Delaware River. This would have delivered Gould's railroad directly to the busy Philadelphia waterfront, connecting it with the city-owned Philadelphia Belt Line Railway, which served the entire Philadelphia waterfront. P&W announced that it would operate high-density rapid transit within the city as well as a network of high-speed interurbans connecting the city with the suburbs. Freight and mail would also be carried directly into the city.

Five days later the Philadelphia newspapers reported that Kobusch had met with the holders of a Camden-to-Atlantic City franchise, and that the P&W planned to run service directly from Parkesburg through Philadelphia, under the Delaware River to Camden and on to Atlantic City. The Camden-Atlantic City train service was an extremely lucrative business for the Pennsylvania Railroad, but passengers from Philadelphia had to cross the river on ferries.

While the city's business groups and its newspapers seemed overjoyed by the P&W's subway-elevated plan, Mayor Weaver moved cautiously and ultimately used the threat of competition to wrest concessions from the PRT. All this was not to be. Both PRT and PRR, a powerful combination, prevailed on Philadelphia's city councils to defeat the P&W proposal. This prompted PRT to speed up completion of the Market Street Elevated. And it undoubtedly caused a great deal of anxiety in the nearby Broad Street Station headquarters of the Pennsylvania Railroad.

The 1906 announcement that P&W would build its own subway-elevated line appears to have been a last-ditch effort by Gould and Kobusch to attract new capital to the struggling railroad. This conflicted with an agreement between P&W and PRT to permit P&W cars to run express directly over PRT's elevated tracks to Center City, terminating next to the Pennsylvania Railroad's Broad Street Station. To accomplish this, the elevated would be built to standard railroad gauge instead of the 5'2¼" gauge that had been planned. (The Philadelphia streetcar network was built to the wider gauge.) But that, too, was not to be. The agreement was never implemented, and the elevated railway was in fact built to the wider gauge.

TERMINAL MOVED WEST

Philadelphia & Western had wanted to begin train service at an earlier date than it actually did, but it faced two problems. Construction lagged because there was often a shortage of cash. A great deal of money had been wasted on right-of-way acquisition and even some grading between Strafford and Parkesburg. There simply wasn't enough cash to complete the entire 44-mile proposed line, hence the decision by early 1906 to concentrate on opening the first section only as far as Strafford.

And there was a second, albeit temporary, problem: the lack of rapid transit connections at the P&W's 63rd Street terminus. Had the line opened in 1905 or 1906, as originally planned, passengers would have had to transfer to streetcars running in the middle of Market Street from 63rd Street all the way to Center City, an interminably slow ride which would have discouraged P&W patronage.

PRT's Market Street Elevated Passenger Railway Company had been granted its franchise in 1903. It was to open in 1906, but it, too, was delayed. It finally opened on April 30, 1907, providing a 15-minute ride to City Hall and a frequent and speedy connection for P&W passengers. Had the P&W opened earlier than the elevated, its patrons would have been virtually stranded at the city's western boundary.

It was the original plan to build a joint terminal at 63rd and Market Streets for the elevated road, the P&WCT trolleys from West Chester, Ardmore and Collingdale and the P&W. The P&WCT's Taylor, however, preferred a location somewhat further west, and he prevailed. But this left the P&W with inadequate space for a large terminal facility. P&W ultimately built an inexpensive station tacked onto the north side of the main PRT portion of 69th Street Terminal that was supposed to be temporary. The P&W facilities were hemmed in on the south side by the main terminal building and on the north side by the elevated railway's maintenance, car storage and powerhouse area. The space available to the P&W was adequate for a 10-mile route, but would never have sufficed if the line had been extended to Parkesburg or beyond. Drawings in the 1905 Street Railway Journal show P&W tracks continuing further east toward 63rd Street.

The P&W's new 69th Street terminal was distressingly spartan and didn't even contain a waiting room because it was expected the structure wouldn't last very long. There was one unloading track on the upper level and two loading tracks, one on the same level and one slightly lower. The upper loading track was used chiefly for car storage. The P&W's dispatcher's office and trainmen's room were located in the temporary terminal, which had wooden platforms and corrugated iron walls.

FORECLOSURE AND REORGANIZATION

In early 1905 a hard-pressed Kobusch had solicited the New York City investment firms of William C. Sheldon & Company and Mackay & Company to find new sources of money. Sheldon's company was headed up by George R. Sheldon, a prominent New York City banker and president of the North American Company, a holding firm that controlled a number of traction lines including the Milwaukee Electric Railway and Light and streetcar lines in St. Louis and Detroit. A business associate of Kobusch, the influential Sheldon was involved in major steel companies, the American Locomotive Company, and was a member of the Republican National Committee.

Plunging right in, the two firms purchased $1.6 million of P&W's first mortgage bonds, out of a total authorized issue of $15 million. Kobusch advanced additional funds, but there still wasn't enough to complete the road. P&W defaulted in the payment of the interest on its bonds, so in the spring of 1907 the two firms organized a syndicate to fund the first section of the line, and reorganize the P&W so that additional stock and bonds could be sold. The next step was a foreclosure sale, held at the Chester County Court House on May 20, 1907. The property was sold for $1 million to Randolph Rodman and James H. Brewster, Jr., both P&W directors and representatives of the syndicate. The name of the company was then changed from Philadelphia & Western Railroad Company to Philadelphia & Western Railway Company, with Sheldon as its president.

The day after the reorganization—on May 21, 1907—a formal inspection trip of the P&W took place. Among the guests were P&WCT's Taylor, three officers of the PRR, including William W. Atterbury, general manager and later president; six PRT officials, including George D. Widener, first vice president, and numerous financial men from Philadelphia and New York. PRT operated a special subway train from 15th Street to 69th Street for the ceremonies, and lunch was served in the new carbarn.

Regular passenger service began the next day, and on June 7 P&W was recapitalized at $7.3 million, which included $4 million in common and preferred stock. A total of $20 million in stock was authorized, the balance of $16 million to be issued in the future for "extensions, betterments and permanent improvements."

Gould appears to have lost interest in the P&W by this time, finally giving up forever his dream of a coast-to-coast railroad that would challenge the mighty Pennsylvania Railroad. He of course left Kobusch holding the bag, a popular tactic of both George Gould and his father, Jay. Kobusch resigned as P&W president in April, receiving $109,600 for his interest in the Southeastern Construction Company. His temporary replacement was W. Robinson Molinard, a company director and its vice president. Kobusch did not deign to attend the opening day ceremonies.

THE PHANTOM CARS

The first cars that P&W ordered never arrived. In July, 1905, the railroad placed an order for 22 passenger cars with the St. Louis Car Company. At that time the railroad anticipated an opening date during the fall of 1905. The cars were ready on time, but the financially strapped railroad wasn't. Since the carbarn and yard tracks hadn't yet been built, there was literally no place to put the cars even if the P&W could have paid for them.

The big cars remained at the builder's St. Louis plant waiting for the P&W to get its act together. Eventually the P&W canceled the order. This must have been particularly embarrassing to George Kobusch, who was president of both the St. Louis Car Company and the P&W. Buyers were eventually found for all of them.

UNITED RAILROADS OF SAN FRANCISCO

Due to the disastrous San Francisco earthquake of April, 1906, the city's public transportation system was a shambles, with many trolleys and interurbans destroyed by the earthquake. Patrick Calhoun, president of United Railroads, hurried east to purchase whatever replacement cars he could. While visiting the St. Louis Car Company he spotted the big P&W interurbans and immediately bought them for use on the United Railroads' San Mateo line.

Calhoun paid $12,500 each for 12 of the cars. Numbered 1-12 for the P&W, the same numbers were retained by United Railroads and were the largest and fastest to operate in the San Francisco area. Known as "Big Subs" the cars ran with only minor modifications until withdrawn from service in 1923. Cars. 2, 3, 6, 7, 9 and 11 were scrapped in 1933 and the others in 1935.

One of the original P&W cars on the San Mateo line in San Francisco. Twelve were purchased from St. Louis Car Company. *Collection of Harre W. Demoro.*

VISIONS OF GRANDEUR

SACRAMENTO NORTHERN RAILWAY

Four of the cars, Nos. 13-16, were acquired in 1907 by Northern Electric Railroad, later a part of the Sacramento Northern Railway in California, where they were operated as trailers 250-253, before being remotored. Car 250 was rebuilt into combine 107 in 1913. No. 251 was rebuilt into combine No. 10 for subsidiary Marysville & Colusa Railroad in 1912, and was renumbered Northern Electric 109 in 1915. Both cars remained in service until 1940. No. 252 was rebuilt into combination car 1 of the subsidiary Sacramento & Woodland Railroad in 1912. In 1915 it became Northern Electric 108. It was rebuilt again to a full passenger coach for service in the deluxe "Meteor" train, which included a parlor car. The car was put into storage in 1935. No. 253 was rebuilt to Northern Electric combine 106 in 1911, converted to a freight switcher in the mid-1920s and retired in 1935. All were scrapped in 1941.

ERIE RAILROAD

The remaining six cars, P&W 17-22, were sold to the Erie Railroad in 1907, where they became 3100-3105. These vehicles were for use on the Erie's pioneering 25-cycle 11,000-volt alternating current electrification of its 34-mile Rochester-Avon-Mt. Morris branch in New York State, which opened in June 1907. The first four of these cars remained as coaches, but the last two were rebuilt into combines. The cars were equipped with Westinghouse alternating current traction equipment and used pantographs instead of trolley poles.

Electric operation on the Mt. Morris branch ceased on November 29, 1934, replaced by gas-electric cars, and all service ended on September 30, 1941. The four coaches were scrapped in 1934. The two combines were de-electrified and converted to work cars, renumbered X01845 and X01846.

One of the original P&W cars in service for the Erie Railroad. *Collection of Fred W. Schneider.*

One of the four original P&W cars that operated for the Sacramento Northern. *Collection of Harre W. Demoro.*

Historians do not treat George Gould kindly. While his goal was to carry out his father's dream of a transcontinental rail empire, he "proved unequal to the enormous responsibility thrust upon him," according to Maury Klein in his biography of Jay Gould. "George lacked not only his father's genius but his appetite for work," according to Klein. "Where Jay learned everything and revealed nothing, George seldom bothered with homework and was careless with details. George preferred parties and vacations in Europe to the hard grind of work, but the Gould empire was too vast and intricate to be run on a part-time basis."

Thus it was that Gould's mounting financial problems forced him to abandon his dreams of eastward expansion. When the Panic of 1907 struck, it found Gould grossly overextended and with a host of powerful financial enemies. Some of his railroads filed for bankruptcy within a year. After 1907 he rapidly lost control of his empire. He did retain enough money to continue playing polo, a favorite interest, and to live comfortably at his estate in Lakewood, New Jersey. When he died in 1923 at age 59 he had long ceased to be an important player in American railroads.

CHAPTER TWO

Settling In
1907-1910

BECAUSE OF its promise as the proposed connection for a long-distance steam railroad, the little Philadelphia & Western was absurdly overbuilt. Few interurban electric lines anywhere in the world equaled the P&W's standard of construction or its cost, and none in 1907 excelled it.

The opening of the P&W "marks another noteworthy step in the development of heavy electric traction for high-speed transportation in the suburbs of our large cities," said the Street Railway Journal. "The operating results of the new line...may well be expected to demonstrate anew the superiority of electricity for suburban service."

Only experienced motormen and conductors were hired at what P&W called "liberal wages" of 25 cents an hour. Originally 14 train crews were enlisted, but within two years there were only eight motormen and nine conductors because of the low ridership. Crews worked 10 hours a day and six days a week.

The P&W was built under a Pennsylvania law that gave it the right of eminent domain and a perpetual franchise. This law required that there be no grade crossings with highways or rail lines and that the P&W offer freight service. Without the right of eminent domain, it is unlikely that the railroad would have been able to obtain all of the land it needed in such close proximity to the influential Pennsylvania Railroad.

A FIRST CLASS INTERURBAN

Typical electric railway construction of the day included numerous grade crossings, often side-of-the-road construction, street running through the towns, sharp curves, significant grades and street-level station platforms. Even the neighboring Philadelphia & West Chester Traction Company's Sharon Hill and Media lines, built between 1906 and 1917 and considered high quality trolley construction, possessed most of these attributes.

Had the P&W ever constructed the four tracks it was originally designed for, it would have been even more unusual. In anticipation of adding two more tracks, the original P&W right-of-way was 230 feet wide.

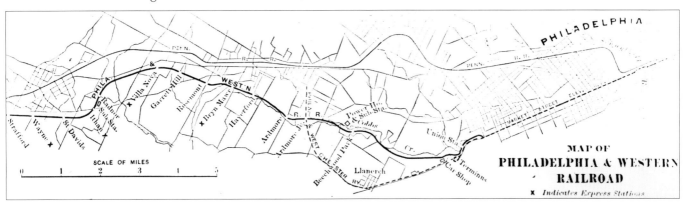

Above: As built, the P&W was a mere shadow of its original proposal. *Collection of Ronald DeGraw.* **Left:** Two of the early cars pass near Ardmore Junction Station. Note the under-running third-rail and the heavy ballasting. *Collection of Roger Prichard.*

P&W's track was protected by automatic semaphore block signals. The lack of grade crossings made high-speed operation feasible and safe. Grades on the entire line never exceeded 2.5 percent and curves were a maximum of five degrees. Ballast for the line came from a company-owned quarry in Wayne. This resulted in construction costs far higher than nearly any other interurban line in the country, but it was doubtless the finest interurban built up to that time. The line to Strafford cost nearly $400,000 per mile to build, an astonishing ten times higher than the average.

The high construction standards of the P&W required many cuts and fills, and what the Street Railway Journal called "an extraordinary number" of bridges, arches and culverts. One million cubic yards of earth were moved. The short 10.6-mile route required 11 overhead bridges for public highways, four overhead bridges for private crossings, two arches, including a 33-foot diameter span at a high fill over Conestoga Road in Rosemont, 15 rail bridges over highways, two rail bridges over other electric rail lines and six footbridges at stations, amounting to more than three bridges per mile.

All station platforms were built to the same height as the car floors. This provided easier and safer boarding for passengers, and it decreased dwell time. The P&W's entire right-of-way was lightly fenced, largely to keep animals off the tracks but also to discourage passengers from attempting to cross. Passengers got across the

The subway-elevated terminal was immediately adjacent to the P&W terminus at 69th Street Terminal. The three-track subway trackage is still intact. The P&W terminal has been completely rebuilt. P&W cars are in midday storage at top right. *P&W photo. Collection of Bob Foley.*

A view from the other direction shows an overhead employee bridge connecting with the P&W terminal which was removed in the 1930s. The P&W cars are in midday storage. The track in the middle of the photo is the connection to the Pennsylvania Railroad"s Cardington Branch, which survived into the 1960s. *P&W photo. Collection of Bob Foley.*

tracks by using either footbridges or stairs up or down to adjacent highways. Beechwood Park Station, where the railroad's amusement park was located, had a pedestrian underpass and a footbridge connecting the station with the park.

The $3000 stations were inexpensively constructed of wood with corrugated iron roofs. Most included a heated waiting room on the inbound side, and originally nearly all had ticket agents. Within the first year or two the agents were eliminated for lack of patronage, except at 69th Street Terminal, Bryn Mawr and Strafford. All of the platforms were covered with canopies so passengers could wait for and board trains without getting wet.

Garrett Hill was a typical station. The adjacent highway bridge obviated the need for a pedestrian bridge. *Collection of Robert Goshorn and Tredyffrin-Easttown History Club.*

At Strafford a loop was constructed on the east side of Sugartown Road, utilizing an old farm house as the temporary terminal until the tracks could be extended further westward toward Parkesburg. Third tracks were constructed at Bryn Mawr and at Beechwood Park, with two tracks straddling the inbound platforms. The Beechwood Park turnback track was installed to handle pleasure seekers who never materialized. The Bryn Mawr turnback track was designed so that local trains could be operated during peak periods only as far as Bryn Mawr and express trains could skip most stations between Bryn Mawr and 69th Street Terminal. The Beechwood Park turnback track was seldom used, and the Bryn Mawr track was not used regularly until 1911. There was also a siding at Strafford to permit car storage, but this, too, was never needed. A private telephone system connected all stations with the dispatcher at 69th Street Terminal.

The original Strafford Terminal was in an old converted farmhouse on a loop at the end of the line at Sugartown Road. The farmhouse served from 1907 until 1911, when the line was extended to the Pennsylvania Railroad Station. The crew relaxes on the porch during their brief layover. *Collection of Robert Goshorn and Tredyffrin-Easttown History Club.*

SETTLING IN

The Strafford loop viewed from the railroad's main line. The farmhouse-station is in the background. *Collection of Robert Goshorn and Tredyffrin-Easttown History Club.*

A train negotiates the Strafford loop. The bathroom window is clearly visible at the car's rear. *Collection of Robert Goshorn and Tredyffrin-Easttown History Club.*

P&W's original signal system consisted of semaphores. They were changed in the 1930s. *Collection of Howard L. E. Price.*

32 CHAPTER TWO

P&W's semaphore block signal system was furnished by General Railway Signal Company. Most interurban lines of the time did not think signals necessary, even on a single-track route, relying instead on train orders via company telephones.

The carbarn was built just outside 69th Street Terminal. It contained six tracks, two of which were for car maintenance and the others for indoor storage and routine inspections. The big concrete structure cost $100,000 and was designed so that at least two additions could easily be built, nearly doubling its size, but these additions never materialized. Skylights over all of the tracks made it an extremely well lighted facility.

THE THIRD RAIL

Trains were powered by an unusual under-running type of third-rail system, different than that used by the Market Street Elevated trains. It was an inverted U-shaped third-rail built by the Farnham Company of Chicago. The New York Central used the Farnham system, and the stillborn Chicago-New York Electric Air Line interurban was projected to use it. Most other properties equipped with under-running third-rail usually adopted the over-running Sprague-Wilgus system.

Anticipating the need for long and fast trains, P&W used third-rail current collection instead of overhead wire to enable it to run high-speed multiple-unit trains. It had not yet become possible to operate fast, multiple car trains with direct current using overhead wire, because insufficient power reached each car. Up to that time, all successful multiple-unit operations, such as subway and elevated systems, used third-rail. This could carry heavier currents directly to each car in a train, boosted by the use of two pickup shoes on each car as opposed to one trolley pole for overhead wire.

Most interurban lines couldn't choose third-rail because they had much side-of-the-road and street trackage. The first interurban to successfully employ trolley poles with overhead wire for fast multiple-unit operation was the Lake Shore Electric Railway in Ohio in 1906.

P&W used 625 volts direct current, which was the same as most other electric railways.

ROLLING STOCK

Unsurprisingly, P&W's first cars were built by the St. Louis Car Company, since they had been ordered while George Kobusch was still president of both the P&W and St. Louis Car. They were Nos. 25-46, reflecting the fact that the first group of cars actually ordered were

The first cars were built for fast service but had a top speed of only 45 miles an hour. They were wood cars with spoked wheels which made them look even older. This pair sits in front of the carbarn. Note the overhead poles and the lack of third-rail in the carbarn area. *Collection of Fred W. Schneider.*

supposed to be 1-22, but never arrived in 1905 because the P&W wasn't completed and was having financial problems. Two freight motors, which were also part of the 1905 order, were to be 23 and 24. They were accepted by the P&W in 1905, but were renumbered 101 and 102.

Wooden. 51-foot, 54-seaters 25-46 were painted dark green with maroon window trim and gold lettering. The interiors were done in mahogany with a marquetry inlay design. Fifteen cars had smoking compartments and seven were full coaches. All had restrooms. The cars had high-back walkover seats with headrests that were upholstered in green leather. They cost $12,300 each and weighed nearly 39 tons. A conductor staffed the rear door, from which passengers entered and departed.

While the cars were powered by the third-rail, they also contained an unusual sliding bow system for use under wires in the carbarn and the yard area. It was originally deemed unsafe to place third rail in these areas. Two small poles were installed on one end of each car, permanently upright, and a wire connected them. This wire made contact with the overhead wire in the carbarn area. This system was used in Germany, and a major advantage was that it worked well on sharp curves. The carbarn and yard track were connected to P&W's main line by an awkward curve on which the bow system functioned smoothly.

HISTORIC AREA SERVED

The P&W's route passed several historic sites. An historic mansion called The Grange, built in the early 1700s on property settled by a Welsh Quaker, is next to the tracks 1.6 miles from 69th Street Terminal. Its founder, Henry Lewis, was one of the first three Europeans to settle in Haverford Township in 1682. Just east of Beechwood Park Station were some early mills that made gunpowder for American troops in the War of 1812. One of them was in the way of the P&W, so the railroad purchased it but only tore down a corner of the old mill because of its historic value. The mill is still standing, but has been empty for a century.

Three very old colleges were served. Haverford College, a men's school with a national reputation, had its own

The Farnham Company designed P&W's unusual under-running third-rail. *Collection of Andrew W. Maginnis.*

station. Bryn Mawr College, a prestigious school for women, was within walking distance of the P&W but was much closer to the PRR station. A great many Villanova College students and employees used the P&W, whose station was adjacent to the school.

At Bryn Mawr, the P&W came within 150 feet of a portion of the old Philadelphia & Columbia Railroad. The Columbia line's White Hall Station still exists adjacent to the north side of the P&W. This portion was abandoned in 1871 when the Pennsylvania Railroad straightened out the route to run through Humphreysville, renamed Bryn Mawr. The old station building was acquired by Bryn Mawr Hospital, which first used it as a contagion ward. It is now the hospital's thrift shop. Employees of the hospital have always been an important source of business for the P&W.

Colleges and historic sites aside, despite its extraordinarily high level of construction, the P&W had a truly major problem: it didn't really go anywhere.

Running on its alignment south of Lancaster Pike and south of the Pennsy, the P&W served a sparsely populated territory. Only 12,000 people lived within a mile of the railroad, and the only towns of more than 2,000 souls were Ardmore, Bryn Mawr and Wayne. The P&W ran reasonably close to Bryn Mawr, but was too far away to easily walk to Ardmore and Wayne. With very few houses and no towns along the line, it did not appear that the P&W was going to be a success as a 10-mile passenger railroad. Business was so meager that half of the car fleet was rarely used and sat in temporary storage.

REVENUES FALL SHORT

The first three years of operation produced revenues of $344,000, but an operating profit of only $19,000. While business each year was up slightly, it was not rising nearly fast enough to make the P&W profitable and there was a large bond issue on which to pay interest. The line originally had 167 employees, including 10 ticket agents, seven powerhouse engineers, five firemen for the powerhouse, 14 conductors, 14 motormen and numerous

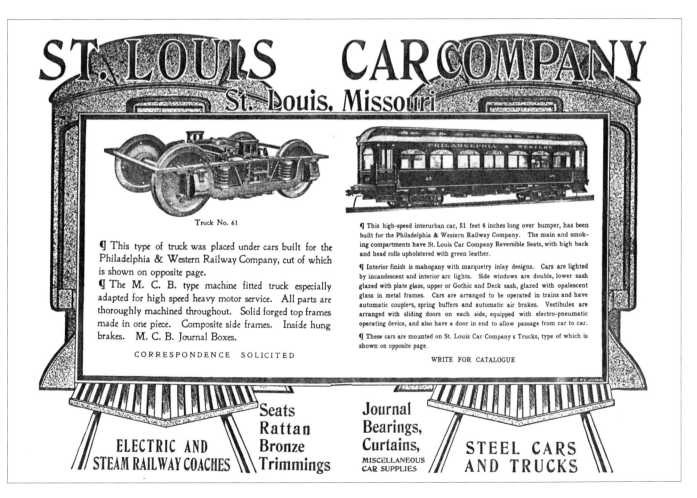

St. Louis Car Company ran ads touting its P&W cars in the trade journals. *Collection of Andrew W. Maginnis.*

The first fleet remained in service for only about 20 years. They mostly ran in single car service due to a lack of passengers. *Collection of Robert W. Lynch.*

The P&W's stations were built mostly of wood and corrugated iron. This is Ardmore Junction Station, where the P&W crossed over top of the Philadelphia & West Chester's Ardmore Line. *P&W photo. Collection of Bob Foley.*

car mechanics and maintenance men. This staff was quickly trimmed, and within a year most of the ticket agents were gone, the train crews had been reduced by half a dozen and there were far fewer car mechanics and track maintenance men. By 1910 the staff was down to 63, but even that wasn't enough.

Philadelphia & Western was sailing against stiff winds. As a result of the financial reorganization that had occurred two days before the P&W opened for business, George Sheldon had been elected president and Thomas Newhall vice president. Over the next two years, Sheldon met several times with officials of the Western Maryland Railroad hoping to revive interest in a westward extension of the P&W to York. The West Chester Daily Local News reported in early 1909 on new speculation that an extension to West Chester and Parkesburg was likely. But the financial depression of 1907 had made this improbable.

Sheldon also was still negotiating with the PRT, and in early 1910 announced a deal to permit P&W trains to run over the elevated directly to Center City. It was suggested that a third running rail could be laid on the Market Street Elevated to create dual-gauge trackage, but nothing was mentioned about the difference in the type of third-rail current collection. Again P&W officials mooted the possibility of building under the Delaware River to Camden, but it all remained just a dream. About the same time, PRT officials admitted that they had been attempting to lease the P&W.

Car 45 pauses at Bryn Mawr station in this postcard view dating from 1910. *Collection of John R. Nieveen.*

Bryn Mawr was originally built for three tracks, although short-turns were not scheduled until 1911. This view looks toward 69th Street Terminal. Note the old-style semaphore signal. The waiting room is on the upper left. *Collection of Harry P. Albrecht.*

A view from the other direction shows the trackage at Bryn Mawr Station. *P&W photo. Collection of Bob Foley.*

SETTLING IN

P&W files showed that its subsidiary, Southeastern Construction Company, was by 1908 "hopelessly insolvent," and it was soon abandoned. Feeble attempts were made to increase revenues. Another subsidiary, Homestead Real Estate Company, built a few houses along the line and sold some building lots. A new subsidiary, Villa Nova Sewage Company, was created in an unsuccessful attempt to develop the area.

COMPETITIVE ADVANTAGES

Motor and rail excursion service began in 1910 from Strafford to Valley Forge State Park by Norris City Company with five 20-passenger open touring cars. The tour covered 14 miles and included lunch at an old inn. The fare, including a round-trip on the P&W, was 95 cents. Valley Forge Park, where Washington's army had endured the winter of 1777-1778, had been created by the state on 472 acres in 1893. It was a popular tourist attraction and generated some traffic for the P&W, particularly in the summer.

The P&W did have some competitive advantages over the Pennsy. P&W operated about twice as many trains as the steam railroad, and its fares were cheaper. A one-way fare on the P&W and PRT from Bryn Mawr to Center City was only 16 cents, compared to 26 cents on the PRR. From Strafford, the combined P&W-PRT fare was 27 cents and on the PRR it was 39 cents. The travel time to Philadelphia, including the transfer at 69th Street Terminal, was only about two minutes longer than the PRR.

In addition, passengers on the P&W-PRT could detrain at numerous stations within the city. In 1908 the elevated was extended eastward to serve the city's principal shopping district and to make connections with the ferries to New Jersey, giving the elevated line 16 stations in the city. The PRR only offered stops at 32nd and Market or 15th and Market Streets, and traveling to the department stores or the ferries required a transfer to local trolleys or a long walk.

Four new stations were added to the P&W in 1908. West Overbrook was built at City Avenue a mile and a half from 69th Street Terminal. Penfield Station, east of Beechwood Park Station, served a new residential district along Manoa Road. Wynnewood Road Station also served a few houses as well as St. Denis Roman Catholic Church, one of the oldest Catholic parishes in the area. Haverford College Station, while only one-tenth of a mile from Haverford Station, was more convenient for students.

REORGANIZATION

P&W Vice President Newhall was a partner of Edward B. Smith & Company, one of the largest banking firms in the city. A descendant of Robert Morris, financier of the American Revolution, Newhall later became a partner in the J. P. Morgan firm. Newhall became a director of the P&W when the railroad was reorganized in May 1907. He persuaded Smith & Company to become interested in the P&W, and within the first three years of the railroad's operation it had acquired a

The entire 69th Street Terminal complex is shown in this 1907 view. The P&WCT section is on the right, the P&W section on the left. A St. Louis car is loading for Strafford. *Collection of Robert Goshorn and the Tredyffrin-Easttown History Club.*

View looking west at St. Davids Station, later renamed Wayne-St. Davids, in 1908. This station later became the end of double-track on the Strafford line; the footbridge was then eliminated. *Collection of Radnor Historical Society.*

majority of the stock. The Sheldon-Mackay Syndicate was happy to bail out, and the Smith Company announced on April 12, 1910, that it would take over. Newhall was elected president on the same day, and things quickly began to change.

"The present management assumed control and found the physical condition had been allowed to run down," Newhall reported to the board. "Heavy expenditures were necessary for renewals of ties, for repairs to motors and cars and for repairs to power house machinery. The principal item of expense was for the complete reconstruction of the third-rail; not only had the insulators not been maintained but their design was found to be defective and the clearance [for freight cars] insufficient."

Importantly, Newhall decided to scrap forever the dreams of westward expansion to Parkesburg, and the entire line beyond Strafford was officially abandoned on March 22, 1912. And he took immediate steps to forever change the destiny of the Philadelphia & Western.

Thomas Newhall, president of the P&W and the man most responsible for its early growth. *Collection of John Newhall.*

A two-car train passes a typical station on the Strafford line. *Collection of Chester County Historical Society.*

SETTLING IN

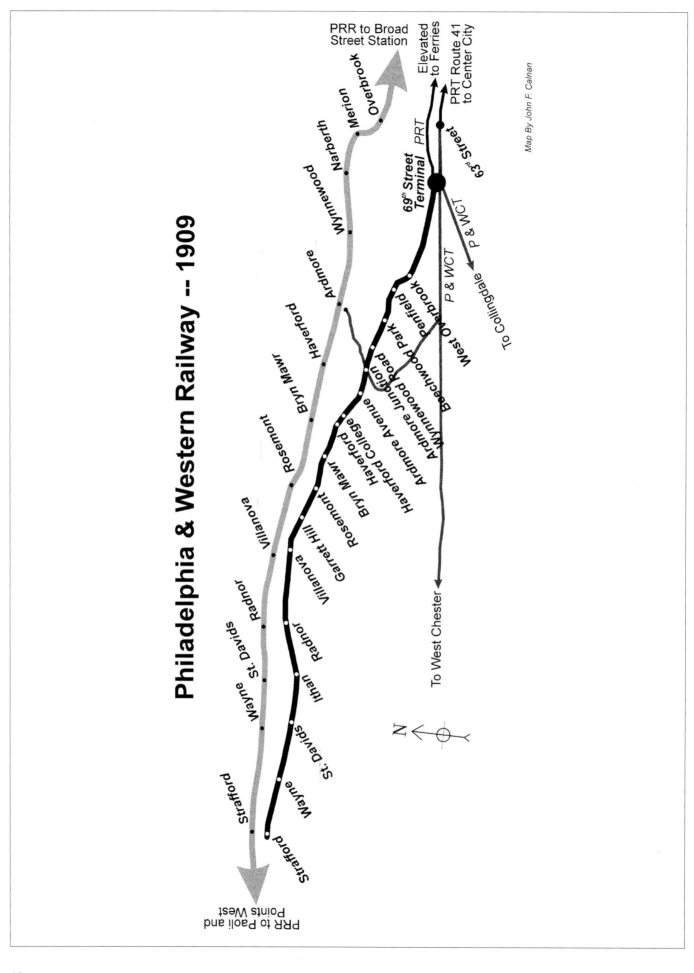

SERVICE PATTERNS, 1907-1910

P&W's first public timetable established a uniform 15-minute frequency, with the first train leaving 69th Street Terminal at 5:30 A.M. and the last train at 1:00 A.M. The same schedule applied on Sundays, except that there was only half hourly service before 7:30 A.M.

The first schedule turned out to be optimistic, and a new one only two months later reduced service before 1:00 P.M. to every 20 minutes. On October 7, 1907, trains began running every 10 minutes in peak periods. All trains ran to Strafford, but every other train operated non-stop between 69th Street Terminal and Haverford. The express schedule was also apparently premature, and effective January 1, 1908, trains ran every 15 minutes during the morning and afternoon peak periods and every 20 minutes in the midday and evening.

By mid-1909 the entire railroad was back to a 15-minute service, essentially the same schedule that had begun service on May 22, 1907, and this pattern continued through 1910. Most trains were operated with single cars.

THE STATIONS

This is a listing of the stations that existed in 1909, including mileage and running times from 69th Street Terminal as well as the cost of one-way fares and 60-trip monthly tickets. Ticket agents had by 1909 been eliminated at all stations except 69th Street Terminal, Beechwood Park (summer season only), Bryn Mawr and Strafford.

This sign appeared for many decades on the unloading platform of the Market Street Subway-Elevated platform at 69th Street Terminal. *Photo by Harre W. Demoro.*

Stations	Miles	Minutes	One-Way	Monthly
69th Street Terminal	0.0	—	—	—
West Overbrook	1.5	2	.05	2.10
Penfield	1.9	3	.05	2.30
Beechwood Park	2.6	5	.05	2.30
Wynnewood Road	3.2	6	.05	2.40
Ardmore Junction	3.5	7	.05	2.40
Ardmore Avenue	3.9	9	.08	2.40
Haverford College	4.5	10	.08	2.40
Haverford	4.7	11	.10	2.40
Bryn Mawr	5.4	13	.10	2.70
Rosemont	5.8	14	.12	3.00
Garrett Hill	6.3	16	.13	3.15
Villanova	7.0	17	.13	3.30
Radnor	8.2	20	.15	3.60
Ithan	8.8	21	.18	3.75
St. Davids	9.4	23	.18	3.90
Wayne	10.0	24	.20	4.05
Strafford	10.6	26	.22	4.35

Southbound Ardmore Junction Station as it appeared in the 1960s. The little stations originally had electric heaters for the comfort of passengers. *P&W photo. Collection of Bob Foley.*

BEECHWOOD POWERHOUSE

At the time that the P&W was built, railways could not simply purchase electric power from a nearby utility company. The railroads were forced to build their own power generating stations, a very expensive proposition.

P&W chose a spot 2.6 miles west of 69th Street Terminal and adjacent to Beechwood Park Station. Beechwood Amusement Park sat on a hill next to the station on the south side of the tracks. The powerhouse was built on the north side, slightly below the station and adjacent to Cobbs Creek. The big powerhouse structure was divided into two parts, the biggest portion for the boilers, turbines and superheaters and the other for a substation containing the transformers and rotary converters. The power station produced electricity at 25-cycle, 625-volts direct current for distribution to the railway. Feeder cables connected the powerhouse to a second substation just east of Ithan Station.

The original plans called for three additional powerhouses at Wayne, West Chester and Parkesburg to provide sufficient electricity for the proposed four-track, 44-mile railway. Beechwood Powerhouse was reportedly big enough to generate whatever power would be needed for extensions that had been considered to Norristown and Wilmington.

Ironically, the P&W depended upon the PRR for its lifeblood. A siding from the P&W's northbound main line just north of Beechwood Park Station included a concrete trestle alongside the outer boiler room wall that permitted coal to be dumped through chutes either directly into the boilers or into an outside storage area under the trestle. The fuel arrived regularly in standard hopper cars from a connection with the Pennsylvania Railroad just east of 69th Street Terminal. Ashes were removed in side-dump cars on a narrow gauge track running alongside the boilers.

The powerhouse was large enough to provide electricity for the proposed P&W extensions. *P&W photo. Collection of Bob Foley.*

A dam was constructed on Cobbs Creek a few hundred feet below the powerhouse, and a connection was made with Springfield Water Company half a mile away for periods when the creek was low or muddy.

The brick Ithan No. 1 Substation was six miles way. It contained two 500-kilowatt rotary converters, with room for a third which was never added. The Norristown extension, opened in 1912, included an additional substation located under the Bridgeport-Norristown viaduct just north of the Bridgeport Station at 4th Street.

World War I created a serious shortage of coal, causing the P&W's coal bill to increase by $44,000 in the year ending June 30, 1918, and another $45,000 following year. Overall, fuel for the Beechwood Powerhouse was now costing $165,000 a year, triple what it had been only three years earlier.

Recognizing this problem as early as 1917, P&W signed a contract to purchase cheaper electricity from Counties Gas & Electric Company. The conversion plan required the change from 25-cycle to 60-cycle operation, rendering the existing rotary converters useless. New substations were built at Beechwood and Villanova, and another was set up on the property of Counties Gas & Electric's generating plant in Norristown. The old substations at Beechwood, Ithan and Bridgeport were abandoned, along with the powerhouse.

The railroad began buying power on July 20, 1919. The huge powerhouse was closed and dismantled, although remnants of it remained standing for another 60 years and portions of the old Cobbs Creek dam are still visible. Although the total cost of the conversion project was $165,000, about $105,000 was recovered through the sale of abandoned equipment. Most of the powerhouse staff was eliminated, producing substantial annual operating savings.

After the powerhouse was abandoned in 1919, many concrete pillars stood in the valley for decades. *P&W photo. Collection of Bob Foley.*

SETTLING IN

CHAPTER THREE

Beechwood Park

MANY TROLLEY and interurban companies around the turn-of-the-20th century built amusement parks in order to draw additional passengers. They were enormously popular in the days before radio, television or automobiles. The secret was to build a park in a remote location that was difficult to reach except by trolley. Most people then worked six days a week, and on Sundays families would take a picnic lunch and spend the whole day at the place.

The largest and most successful park in the Philadelphia area was Willow Grove Park, built in 1896 by the predecessors of Philadelphia Rapid Transit several miles north of the city. John Phillip Sousa and his famous band performed regularly at Willow Grove. Another busy park was Woodside Park, constructed by the Fairmount Park Transportation Company in 1897 in Fairmount Park, within the City of Philadelphia. Both parks outlasted the trolleys that served them.

Neighboring Philadelphia & West Chester Traction Company, attempting to capitalize on the growing trend, opened Castle Rocks Park in 1899 about half way out its West Chester trolley line. It was largely a picnic park, with a few rides and a restaurant built among large rock formations adjacent to the tracks. But Castle Rocks was a long way out, and it suffered badly from the competition of Willow Grove and Woodside, both much bigger. The amusements at Castle Rocks closed in 1905, but the area remained a popular spot for Sunday School picnics into the mid-1920s.

Above: The entrance to Beechwood Park was impressive. This photo was taken in 1906 while the station and the park were still under construction. All aspects of the park were demolished within 10 years, and homes were built on the property. *Collection of Ronald DeGraw.* **Left:** Station as it appeared in the 1920s. The turnback track has been converted to the southbound main track. The Beechwood Substation is in the upper right. *Collection of Warren Speegle.*

About the same time that Castle Rocks was being abandoned as an amusement park, the Philadelphia & Western was formulating plans to build its own park at Beechwood, a five-minute ride out of 69th Street Terminal. This park opened with great fanfare on May 30, 1907, a week after the railroad began running. Five thousand visitors attended the ceremonies, which featured the Royal Imperial Italian Band, decked out in red and green uniforms. The nickelodeon played The Great Train Robbery and European acrobats performed for the breathless throngs.

P&W ran special trains from 69th Street to Beechwood, where a third track permitted trains to turn back. Beechwood Park Station was the biggest one on the railroad, costing $16,000 to build, the same as the P&W's portion of 69th Street Terminal. Judging from its opening day, the park had a brilliant future. But as it turned out, Beechwood Park would make Castle Rocks Park look like a raging success.

Some 15,000 visitors could be accommodated at the park, which offered a roller coaster, a ferris wheel, a big midway with a 32-foot wide boardwalk, a tunnel-of-love, a crazy house, games of chance, a bandstand, a merry-go-round, swings, a Japanese garden, a restaurant, a dance hall and several other amusements. Fireworks were a big attraction on Friday nights. An artificial lake created by the dam constructed for the P&W's powerhouse across the tracks from the park featured rowboats that could be rented for 25 cents.

William C. Sheldon, P&W's president, told newspapers that "the many new attractions offered at Beechwood Park are certain to draw large crowds, particularly on holidays and evenings, when a fast, clean, cool ride on the elevated and on our line will be a great relief to many persons."

An enterprising real estate company promoted "choice sites" for homes in "beautiful Beechwood," just across the tracks from the park. "On the wooded highlands skirting historic Cobbs Creek, Beechwood is the choicest and most picturesque location on the line of the new Electric Road, which is bound to cause a remarkable rise in values soon," touted its advertisement. Prices for house lots ranged from $120 to $390, with a $2.00 down payment and weekly payments of $1.00 to $2.00.

DISAPPOINTING ATTENDANCE

But the weather was bad that first summer, and a riot in front of the gypsy fortuneteller's tent required the intervention of state police and damaged the park's reputation. A depression in 1907 also caused potential visitors to stay away. Less than two months after the park opened, it went into receivership. The park owed $30,844 to its bondholders and had been losing $700 a week. Treasurer Loren N. Downes of the P&W was named receiver.

The passenger platforms were wide and the overhead pedestrian bridge was spacious enough to handle the expected crowds that never materialized. The park entrance was on the right. There were three tracks at the station to accommodate short-turn trains. *Collection of Ronald DeGraw.*

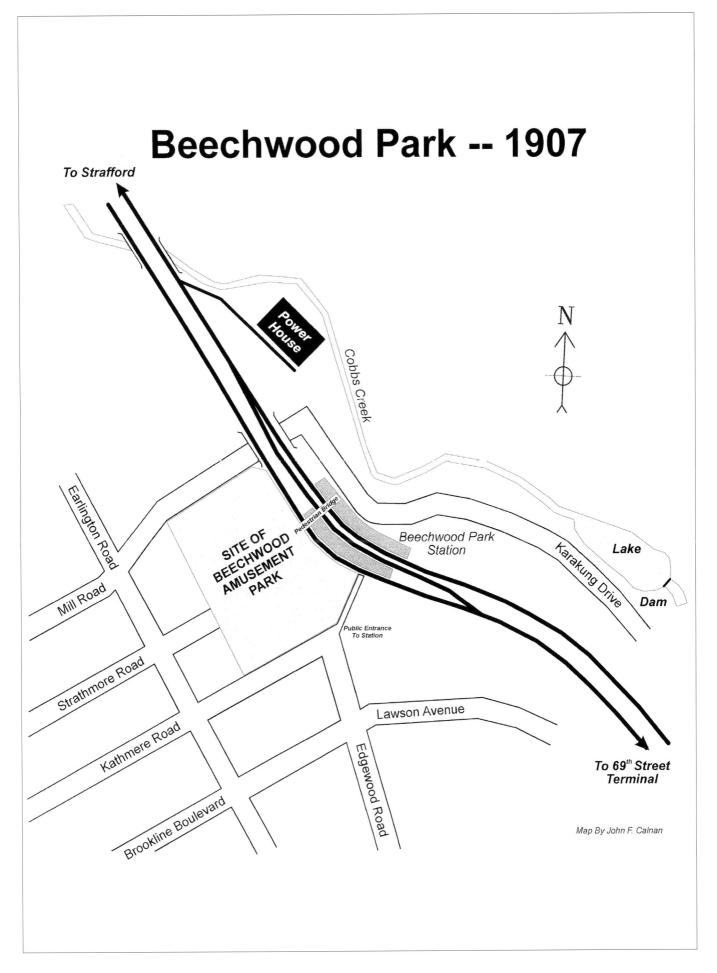

Frank H. Libbey, a park company bondholder and treasurer had petitioned for the receivership, and he attributed the financial problems to "bad weather and poor management." The park had been capitalized at $300,000, and 3,000 shares of stock were issued. Some 150 bonds were offered for sale at $150 each, but there were no takers for 108 of them. Hugh Kyle, a representative of the park, promised it would carry on. Reconstruction work would be commenced immediately, more amusements added, and the officers changed, he said.

But Kyle was an optimist. The park survived the 1907 season, reopened for Decoration Day (now Memorial Day) through Labor Day in 1908, and opened again on Decoration Day of 1909. But it closed for good in early August of 1909. The amusements were dismantled, the buildings crumbled, and the land was sold a decade later. Houses were constructed in the 1920s. In 1919 the powerhouse across the tracks from the park was also abandoned when the P&W began purchasing its electric power. The railway generating plant had also produced the electricity for the park.

The extra track was removed from Beechwood Park Station, and even the station's name was changed in 1923 to Beechwood-Brookline.

Nearly all traces of the park disappeared, but numerous concrete pillars which had supported the powerhouse, the large station platforms and the entrance to the park, remained standing for several decades. A few of the old concrete stanchions can still be spotted. The original wooden station endured until 1958, its platform narrowed with the elimination of the third track. It was then replaced by a concrete and brick structure.

The subsidiary company formally went out of business in 1910, but for more than 80 years its name remained, painted in gold leaf outlined in red on the door of a big walk-in vault inside the P&W carbarn: "Beechwood Park Amusement Co." The door was finally repainted in 1992.

The outbound Beechwood Park Station platform had a smaller shelter and platform. Opposite to it was the railroad's Beechwood Power House, which generated electrical power for the P&W until 1919. *Collection of Ronald DeGraw.*

Newspaper advertisement selling house lots in Beechwood. *Collection of Ronald DeGraw.*

After the collapse of Beechwood Park, the third track was removed and the station received a name change to Beechwood-Brookline. *Collection of Ronald DeGraw.*

The narrowed station became just another residential station, but with interesting concrete pillars all around. Roger and Jeffrey Prichard lived nearby; both youngsters later became avid railfans. *Collection of Roger T. Prichard.*

CHAPTER FOUR
Building for Survival
1911-1912

SOMETHING HAD to be done about P&W's disappointing ridership. New president Thomas Newhall had two ideas about this, and both included extensions. Newhall had ceased to believe that any future westward expansion of the P&W had any merit, and he had no trouble persuading his board of directors. He also convinced the board to extend the Strafford line half a mile beyond Sugartown Road (now Old Sugartown Road). The "temporary" end of the line in Strafford was unsatisfactory. Because only a few large homes surrounded the station, ridership was low.

Newhall's proposal extended the railroad in a giant half-circle ending adjacent to the Pennsylvania Railroad's Strafford Station on Old Eagle School Road. Work on the $100,000 half-mile extension began early in 1911 and it opened on October 11 of that year. This brought the total mileage on the Strafford line to 11.1. It meant that trains traveling west from 69th Street Terminal were facing east by the time they finished their run.

The extension required bridges over Sugartown Road and Lancaster Avenue. The old Strafford loop was abandoned, and the temporary farmhouse terminal was sold. A smaller station was constructed on the east side of Sugartown Road. The double track continued across Lancaster Avenue, then went into single track, then branched into a wye. One leg of the wye went east to the new Strafford terminal, whose station included a ticket agent, a waiting room and two tracks. Conveniently, it was connected by a stairway to the inbound platform of the PRR's station. The other leg of the wye curved west and met the Pennsy's tracks for the interchange of freight cars, although it never received much use.

Newhall believed that more riders would show up if passengers could transfer between P&W and PRR trains. But business increased only slightly.

The P&W president's second idea was much better. It changed the entire future of the P&W—indeed, caused the P&W to have a future. It would be the extension to Norristown.

Above: The new Strafford Station, immediately adjacent to the Pennsylvania Railroad's Strafford Station, opened in 1911. It contained two tracks and a ticket agent. *Photo by Aaron Fryer.* **Left:** The Norristown line under construction near Gulph Mills. *P&W photo. Collection of Bob Foley.*

BUILDING FOR SURVIVAL

THE LIBERTY BELL ROUTE

Providing the key to the P&W's ultimate success and survival was a country trolley line that wandered for 46 miles from the city of Allentown, in the Lehigh Valley, to Erdenheim, just over Philadelphia's northwest city boundary of Chestnut Hill. Like the P&W, the Lehigh Valley Transit Company's creators dreamed of bigger things. LVT was conceived as a super trolley line running from Allentown to Philadelphia, then up to New York City. Although the New York idea had been buried by 1910, it was replaced by visions of an interurban that would hustle passengers from Allentown to downtown Philadelphia at mile-a-minute speeds. LVT also operated the city and suburban transit routes in Allentown, Bethlehem and Easton. As a whole, LVT's rail network eventually covered 215 route miles.

Edward B. Smith & Company, the large Philadelphia banking house that now owned the P&W, had previously swallowed up the LVT and had the financial resources to carry out such improvements. In fact, it had acquired the P&W with the intent of welding the two electric railways into a high-speed interurban route from Allentown to 69th Street Terminal via Norristown.

P&W train crews looked sharp in their early uniforms. Here, conductor David Kenney and a motorman pose in front of a St. Louis car at the carbarn. *Collection of David Kenney.*

As the largest electric railway system in Eastern Pennsylvania, LVT had always wanted a fast entrance to Center City Philadelphia. LVT's predecessor, the Philadelphia & Lehigh Valley Traction Company, opened its line to Erdenheim in 1903. It was a slow, meandering trolley route that offered little competition for the rival Philadelphia & Reading Railway's steam trains. The Reading served many of the same towns as the Lehigh Valley trolleys, and it ran directly to downtown Philadelphia. The one-hour ride on slow Philadelphia Rapid Transit Company streetcars from Erdenheim to downtown Philadelphia discouraged through ridership on the LVT. Knowing this, LVT had vainly attempted to make the short connection from Erdenheim to the Chestnut Hill stations of the Reading or the Pennsylvania, to speed up the connection to Center City.

Albert L. Johnson consolidated and expanded electric railway companies in the Allentown area and envisioned a 250-mile interurban network running from Allentown to Scranton, Reading, Bangor, New York and Philadelphia, in addition to a line from Philadelphia to New York. Johnson died prematurely, but he did manage to put most of the trolley lines in the Lehigh Valley into a single management and to build the long Erdenheim line. The Johnson properties changed ownership in 1905 and acquired a new name, the Lehigh Valley Transit Company.

The Erdenheim line was dubbed the "Liberty Bell Route" because it followed a routing similar to the one used by patriots to move the Liberty Bell to Allentown when the British invaded Philadelphia in 1777. It was a catchy name, and it stuck. Daylong excursions plied the Liberty Bell Route from Erdenheim through Allentown to the Delaware Water Gap, a popular tourist attraction, beginning in 1908.

THE P&W REACHES FOR NORRISTOWN

Since the Smith company now controlled both the LVT and the P&W, it became possible to build the high-speed entrance to Philadelphia that Johnson had envisioned. Much of the planning had already been done by the time Smith officially acquired control of the P&W on August 12, 1910. LVT would spend $5 million to relocate and rebuild much of its trackage between Allentown and Lansdale and construct a new route from Lansdale to Norristown, the county seat of Montgomery County. The new high-speed service would reduce the trolley trip time from Allentown to Center City Philadelphia by one hour and 15 minutes.

Montgomery Traction Company's original line ran down DeKalb Street past Norristown's City Hall. *Collection of John R. Nieveen.*

Montgomery Traction ran four-wheel cars from Lansdale to Norristown, which were acquired by Lehigh Valley Transit Company. *Collection of Ronald DeGraw.*

However, the original plan called for the P&W to build north from Villanova to meet up with the LVT at Lansdale. One of the first routings under consideration ran via West Conshohocken to Norristown, serving the huge Alan Wood Steel Company in Swedeland. P&W even filed papers to create the West Conshohocken Transit Company. It hired Stone & Webster Engineering Corporation of Boston, a major electric railway construction company, to design and build the connection with the LVT. In all, seven different routings were considered, including two from Strafford to Norristown.

The path via Gulph Mills was selected, and the plan called for P&W to purchase the faltering Montgomery Traction Company, which had a slow 12-mile trolley route from Norristown to Lansdale. Montgomery Traction was to be upgraded and realigned to provide high-speed service. MT had begun operating in 1902, but it was not making money. Nevertheless, P&W was prepared to pay $200,000 in cash and $17,500 in bonds for Montgomery Traction.

With the extension north to Norristown or beyond, serious consideration was given to changing P&W's name to the Philadelphia & Northern Railway Company.

THE NORRISTOWN TRANSIT COMPANY

There appeared to be some doubt, however, over the legal right of P&W—which had a steam railroad charter—to construct a new line that would use a street railway charter from Norristown to Lansdale. The more the plan was refined, the higher the cost went, and there was fear P&W wouldn't be able to finance construction of the entire spur. Just the extension of the P&W to Norristown would cost $2 million.

So the plan was modified, with P&W building only the six-mile branch from Villanova Junction to Norristown and LVT constructing the portion from Lansdale to the northern borough limits of Norristown. A paper entity—Norristown Transit Company—was created to build and own the single-track line running for two miles through the streets of Norristown. But not everyone was happy. The Norristown Chamber of Commerce and local businessmen opposed the construction of an elevated structure over Swede Street between the Schuylkill River and Penn Street. In June 1910, P&W officials implied that they were going to build the LVT connection by way of Conshohocken instead of Norristown. Hearing this, Norristown Town Council voted approval on June 21, with Norristown Transit agreeing to pay $65,000 for street paving over the next few years.

P&W and LVT each owned half the stock of the new subsidiary, but LVT always operated and maintained Norristown Transit as an integral part of its Allentown to Norristown route. Newhall was appointed NT's vice president. Bridgeport Town Council officially endorsed construction of the P&W on October 3, 1911, but only after the railroad agreed to pay the borough $5,000. Not bothering to wait, P&W had begun construction before receiving the actual approval.

The Philadelphia & Reading Railway, which carried most Norristown passengers destined for Philadelphia, was now worried. The Reading promised to run faster trains to Philadelphia, cutting eight minutes off of the existing 29-minute express time.

Showing how much times had changed, the august William W. Atterbury, general manager and later president of the Pennsylvania Railroad, had warmed to the P&W and began to buy its stock. While the PRR never officially held P&W stock, Atterbury himself would later become the fourth largest P&W shareholder and he bought $30,000 in P&W bonds. Atterbury and Newhall, it seemed, both lived near the P&W in Ithan, and Atterbury's interest was proof that relations between the PRR and the P&W were now amicable. The PRR now fully cooperated when the Norristown branch twice needed to cross under its tracks. The freight connection between the P&W and the PRR at Strafford permitted much of the construction material for the Norristown line to arrive by railroad freight cars.

ENGINEERING CHALLENGES

P&W's Norristown spur called for some unusual engineering feats, and the experienced Stone & Webster lost no time in getting the project underway. The line branched off from the Strafford route a quarter mile west of Villanova Station. It curved through hilly land occupied by large estates and involved two miles of deep cuts. The largest cut was 2,100 feet long and 50 feet deep. The biggest fill was 3,300 feet long and 54 feet high. A half million cubic yards of earth and rock had to be moved. There were seven highway bridges over the tracks and nine railway bridges over highways or farm lanes, in addition to the two crossings under the PRR. The bridges were all built by the Pennsylvania Steel Corporation. An electric substation was constructed under the viaduct adjacent to the Bridgeport Station, supplementing the powerhouse and substation at Beechwood Park and the other substation at Ithan.

The going was tough. A report prepared by Stone & Webster in 1911 admitted that "the work of surveying was one of great difficulty. The property owners were very much opposed to the line, and in order to avoid any possible damage suits...the owners placed the strictest of instructions on the locating engineer. The placing of stakes became a misdemeanor, trimming of bushes criminal, and such an act as placing a benchmark on a tree assumed the proportions of capital crime."

Once again the railroad battled Mary Chew and Martha Brown for land it needed north of Villanova Junction, and the two women kept up another court fight for several years, no doubt encouraged by a court award of $75,000 in their original suit. Several wealthy Main Liners formed an association to try to block the extension on grounds that it would reduce property values. Even Radnor Township's commissioners entered the fray in opposition to the Norristown extension. But nothing delayed construction of the line.

As planned, the entire Norristown branch except for the Schuylkill River Bridge was double-track to the same high standards used in the construction of the Strafford line. There was no longer any need to expect long freight trains, so the branch had many more curves, albeit most of them minimal.

The contract with Stone & Webster was signed on April 20, 1911. Construction began in May and was completed in only 15 months, including the three-quarter-mile long bridge at Norristown. A subsidiary, DeKalb Realty Company, was formed to acquire the right-of-way. DeKalb had about 200 acres of land left over, some of which was sold and some developed into housing adjacent to King Manor Station, where it built a few houses and sold several lots to individuals.

Five hundred workmen, most of them Italian immigrants, began to build the line simultaneously at four locations. Crews began working from Villanova Junction northward and from Bridgeport southward. Construction began on the piers for the Norristown Bridge and on track in the streets of Norristown. A month after construction began, 25 laborers building the Norristown Transit line on Markley Street went on strike. They were making $1.50 a day and demanded $1.75. Local police were called to restore order, wages were not raised and the recalcitrant workers were quickly replaced.

A view of the cut around Rebel Hill. South Gulph Road appears below. Hanging Rock is just out of the photo at the bottom left. *P&W photo. Collection of Bob Foley.*

Workers laying the track adjacent to Yerkes Road in Upper Merion Township had an especially hazardous job. They had to dodge rocks as big as footballs that flew out of an adjacent quarry. The railroad took court action to limit the size of the quarry's blasts and forced the erection of a 20-foot screen fence.

Another place where rocks caused a problem was at Gulph Mills, where the railroad had cut a shelf into the side of Rebel Hill. Small rockslides menaced the workers so the company built a shanty and a night watchman was hired to report on rockslides. Crossovers were installed at Gulph Mills Station and at Matsonford Road so that trains could operate single-track through the area if rocks fell on the track nearest the mountain. Two days after service on the Norristown line began, the watchman sat on the third-rail coverboard at Gulph Mills to rest, fell asleep and was killed by a train.

Two fatalities marred the line's construction. A riveter fell from the viaduct in Bridgeport and broke his neck. Another died after being struck by a small construction locomotive south of Gulph Mills.

Just north of Villanova a bridge was needed to carry the P&W under the Pennsylvania Railroad's four-track main line. Halfway to Norristown the route was blocked by a range of high hills with only one small creek valley cutting through them. Next to the creek was Gulph Road, leaving no additional room for tracks. Stone & Webster chose to carve into the side of Rebel Hill, adjacent to and above the highway. This expensive project retained the P&W's minimal grades, made any highway grade crossings unnecessary and assured high speeds.

A bridge to take P&W under the PRR's Trenton Cut-Off had to be built two miles south of Norristown. This line had opened in 1892 between Morrisville, near Trenton, and Frazer, west of Paoli, as a Philadelphia bypass for Pennsy freight trains running between New York City and the west. The P&W crossed the Trenton Cut-Off nearly a mile south of King Manor Station at an area that the PRR called Rambo.

The greatest challenge to Stone & Webster was the section between Bridgeport and Norristown. The towns were separated by the Schuylkill River which had a canal on each side of it, and numerous railroad tracks along both banks. On the Bridgeport side was the Reading's main freight line to the west and a large locomotive roundhouse. On the Norristown side was the Reading's main passenger line to the west, the PRR's Schuylkill Branch and the double-track streetcar line of Schuylkill Valley Traction Company on Main Street. A spectacular bridge 3,850 feet long was designed to carry the P&W over all of these obstacles. It was built to steam railroad standards so that it could withstand the weight of a train of cars each weighing 50 tons. P&W's steelwork arrived on PRR flatcars and was dragged to Swede Street by 14-horse teams as local residents gathered to watch.

P&W #45 traverses "Brown's Cut" southbound on the Norristown Line in 1912. *Collection of Joel Salomon.*

On the Norristown side, the large Wyoming Cotton Mill stood right next to the river and obstructed a direct entrance to Swede Street. Rather than pay to purchase the building, the P&W simply built an eight-degree reverse curve in the bridge to go around the mill, reducing the speed of trains slightly. The big brick building burned about 1930 and was demolished, but the kink was never straightened out. There is also a 2 percent ascending grade outbound on the Norristown side of the bridge.

THE NORRISTOWN TERMINAL

The Schuylkill River Bridge was designed for double-track, but this was simply too expensive. So the last three-quarters of a mile of the extension was single-track. Costly bridge piers wide enough for a future second track were considered, but rejected. The bridge structure on the Norristown side continued as an elevated railway alongside Swede Street. After it crossed over Main Street, the structure began to descend to meet Swede Street, running uphill. The track entered the roadway at Swede and Penn Streets and swung into the middle of Swede. P&W trains terminated 160 feet further in front of the Montgomery County Court House.

Norristown Transit owned the street trackage, although it was operated as a part of the Lehigh Valley Transit Company. It began at the northern end of the viaduct.

Just beyond the courthouse, the track curved to the west into Airy Street and ran three blocks to Markley Street, thence to the borough limits at Johnson Highway. Norristown Transit's single-track line was 1.9 miles long. LVT trackage officially began at Johnson Highway, curving off onto private right-of-way heading for Allentown.

The only passing siding on the Norristown Transit line was in Airy Street near Swede Street, where P&W operators switched cars with LVT men from 1912 until about 1926. After 1926, the siding was moved to Markley and Marshall Streets.

P&W cars had to raise and lower trolley poles for the last block of street running, and that was awkward and time-consuming. To avoid this, P&W had originally designed an ornate terminal to occupy the block of Swede Street between Main and Penn Streets. This would have established the terminal building on the north end of the elevated structure where there was third rail. But as the cost of the Norristown extension continued to rise, plans for the ornate terminal were postponed, especially after Norristown Town Council demanded a $25,000 fee for the use of the portion of the public square that would be occupied by the building. Instead, an old hotel on Swede Street was utilized as the Norristown ticket office and waiting room.

Interestingly, the Rambo House was a small hotel and tavern that had been built in 1810. It was immediately across from the front door of the court house and adjacent to the P&W terminus on Swede Street. P&W and LVT had a joint ticket office and waiting room on the ground floor of the hotel, which was about half a story below the sidewalk level. It was a cheap alternative, but it meant that for the next 19 years P&W conductors had to

The signal tower was constructed over Aldwyn Lane at Villanova when the Norristown branch was built in 1912. The building survived for 80 years. *Photo by Aaron Fryer.*

A rockslide has closed the northbound track on Rebel Hill in 1932. A work train is removing the debris. *P&W photo. Collection of Bob Foley.*

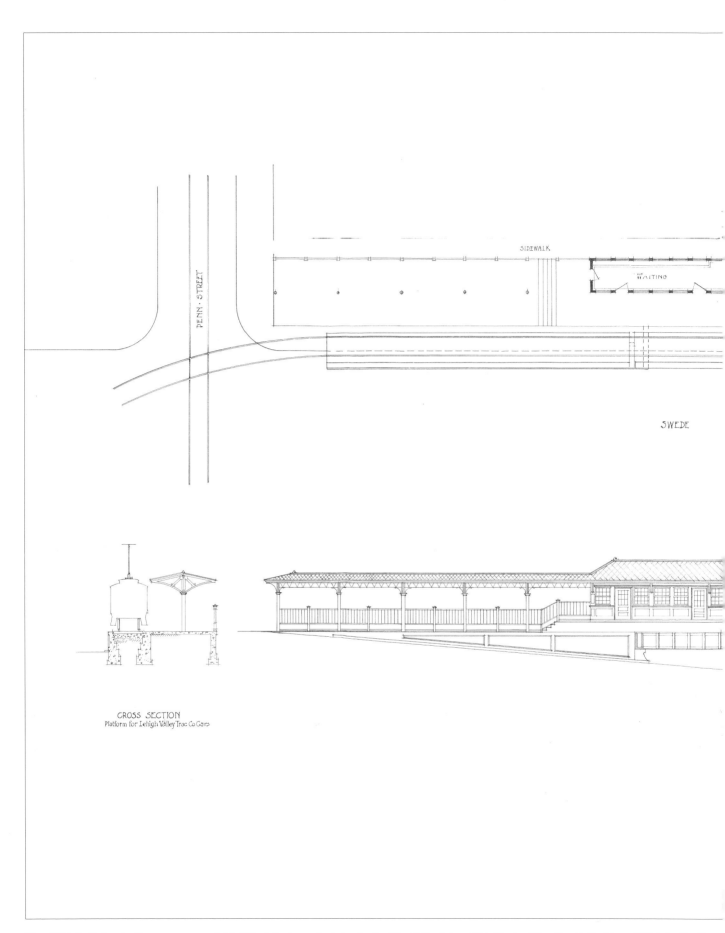

Stone & Webster Engineering Company recommended that this station be constructed on the Norristown bridge between Main Street and Penn Street in Norristown. P&W shelved the idea for financial reasons, opting instead to use Swede Street, which caused traffic congestion for the next 20 years. *Collection of Ronald DeGraw.*

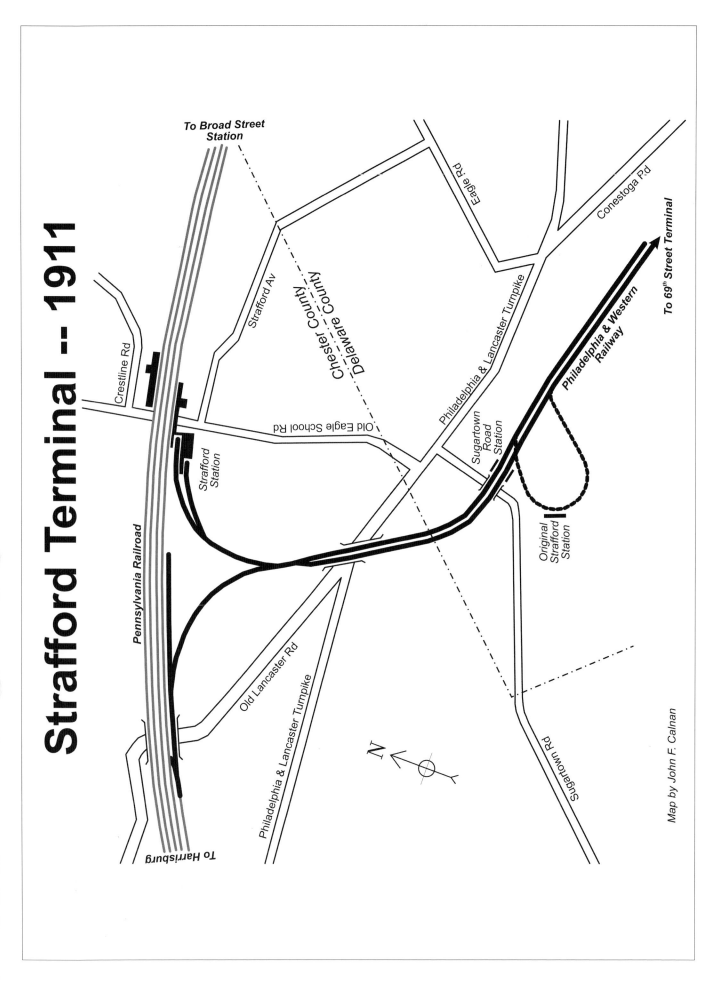

THE NORRISTOWN BRIDGE

The long Norristown bridge was a major accomplishment. It spanned two canals, four railroads, a trolley line, the Schuylkill River and several highways. Construction has just begun in this photo. *Collection of Ronald DeGraw.*

A huge McClintock Marshall Co. steam crane clears the right-of-way approaching the Norristown Bridge. It was also used in the construction of that structure. *Collection of Ronald DeGraw.*

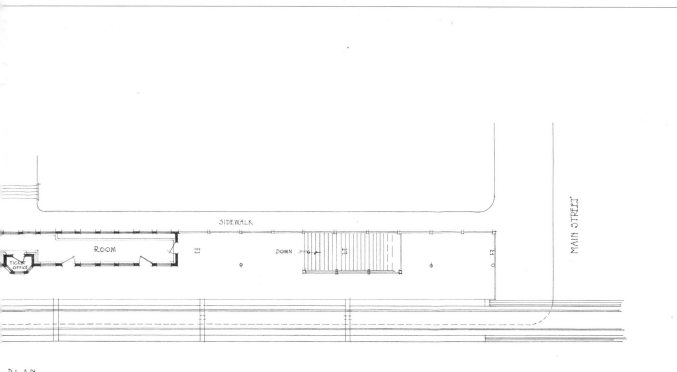

PLAN

STREET

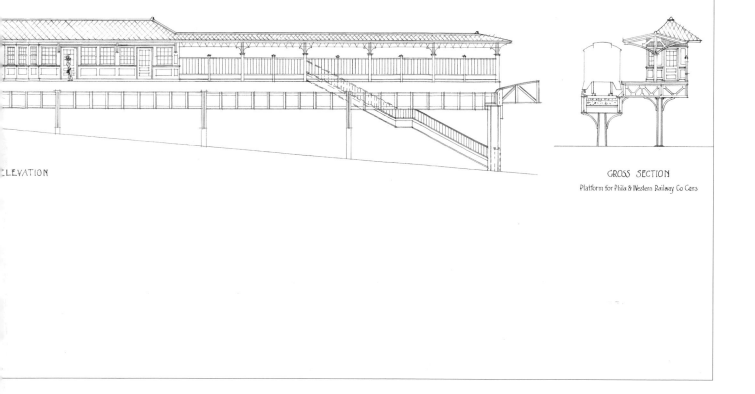

ELEVATION

CROSS SECTION
Platform for Phila & Western Railway Co Cars

CHAPTER FOUR

The bridge had a major kink in it at the Norristown end, built to bypass the Wyoming Cotton Mill factory which stood on the river at Norristown. The factory burned down a few years later, but the kink remained. *Photo by James H. Bean.*

A St. Louis car crosses the completed Norristown bridge, which was impressive, massive and very sturdy. *P&W photo. Collection of Bob Foley.*

P&W's derrick car and a flatcar aided in construction of the Schuylkill River bridge. *Collection of David Biles.*

The bridge is being built over top of Main Street in Norristown. *Collection of Montgomery County Historical Society.*

The bridge over Main Street featured two large clocks which became town landmarks for the next 40 years. It even was featured on a postcard. The photo was taken about 1915. *Collection of Harry P. Albrecht.*

BUILDING FOR SURVIVAL

lean out the back door of their trains to raise or lower a trolley pole in order to serve the Norristown terminal. Standard spring-loaded trolley poles had long since replaced the early sliding bows on the roofs of the cars.

Third-rail shoes on both the P&W and LVT cars were automatically lowered or raised as cars approached or departed from the elevated structure in Norristown. The P&W's general manager and chief engineer, H. S. Farquhar, devised a simple, non-mechanical means of accomplishing this. But the trolley poles on the cars could only be raised or lowered manually. There was a very short stretch of overlapping third rail and overhead wire, and it was possible for trains to make the changeover without stopping.

Controversy arose over the P&W's selection of Swede Street, in the heart of Norristown's business district. Many businessmen didn't want an elevated line crossing Main Street because they didn't think it would look attractive, and there was pressure on the railroad to choose a street other than Swede. But the P&W persisted and won the right to have a terminal station right in the heart of downtown Norristown.

SERVING A LANDMARK REGION

The Norristown branch was 6.3 miles long and was built for maximum speed. The only restrictions were at the Villanova Junction curve, around Rebel Hill and on the Norristown Bridge. On the rest of the branch, cars ran as fast as they could go. And there were few passenger stops along the way to slow them down. Leaving Villanova going north, the first station was at Gulph Mills (then called Gulph), a distance of 2.7 miles. It was a sleepy little village with a few houses, a small inn and some flour and grist mills that dated back as early as 1747. There were few passengers, so trains did not often have to stop there.

Near Gulph Mills Station, which at that time was where Gulph Road (now Trinity Lane) crosses underneath the railroad, was a famous local landmark, Hanging Rock (then called Overhanging Rock). This icon was on the highway below where the P&W clung to the side of Rebel Hill through the only pass for miles around. George Washington's Revolutionary Army camped here from December 13 to 19, 1777, on its way to winter quarters at Valley Forge after the British had taken Philadelphia. A few feet from the P&W right-of-way was an old home that served as the headquarters for the Colonial Army's picket line protecting Valley Forge from a British attack. Lieutenant Colonel Aaron Burr, in charge of the picket line, was stationed here. The building survives as—what else?— a restaurant.

North from Gulph Mills, it was another 2.3 miles before the next station, originally called DeKalb Street but soon changed to King Road. This served the upper part

The northern end of the bridge declined to reach Swede Street, on the left. Tracks then turned into Swede Street, where the terminal was directly in front of the Montgomery County Court House. *Collection of Railroad Avenue Enterprises.*

The ramp from the bridge looking south. Swede Street is on the right. *P&W photo. Collection of Bob Foley.*

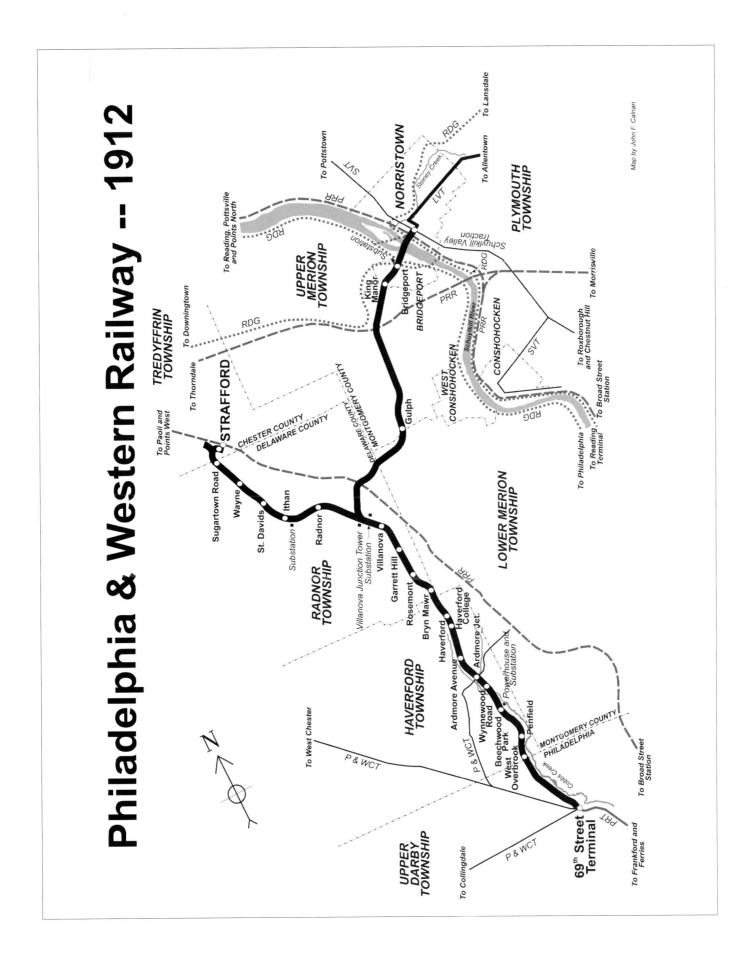

of Bridgeport, and was well patronized. Its name was changed in 1926 to King Manor. Bridgeport Station was a half-mile further. Situated over 4th Street on the single-track approach to the long Norristown Bridge, it much resembled a junior version of one of the Market Street Elevated's stations in West Philadelphia. The Norristown terminal in Swede Street was another eight-tenths of a mile north.

Trains covered the distance from Villanova to Norristown in 13 minutes, with the entire trip from 69th Street Terminal taking 26 minutes.

Indeed, the Borough of Norristown made an excellent terminus for the P&W. Even without the LVT connection, Norristown generated much traffic for the new electric railway. The land that became Norristown was sold in 1704 to Isaac Norris for 50 cents an acre by William Penn, the founder of Pennsylvania. Montgomery County was formed in 1784, and the courthouse was built at Norristown, which became a separate municipality in 1812 and had a population of 30,000 when the P&W opened. Its status as county seat was in itself enough to generate a great many riders.

Norristown was served by trolleys from the east (as far as Roxborough and Barren Hill) and from the west (Pottstown and Boyertown), as well as local cars to Conshohocken, Bridgeport, Swedeland and Norristown State Hospital. Railroads had served Norristown since 1835; it was on the Philadelphia & Reading's main line from Philadelphia to Reading, Harrisburg and Pottsville, as well as a branch line—the Stony Creek line—that ran to Lansdale. Norristown was also on the Pennsy's Schuylkill Branch, which virtually paralleled the Reading's main line. The P&W's Norristown extension opened just a little over three months after the Borough of Norristown's official centennial celebration, held May 5-11, 1912.

SIGNALS AND THE THIRD RAIL

For this new electric line, an automatic three-position upper quadrant semaphore block signal system was installed by General Railway Signal Company. The double-track portion of the line was originally divided into only three blocks in each direction, with the single-track Norristown Bridge established as a separate block. An interlocking tower was built at Villanova Junction. The junction was immediately west of where Aldwyn Lane (then Villa Nova Road) crossed underneath the original Strafford line, and the tower needed to be located exactly at Aldwyn Lane at the beginning of the junction turnouts. Rather than move Aldwyn Lane and pay to build a new highway bridge under the tracks, P&W took the unusual step of constructing the interlocking tower over the top of the street.

As we have seen, the third-rail on the P&W was originally a bottom-contact type of system. Power pickup shoes attached to the trucks of the rail cars had a spring mechanism that pressed up against the underside of the third-rail. This method may have originally been chosen by P&W because it did not require the payment of patent royalties and was therefore cheaper. But it was soon deemed unsatisfactory because the insulators cracked, causing power loss, and because its clearances were insufficient for standard railroad freight cars.

Management now seized the opportunity to invert the third-rail, turning it into an over-running system. The Norristown extension was built with the new type of third-rail, and the original line to Strafford was converted. This was efficiently accomplished under traffic. The third-rail shoes on the cars were temporarily modified to permit top or bottom contact so that trains could continue operating during the conversion. A wooden coverboard provided protection for maintenance workers.

When the Norristown branch was designed, some consideration had been given to converting the entire railroad to overhead trolley wire, but the board of directors vetoed this suggestion.

The Bridgeport Station was built over top of 4th Street, closely resembling a miniature elevated station on Market Street. Adjacent to it was the Bridgeport Substation, abandoned in 1919. *Collection of Ronald DeGraw.*

Villanova Junction as it appeared in 1912. The Strafford branch goes straight ahead. The Norristown branch curves off to the right. *P&W photo. Collection of Bob Foley.*

Villanova Junction view from the other direction in 1920. *P&W photo. Collection of Bob Foley.*

The single-track P&W bridge spanned the Pennsylvania Railroad's Schuylkill Division, which then ran at grade across Swede Street on the right. *P&W photo. Collection of Bob Foley.*

BUILDING FOR SURVIVAL

Two months before the Norristown branch was ready to open, the question of direct service to Center City Philadelphia again arose. But this time it was Philadelphia Rapid Transit Company that did the proposing. Alert to the expanding network of suburban electric rail lines, PRT developed a plan to run its subway-elevated trains directly from Center City to Norristown, Strafford and West Chester. The plan called for P&W to lay a third running rail for dual gauge track on PRT's structure. Upon reaching 69th Street Terminal, one car of each elevated train would be uncoupled to run to Norristown. Another would run to Strafford and another out the 19-mile West Chester line of the Philadelphia & West Chester Traction Company, which was the same wide-gauge as the elevated. But the plan died of its own weight, particularly after the P&W had changed its third-rail to over-running.

SALVATION AT NORRISTOWN

P&W trains began running to Norristown on Monday, August 26, 1912, four months before the LVT connection was completed. The first train left 69th Street Terminal at 5:20 A.M. and arrived on time at Norristown at 5:46 A.M. Ridership was heavy throughout the day as thousands turned out to view the new interurban.

The one-way fare was 25 cents, and a 10-trip ticket was $2.00. With 60-trip tickets, however, commuters wound up paying only 11 cents per ride, less than a penny a mile. To these fares had to be added the five-cent charge on the elevated. Initially, all Norristown trains consisted of two cars, one of which was used as a smoker. There had been no need to purchase any new cars for the new branch, since only half the original fleet of 22 cars was required for Strafford service.

A St. Louis car loads at the Norristown terminal. The court house is in the background. *Collection of Montgomery County Historical Society.*

Frustratingly, the opening of the line caused much traffic congestion on Swede Street at the terminal, a problem that was not resolved for two more decades. P&W had originally sought permission to lay dual tracks on Swede Street, but this was refused, since it would have undoubtedly caused even more congestion for automobiles and horse-drawn vehicles. The single-track, however, made access to the terminal extremely awkward. In addition to being the P&W terminus, it was also the end of the line for LVT local cars and was used by Liberty Bell Limited through trains.

P&W ran 53 round-trips daily to Norristown, compared to 65 daily round-trips by the PRR and the Reading combined. Remarkably, travel time on the P&W and elevated trains combined was faster than most of the steam trains, and the interurban/elevated fares were cheaper The railroads charged 43 cents for a one-way ticket and 69 cents for a round-trip. Ten-trip tickets cost $3.11.

The new electric route was an instant success. Ridership on the P&W boomed. The Norristown line quickly became the main line, relegating Strafford to branch status. All Norristown trains were expresses, stopping only at Ardmore Junction, Bryn Mawr and Villanova on the trunk line. Strafford trains held down all the local service. As ridership soared, the Norristown extension quickly turned out to be nothing less than the company's salvation.

LVT RIDES THE P&W

Both LVT and P&W were atypical interurbans for the eastern United States. Most of the nation's long and fast interurban lines were in the Midwest, where they competed strongly with steam railroads. In the East and in New England, long suburban or interurban trolley lines tended to be slow side-of-the-road affairs that fell easy prey to competing bus lines and automobiles in the 1920s. There were only a few notable exceptions, such as the Pennsylvania's Lackawanna & Wyoming Valley Railroad and the Washington, Baltimore & Annapolis Electric Railroad. The P&W/LVT combination was the only high-speed interurban to ever serve Philadelphia. P&WCT's West Chester trolley line, while reasonably fast and well operated, was certainly not in the same category.

Through service from Allentown was delayed for a few months while LVT continued to realign the Montgomery Traction line between North Wales and Norristown and other parts of its route. Most of the MT route was relocated to high-speed private right-of-

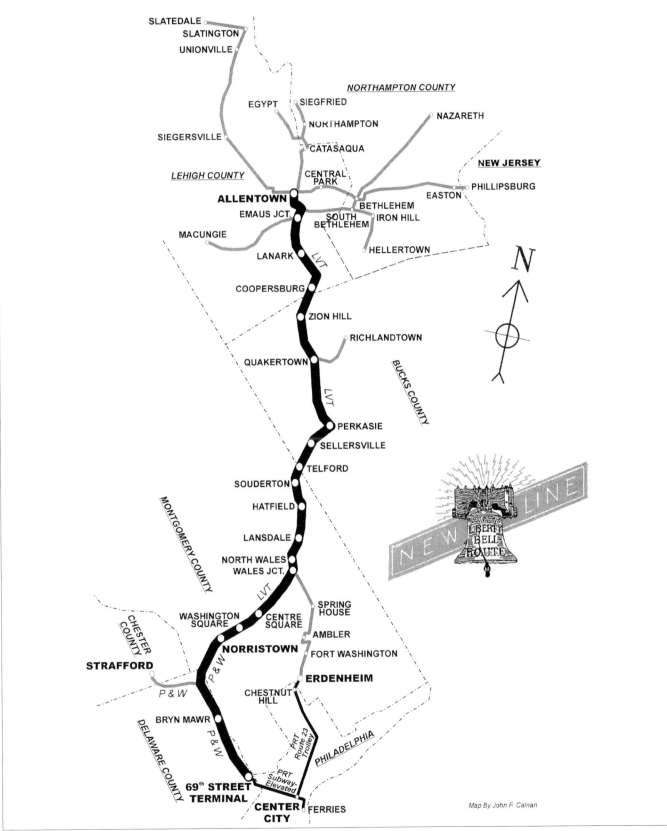

way, and only 1.5 miles of the original right-of-way alongside DeKalb Pike remained in use. At about the same time, the Norristown Transit Company's tracks were completed, and a shuttle car began running on September 19, 1912, from the Swede Street terminal north to Germantown Pike, half a mile north of the Norristown borough limits. Passengers temporarily transferred there to cars of the old wide-gauge Montgomery Traction line to Lansdale.

LVT was spending millions to realign much of its Philadelphia Division trackage to allow high-speed operation. Large portions of the original line were abandoned. Some street trackage was eliminated, and over the next few years even more realignments took place to further speed up the Liberty Bell Route. Two test cars were run for the first time over the entire line from Allentown to 69th Street Terminal on December 9, 1912, and an official inspection tour for dignitaries and the press took place the next day.

Opening day arrived two days later, on December 12, with Liberty Bell cars leaving 69th Street Terminal every hour and roaring virtually non-stop along the P&W and at mile-a-minute speeds across Pennsylvania Dutch farmland, stopping only at the major towns. In their 55-mile run linking the Lehigh Valley with the Quaker City, Liberty Bell cars made only 10 stops. The two hour and 18 minute trip leaving 69th Street at 7:40 A.M. was the "Water Gap Special," and it continued beyond Allentown all the way to the Delaware Water Gap, one of Pennsylvania's major tourist attractions, for a

LVT advertising "Dogwood Excursions" at Valley Forge. *Collection of Ronald DeGraw.*

P&W squeezed an LVT loading track (center) into its cramped 69th Street Terminal layout. The 800-series car on the left sat on the freight track in midday storage. *Collection of Andrew W. Maginnis.*

nearly 200-mile all-day adventure. To handle local stops, LVT operated additional trains once an hour from Norristown to Allentown.

Bursting with local pride, the Norristown Times called the Liberty Bell Route "the finest electric interurban in the East, and the equal of the best in the world." The heavy construction of the lines was certainly the reason that they continued for so long after most other suburban and interurban routes in the nation had died.

Credit for this achievement lay with four men: P&W President Thomas Newhall, Edward B. Smith, whose banking firm financed the project, and R. P. Stevens and Edward C. Spring, LVT's far-sighted managers. Stevens was LVT's president, and Spring was superintendent of its Philadelphia Division. Spring had also been Newhall's assistant for several years before moving to the LVT.

THE LIBERTY BELL FLEET

LVT bought for the Liberty Bell Route the finest, most ornate interurbans cars that could be made. Six heavy

$12,000 steel cars arrived in Allentown in August 1912 from the Jewett Car Company of Newark, Ohio. Renowned as a builder of beautiful interurban cars, Jewett patterned the cars after some it had built for Lake Shore Electric Railway and Lima Route in Ohio.

The cars became Nos. 800-805, and they were more luxurious and offered a better ride quality than the P&W's wooden fleet. They were 56 feet long with a small baggage section, a smoking compartment, a restroom and a drinking fountain. They seated 54 passengers and were capable of 62 miles an hour. Two of the cars initially had leather and mahogany club chairs in the smoking section and seated only 44. The cars were painted a medium shade of green with gold lettering and striping with a yellow roof and black trim. The Philadelphia Inquirer pronounced the equipment "as far in advance of anything ever used in or about Philadelphia."

Like steam railroad cars, the 800s were capable of high-level loading and had steps for serving ground-level platforms. Farquhar's third-rail shoes were attached to both sides of each truck. For the first six months of operation, each Liberty Bell Limited ran on the P&W coupled to a P&W car. The P&W car was always on the south end of the train. They coupled and uncoupled on Swede Street in Norristown, but a difference in electrical equipment and the need for a

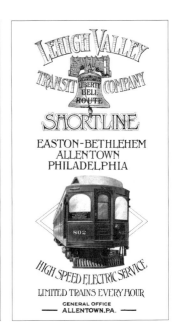

Front covers of P&W brochure dating back to 1912 when Norristown Branch opened. *Collection of Edward Springer.*

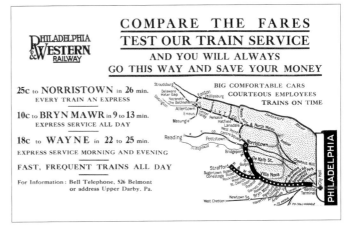

Passenger card advertising how to travel via the P&W and LVT to several eastern Pennsylvania destinations. *Collection of Edward Springer.*

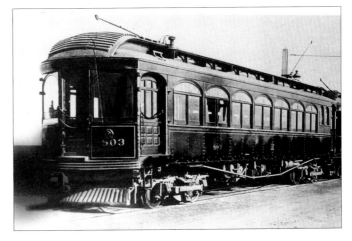

The elegant 800-series cars later ran in three-car trains. *Collection of Ronald DeGraw.*

BUILDING FOR SURVIVAL

The Liberty Bell Route featured 12 of these big, elegant interurban cars, complete with bathrooms and small baggage sections. *Collection of John P. Scharle.*

A newspaper advertisement for LVT's "interurban flyers." *Collection of Ronald DeGraw.*

coupler adaptor made this operation unsatisfactory, it was discontinued in the summer of 1913. After that, LVT trains ran separately over the P&W.

P&W crews staffed the LVT cars while they ran on company property, handing the Liberty Bell cars over to LVT crews at Swede Street. Under the trackage rights agreement, P&W provided the crews and kept the 69th Street-Norristown portion of all LVT fares.

Success crowned the new service, and within less than a month LVT ordered six more of the 800-series cars, which became 806-811. Their arrival permitted the operation of two- and three-car trains.

LVT began with the slogan "Save a Dollar." The round-trip fare on the Reading from Allentown to Philadelphia was $2.86. The fare on the interurban was $1.86, and it drew thousands of passengers away from the steam railroad. The interurban route also provided more convenient stops throughout the Lehigh Valley and on the elevated all along Market Street in Philadelphia. The Reading offered only two Center City stations, at Spring Garden Street and at its terminal at 12th and Market Streets.

SERVICE PATTERNS, 1911-1912

With the opening of the Strafford extension to the PRR station in 1911, P&W's public timetable became more imaginative.

The local running time to Strafford was increased by two minutes—to 28 minutes—and peak period trains again operated express between 69th Street Terminal and Haverford College. They were not true express trains, however, because they did make stops inbound at the local stations for passengers who had boarded west of Villanova and wanted to get off, or outbound at the local stations for any passengers wishing to board at local stations and travel to points west of Villanova. Service to Strafford ran every 20 minutes all day long, with the express trains spanning about three hours in each peak period. While the express trains ran, the local service was operated only between 69th Street Terminal and Villanova.

Express trains made the entire trip in 26 minutes westbound and 23 minutes eastbound. Villanova locals took 17 minutes westbound and 16 minutes eastbound. Trains ran to Strafford—either express or local—every 20 minutes up until 7:00 P.M., when they went to every 30 minutes.

With the opening of the Norristown branch in 1912, local Strafford trains ran every 20 minutes all day long, making all station stops. In rush hours an additional train ran to Strafford every 20 minutes non-stop between 69th Street and Haverford College.

Trains to Norristown ran every 20 minutes all day until 7:00 P.M., when both branches went to half-hour frequency. Norristown trains stopped only at Bryn Mawr and Villanova, then at the three stations on the new branch: Gulph Mills (then called Gulph), King Manor (originally called DeKalb Street) and Bridgeport. Some Norristown trains stopped at Ardmore Junction, but only to accommodate passengers to or from points north of Villanova.

A peaceful scene along the Schuylkill Canal at Bridgeport in 1912. *P&W photo. Collection of Bob Foley.*

This schedule meant that three trains operated every 20 minutes in each direction during peak periods, providing Bryn Mawr and Villanova stations with service on the average of every seven minutes.

Lehigh Valley Transit offered express trains every hour from 69th Street Terminal to Allentown and additional local service north of Norristown. "Limited" trains left 69th Street at 40 minutes after the hour and made the run to Allentown in two hours and 18 minutes, stopping at only 10 stations. On the P&W, the Liberty Bell cars stopped only at Villanova. For the first six months of operation, P&W and LVT cars ran coupled as two-car trains.

STOPPING A TRAIN

P&W had a unique method of stopping for passengers. Most stations were flag stops. The P&W originally used the same method that nearly all steam railroads and other interurbans employed, which required passengers to stand in a location on the platform visible to the motorman during the day or to hold up a light or

A St. Louis car unloads at the Norristown terminal on Swede Street in 1913. *P&W photo. Collection of Bob Foley.*

BUILDING FOR SURVIVAL

a flaming newspaper at night. It was a crude system, but it was maintained by most interurbans during their lifetimes.

Considering itself unique, the P&W soon introduced a greatly improved method whereby intending passengers set a small hand-operated semaphore signal situated above the station roof. If the semaphore was not set, trains did not even slow down. After passengers boarded, conductors were required to step onto the platform and restore the semaphore. These worked quite well, although they were difficult for motormen to see at night. Valuable minutes of running time were gained by not having to slow down and then accelerate at stations where no passengers were waiting.

In the early 1930s P&W Electrical Superintendent William D. Gable devised an even better method for stopping trains. Gable and his staff gradually installed a trip light system at all of the flagstop stations. Passengers arriving at a station pulled a cord near the entrance to the platform. The cord lighted a bulb just above it, so that passengers were assured that it was working. Another light on the end of the platform went on, and so did an advance light along the track about 500 feet before the station. Motormen would see the advance light and know that someone wished to board. If a passenger arrived seconds before the train, then the light at the end of the platform alerted motormen.

A small trip-rail, made from a short piece of third-rail, was installed at each station on the opposite side of the track from the regular third-rail. The trip rail was on a timing circuit. A train pausing at a station for more than about five seconds caused the passenger light to automatically reset itself. An express train running non-stop through a station would not affect a passenger signal because it made contact with the trip rail for less than five seconds.

No. 807 is snug in its 69th Street Terminal loading track. The track was long enough to hold a three-car train. *Collection of Ronald DeGraw.*

This extremely simple and effective system had virtually no working parts and required practically no maintenance. Light bulbs occasionally had to be replaced, which was done by the regular daily station cleaner. A variety of this system is still used on the P&W, with passengers pushing a button instead of pulling a cord.

Most P&W stations were always considered to be flag stops and used this method. Only at Ardmore Junction, Bryn Mawr, Villanova and Bridgeport were all trains required to slow down and look for passengers. Garrett Hill was added as an all-stops station when the Strafford line was abandoned in 1956. A modern version of this system is used today by the South Shore Line interurban connecting Chicago with South Bend, Indiana.

LVT'S ELECTRIC EMPIRE

Lehigh Valley Transit Company at its peak operated a network of city, suburban and interurban rail lines totaling 215 route miles and 280 passenger cars, plus amusement parks, electric power companies and a toll bridge. The empire stretched from Slatedale, west of Allentown, all the way to Phillipsburg, New Jersey, across the river from Easton. It served towns northward to Nazareth and was allied with lines through the

P&W conductor David Kenney stands next to LVT 804 in front of the P&W carbarn, emphasizing the enormousness of the cars. *Collection of David Kenney.*

Delaware Water Gap to Stroudsburg. The Easton Limited operated relatively fast, frequent cars between Allentown, Bethlehem and Easton, the three big cities in Pennsylvania's Lehigh Valley region.

Manifestly the most famous of the LVT services was the Liberty Bell Route. Despite the fact that 69th Street was a mile west of the Philadelphia city limits, Liberty Bell trains were always marked "Philadelphia" as were the P&W's trains. The Liberty Bell route was 55 miles long, including trackage rights over the P&W, and generally operated hourly although half-hourly service was offered during World War II. Liberty Bell cars sped at 60 miles per hour on private right-of-way across farmlands but also traversed the main streets of various little towns. Most towns had station buildings with waiting rooms and ticket agents. A few of these buildings still exist.

LVT's 800-series cars were single-end and the double-end 700-series cars were usually operated from the No. 1 end, so they all had to be turned at the end of a trip. To accomplish this, a wye (turning) track was built opposite the P&W's carbarn just west of 69th Street. When the P&W opened in 1907 a siding had been constructed opposite the carbarn to serve the Garrett Paper Mills. An additional leg was added to this siding to form a wye for the LVT cars. Southbound LVT trains discharged their passengers at 69th Street Terminal, then backed over a crossover at the terminal and ran backwards to the wye. After the car was turned it had to back into the terminal where a separate track was reserved. This turning movement was cumbersome and time-consuming but it endured until the end of Liberty Bell service.

There was another siding track immediately west of the terminal built just for LVT in 1915. The company usually kept at least one spare car at 69th Street to cover breakdowns or major delays.

An aerial view of 69th Street Terminal in 1930 shows the P&W station and tracks in the lower right. All of the residential and commercial development around the terminal occurred in the 1920s. *Dallin Aerial Surveys, collection of Robert W. Lynch.*

Possibly reflecting its Pennsylvania German heritage, LVT was especially concerned about the cleanliness of its cars. Every Liberty Bell train arriving at 8th and Hamilton Streets in Allentown was laboriously backed to the Fairview Carbarn where it was turned around, thoroughly cleaned inside and out and then backed again to 8th and Hamilton to await its return trip.

There were long layovers at 69th Street Terminal, which helped to guarantee that trains would leave on time for their northbound trips and provided time for P&W car mechanics to fix any minor problems that developed on the trip southward.

LVT went to great lengths to foster customer goodwill. There is a story—perhaps apocryphal—that a southbound train operated late one night with its signboard incorrectly reading "Allentown." An elderly woman along the way, perhaps confused as to direction, boarded and promptly fell asleep. When the train reached 69th Street Terminal after midnight, she was startled to find she was at the wrong end of the line. The last northbound train for the night had already left. The crew telephoned the dispatcher for instructions, and the woman wound up riding her own non-stop private train 55 miles to Allentown—with an apology.

Three-car LVT train in storage at 69th Street Terminal. *Collection of Bob Foley.*

CHAPTER FIVE

Prosperity and Competition
1913-1929

PROSPERITY comforted the Philadelphia & Western until the Jazz Age, and the key was the many connections it enjoyed with other carriers, including some newfangled bus lines. It interfaced with a great many other electric railway lines, not to mention the established steam railroads.

But its most important links were with the Market Street Elevated and the Liberty Bell Route. PRT's Market Street Elevated had opened on March 4, 1907, between 69th Street Terminal and 15th and Market Streets at Philadelphia's City Hall. In West Philadelphia it was built as an elevated railway. It had its own bridge over the Schuylkill River and then ran as a subway east to 15th Street. Much of West Philadelphia was then undeveloped land and the construction of the elevated spurred its growth.

The following year the elevated was extended eastward under Market Street, serving the commercial heart of the city. The subway stations at 13th, 11th and 8th Streets connected directly with the basement levels of all the city's six major department stores, and display windows of the stores lined the subway's pedestrian concourses. It was all very cosmopolitan.

East of 2nd Street Station, the line again became an elevated and served the ferries operated by the Pennsylvania Railroad and the Philadelphia & Reading. There was no bridge, so those destined to or from points in southern New Jersey had to use railroad-owned ferries. Swarming the ferries on summer days were tens of thousands of Philadelphians bound for Atlantic City,

Above: A view of "the fill". The track at the right led from the unloading platform; the track near the center dipped down to the principal loading track. The tracks on the far left led to the Pennsylvania Railroad's Cardington branch. *P&W photo. Collection of Bob Foley.* **Left:** A 160-car arrives westbound at Villanova Station. *Photo by Aaron Fryer.*

No. 50 is parked on a storage track at 69th Street Terminal, shown from the east end of 69th Street Terminal. Two St. Louis cars appear on the right. *Collection of Andrew W. Maginnis.*

Ocean City, Wildwood, Cape May and other South Jersey seashore points. The two railroads competed vigorously by offering fast, frequent service to the shore.

P&W could not have survived without the subway-elevated connection. Elevated trains ran so frequently—at least every five minutes—that transferring between the two lines at 69th Street was easy and fast. And for many years the fare was just five cents. Riding the P&W and the elevated, rather than the steam trains, was cheaper and more convenient for many business trips and especially for most shopping trips. It was also the only direct way to reach the Delaware River ferries. Seventeen stations along the elevated provided access to various parts of the city, and most of the stations had connecting PRT trolley routes.

At 69th Street Terminal the P&W also connected with five trolley routes of the Philadelphia & West Chester Traction Company. Four main routes ran to West Chester, Ardmore, Sharon Hill and Media. In addition, a shuttle trolley operated from 1907 until 1911 between 69th Street and 63rd Street. It was replaced by PRT's Route 41 trolley, which ran on Market Street all the way from Front Street to 69th Street until it was cut back to 63rd Street in 1920. The first P&WCT bus route, through a subsidiary, Aronimink Transportation Company, began running from 69th Street Terminal in 1923. It was Route A to Aronimink via West Chester Pike and State Road. For its part, PRT began bus service from 69th Street to Center City on Route D using double-deck buses in 1926.

John Drew Auto Bus Company, a small independent firm, ran from 69th Street to Lansdowne and Darby beginning in 1918. Two other smaller operators also briefly offered bus service to the terminal.

P&WCT trolleys connected with other electric railways near their outer terminals. Passengers could travel from Philadelphia as far as Lancaster and Harrisburg by using the West Chester trolley line, and to Chester and Wilmington via the Media or Sharon Hill lines. These connections opened up many possibilities to P&W riders in a time when automobiles were few and public transportation was the only practical way to get around.

At Ardmore Junction Station, 3.5 miles from 69th Street Terminal, P&W crossed over P&WCT's Ardmore trolley line. This became a popular transfer point for passengers wishing to go from Ardmore to Norristown or further north on the LVT.

Two of the 50-series cars at 69th Street Terminal. *Collection of Kevin T. Farrell.*

At Strafford Station, P&W passengers could change to the PRR main line trains to reach points as far west as Harrisburg, Pittsburgh, Chicago and St. Louis.

There was also another connection planned for Strafford, one that never happened. The Phoenixville, Valley Forge & Strafford Electric Railway Company opened a line in 1912 from Phoenixville to the western edge of Valley Forge State Park, a major tourist attraction. It planned to connect with the P&W at Strafford and also to access both the P&W and Schuylkill Valley Traction at Bridgeport, across the river from Norristown, with transfer possibilities to LVT and the Reading Railway.

Alas, the Phoenixville line was poorly financed and served a sparsely populated territory. And it was unable to obtain permission to run its tracks through the state park. It tried to survive largely on summer tourist traffic to Valley Forge Park and to an amusement park it had built. It also made a little money from Betzwood Film Company, which shot many of the old Toonerville Trolley films along the line in the early 1920s.

P&W conducted its own survey in 1913 for an extension that would diverge from the Norristown branch just south of King Manor Station and skirt King of Prussia, go through the village of Port Kennedy and past

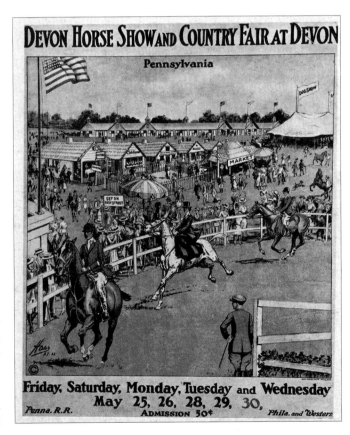

P&W carried a great many passengers to the Devon Horse Show just beyond its Strafford terminal (see bottom right of drawing). *Collection of Ronald DeGraw.*

PROSPERITY AND COMPETITION

Washington's Headquarters in Valley Forge Park to a connection with the Phoenixville line. Nothing came of this.

Thomas Newhall, however, was greatly in favor of the Phoenixville trolley company building a connection to the P&W at Bridgeport. He was so confident that the Valley Forge connection would be good for P&W that in 1915 he offered 4,000 shares of P&W stock worth about $50,000 to the Phoenixville company if it built the link. PVF&S was still distributing maps as late as 1921 showing that its line ran to Strafford and Bridgeport, but no construction ever took place.

The little wide-gauge trolley line stumbled along for a few years, shrinking to only a handful of daily trips, and was eventually put out of its misery in 1923. Had it succeeded in building a connection to the P&W, it would undoubtedly have survived much longer.

TOURIST AND OTHER CONNECTING SERVICES

P&W early recognized the possibilities of Valley Forge State Park as a tourist attraction. The primitive motor buses of Norris City Lines that began meeting P&W trains at Strafford in 1910 were very popular, especially in the summer. During the 1911 season 6,800 Valley Forge excursion tickets were sold. By 1917 the bus route was run by the West Chester Street Railway. A joint timetable showed service from 69th Street to Valley Forge every hour, with a round-trip fare of $1.28. In 1919 the P&W arranged for a shuttle service from Norristown to Valley Forge Park. By the mid 1920s the fare had dropped to a dollar.

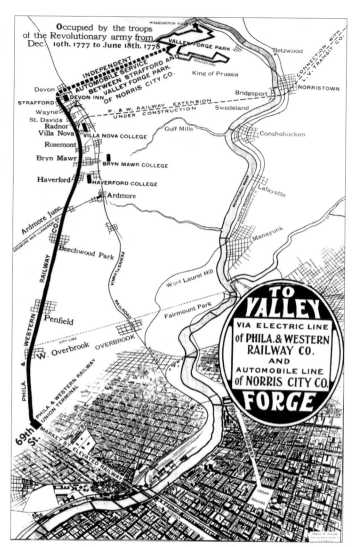

Bus service connected the P&W with Valley Forge Park. Norris City Company promoted the connection with this advertisement. *Collection of Chester County Historical Society.*

Snow sweeper #10 arrived in 1915, but was seldom used. *Photo by Ernest A. Mozer.*

Chester Valley Lines by the mid-1920s had an extensive network of bus routes throughout Chester County. It operated hourly service from Royersford, in Montgomery County, through Phoenixville and Valley Forge to Strafford, Paoli, Malvern, West Chester and Downingtown. The route was later changed to run between Valley Forge and Norristown instead of Royersford, and it provided an important connection for the P&W at Strafford. Chester Valley Lines also ran a bus route from Norristown to Pottstown via Phoenixville and Royersford.

At Bridgeport, P&W passengers who worked at the Alan Wood Steel plant could transfer to the Swedeland trolleys of Schuylkill Valley Traction.

Numerous transfer opportunities existed at Norristown. In addition to LVT, which offered not only connections to Allentown but also to Bethlehem, Easton and many other points in the Lehigh Valley, there were the two steam railroads that ran frequent service to westward points, all the way to Reading, Harrisburg and Pottsville. The local trolley network, which was owned by Schuylkill Valley Traction Company but operated under lease by Reading Transit & Light Company, was extensive. Trolleys ran westward to Collegeville, Pottstown and Boyertown, where transfers could be made to reach Reading and its many suburbs. Eastward, the cars ran to Conshohocken and to the northwestern edge of Philadelphia at Manayunk, Roxborough and Chestnut Hill. Schuylkill Valley trolleys were replaced by buses in 1933.

Another smaller trolley line serving Norristown was Montgomery County Rapid Transit Company, which may have been the most misnamed trolley ever built. It ran—very slowly—to the tiny towns of Skippack, Lederach and Harleysville. After struggling along for 18 years with very little ridership it was abandoned in 1925 with no bus replacement.

These many connections put the P&W in the center of a vast transportation network that helped it to prosper. Within less than a year after the Norristown branch opened, the P&W was carrying 50 percent more passengers and revenue more than doubled. By 1914 the interurban was carrying twice as many people as it had three years earlier and its income had tripled.

Passenger counts continued to climb rapidly for more than a decade. From 1.3 million in 1911, the numbers climbed to 1.5 million in 1912, 2.2 million in 1913, 2.6 million in 1914, 2.9 million in 1915, 3.5 million in 1916, 4 million by 1919 and 5 million by 1924. Edward B. Smith & Company never had cause to regret its investment in the P&W.

By early 1916 Newhall reported to his board that "the physical condition of the property is excellent," and profits for the year climbed to $121,677. That year the company began paying quarterly dividends of one percent on its preferred stock, a practice that lasted until the Great Depression.

PRR'S ELECTRIC COMPETITION

Even a dramatic move by the Pennsylvania Railroad, which should have resulted in draining away many P&W riders, didn't seem to have any affect on the interurban. The PRR had been experimenting with electric propulsion for its trains since the 1890s. In 1895 it electrified a seven-mile branch from Burlington to Mount Holly, New Jersey. Forty-four miles of the Long Island Rail Road, a PRR subsidiary, were electrified in 1905.

In 1906 the Pennsy, through its subsidiary West Jersey & Seashore Railroad, electrified a 59-mile line (mostly third-rail) from Camden to Atlantic City, with a branch to Millville. This 650-volt direct current installation was very successful, offering fast, frequent interurban-type service carrying the summer throngs to the seashore. It was the longest railroad line up to that time to be changed from steam to electric power. The PRR opened its massive Pennsylvania Station in New York City in 1910, and the tunnels leading to it were electrified with 11,000-volt alternating current.

No. 170 is about to leave the Strafford Station, with the Pennsylvania Railroad station in the background. *Collection of Railroad Avenue Enterprises.*

The 60-cars ran primarily in service to Strafford. One poses at the Strafford Station while a Pennsylvania Railroad freight train hauled by a GG-1 roars by. *Collection of Bob Foley.*

PRR was now convinced that electricity was the future for its commuter trains in New York City and Philadelphia, and the four-track line to Paoli became the region's first electrified railroad commuter line on September 11, 1915. This meant that more trains could be run, and they would be faster and cheaper to operate. Running times from Paoli to Broad Street Station in Philadelphia were reduced from 59 to 49 minutes. The PRR spent $4.2 million to electrify and make other improvements to the Paoli line, including the elimination of all grade crossings.

The Paoli improvements should have spelled trouble for the P&W's Strafford line, but the P&W was actually capturing far more passengers from the PRR than the steam road had ever anticipated.

RIDERSHIP KEEPS GROWING

Newhall revitalized P&W's real estate subsidiary in 1920. Homestead Real Estate Company, formed to purchase the original Parkesburg right-of-way, had changed its name to DeKalb Realty Company in 1911 to obtain right-of-way for the Norristown branch. On October 20, 1920, it changed its name again to Philadelphia & Western Home Owners' Association. Two years later it finally did something new by developing the area of King Manor near the P&W station. New houses went up through the 1920s, and several were sold to P&W employees. The company owned a few other houses along the railroad, and leased them to employees for as low as $10 a month. Part of its philosophy was that employees living near the railroad would be able to respond quickly in emergencies or snowstorms.

Flushed with success, P&W reached for even greater heights. Shuttle bus service was operated to the Bryn Mawr Horse Show from Strafford Station beginning in 1910. The popular show was held in Devon, two miles west of Strafford, in late September and proceeds went to Bryn Mawr Hospital. The name was later changed to the Devon Horse Show and it was scheduled for Memorial Day weekend. Special tickets were sold offering reduced train fares and reduced admission.

Weekend riding on the Norristown branch was so heavy by the early 1920s that many two-car trains were required. A few trains had to run with three cars, which was awkward because most station platforms were only long enough for two cars. Conductors attempted to solve the problem by filling the last car only with riders destined for 69th Street or Norristown. On summer

No. 166 stops inbound at West Wayne Station. *Photo by Edward S. Miller.*

Three cars appeared on "the fill", which was the end of the line just beyond 69th Street Terminal's unloading platform. *Collection of Andrew W. Maginnis.*

Sundays and holidays an additional train was scheduled to leave Norristown at 4:30 A.M., before the first regularly scheduled train, for day-trippers going to the seashore resorts.

AMBITIOUS IMPROVEMENT PLANS

To cure the highway congestion at the P&W terminal on Swede Street in Norristown, Newhall in 1915 proposed that a new depot be created on the elevated structure over the top of Swede Street between Main and Lafayette Streets, two blocks south of the street terminal. It would have two tracks, to allow P&W to run Norristown trains every 10 minutes instead of every 20. P&W trains would use a stub-end track at the new station and LVT cars would slide by on the through track. Due to objections, the new station was never built.

Undaunted, Newhall told his board of directors in 1917 that P&W would buy several new cars, enlarge its 69th Street Terminal facilities and build a better Norristown terminal. All of these things eventually happened, although one of them was stalled for nearly half a century.

Newhall proposed two extensions, one to Lansdowne and one to Conshohocken. The Lansdowne extension, proposed in 1913, would have used the Cardington Branch of the PRR, which was P&W's freight connection at 69th Street. Leaving the Pennsy right-of-way at East Lansdowne, the interurban extension would go half a mile further to the Borough of Lansdowne.

The branch from Gulph Mills to Conshohocken was first proposed when the Norristown line was being designed and was resurrected in 1920, as a new highway bridge over the Schuylkill River between Conshohocken and West Conshohocken was being planned. The cost of the two and a quarter mile extension was put at $150,000. Traffic counts showed that the PRR and the Reading combined carried fewer than 1,700 daily passengers to or from Conshohocken, however, so P&W cancelled the project. The Lansdowne extension idea also went nowhere.

The old covered DeKalb Street highway bridge connecting Bridgeport and Norristown was destroyed by fire on April 24, 1924. The 1830 bridge was long in decrepit condition, and when P&W was planning its Norristown extension in 1910 it had proposed that the old wooden structure be replaced by a new highway and railway bridge. The county expressed no interest, so the railroad built its own span over the Schuylkill River.

The other highway bridge connecting the two towns, the old Ford Street Bridge east of DeKalb Street, had been burned in 1883 and rebuilt to include a Reading Railway freight track. Ironically, it burned again on June 11, 1924, only three months after the DeKalb Street Bridge fire. The private owners made temporary repairs and charged one cent for pedestrians to cross it. But the bridge was never again reopened for auto traffic, and was finally demolished in 1939. After the fires, a temporary DeKalb Street Bridge was hurriedly constructed, but for five months the P&W was the only way to get between the two towns. A shuttle car was used to temporarily double the service between Bridgeport and Norristown, and the P&W carried an extra 288,000 passengers during that five-month period. A new permanent DeKalb Street Bridge opened on November 1, 1925.

BOARD MEMBERS PINCH PENNIES

Despite the P&W's increasing ridership and profitability, its board of directors remained frugal, if not downright stingy. Julius L. Adams, the general manager, asked for a $200 gasoline handcar that could carry several men and tools. The board said no.

Adams also sought a fare reduction for Norristown passengers. The P&W's round-trip fare was 50 cents, plus the elevated fares of 10 cents. The steam railroads charged 69 cents. Adams thought this difference wasn't great enough to attract new P&W passengers and he wanted a round-trip fare of 35 cents for the P&W, plus the elevated fares. The board said no again.

Indeed, P&W raised its fares. The advent of World War I, even before the United States officially entered it, forced the cost of supplies and labor to increase rapidly. Effective July 5, 1917, P&W implemented the first general fare increase since it had opened a decade earlier. Fares to Strafford were raised from 20 to 25 cents and to Norristown from 25 to 30 cents. A newly formed Philadelphia & Western Commuters' Association unsuccessfully opposed the fare hikes. The Beechwood Civic Association challenged the 40 percent increase at Beechwood Park Station from 5 cents to 7 cents. After extensive hearings before the Public Service Commission, the railroad won.

A 160-car arrives westbound at Villanova Station. Photo by Aaron Fryer.

Rates went up again on June 14, 1923, establishing a minimum base fare of 10 cents cash or four tickets for a quarter, although the Strafford and Norristown rates remained the same.

Ever attempting to generate higher profits, Newhall in 1920 moved the P&W's general offices from space

No. 163 leaves Ithan Station, which was built literally in Thomas Newhall's backyard. Photo by Richard S. Short.

leased from PRT in 69th Street Terminal into the ground floor of the Rambo House in Norristown. The monthly rent for the new facilities, including a new waiting room and ticket office, was almost completely offset by rentals paid to P&W by newsstand and luncheonette concessions at the Norristown terminal.

Newhall never worked out of the 69th Street or Norristown offices. The corporate office of the company was in the Franklin Bank Building at Broad and Chestnut Streets in Center City. The offices of Edward B. Smith & Company were half a block away at 1411 Chestnut Street, and the interurban's executive office was later moved to the same building.

Conshohocken Road Station was opened in 1920 on the south side of Rebel Hill at Matsonford Road, which led to the boroughs of West Conshohocken and Conshohocken. Local residents contributed $2,623 towards its construction.

A mile south of King Manor Station a private developer built homes along the P&W, so a new station called Hughes Park was opened there in August 1925. The station was named after John Hughes, whose family members were early settlers in Upper Merion Township and owned much land in the area. When the Norristown branch was constructed, it severed a Hughes farm.

A private crossing under the tracks was built to reconnect the two parts. Another stop, more than a mile north of Villanova Junction called County Line Station was opened in August 1929. It, too, was built by contributions from local residents but never generated much traffic. Some station names were changed on the Strafford line, ending a long-standing feud between the P&W and local civic groups. The St. Davids Station was changed to Wayne-St. Davids on April 29, 1928, and the old Wayne Station was then called West Wayne.

MODERN CARS FOR A MODERN RAILWAY

With ridership still climbing, Newhall moved to supplement the original wooden passenger car fleet. The railway's first all-steel car, No. 50, arrived in May 1920, built by the J. G. Brill Company of Philadelphia. The 56-foot car had a third door on each side behind which the conductor stood. The shorter section was a smoking compartment. It cost $23,000 and was wider and higher than the old St. Louis cars. Although it was certainly more modern than the 22 wooden cars, its rattan seats were not as comfortable. Car 50 did not include steps, so it could not be used in Norristown service. It did, however, have trolley poles.

Not overjoyed with No. 50, P&W entertained a suggestion from the Cincinnati Car Company to re-equip the

The first of the 50-series cars arrived in 1920. This all-steel car was wider than the old cars, but was not as fast. They seldom ran to Strafford, being used instead for Bryn Mawr short-turns. *Photo by Anthony Krisak.*

The 50-series cars contained a center door, where the conductor sat. His collapsible seat is visible at the door. The smaller compartment on the left was for smoking. The cars had trolley poles but no steps, so they could not be used in Norristown service. *Collection of Historical Society of Pennsylvania.*

entire railroad with a fleet of lightweight interurban cars that would cost only $15,000 each. It was decided that 23 cars would be needed, and that replacing the entire old fleet would save $134,000 annually in maintenance and power bills. It was also found that the elimination of conductors would save another $24,000. There was, of course, a catch. The lightweight cars did not offer the same ride quality as the heavier P&W cars and their wheels were smaller, so all the station platforms would have had to be lowered by several inches.

P&W finally rejected the Cincinnati offer and instead ordered from Brill two more cars nearly identical to No. 50. Nos. 51-52 arrived in 1922. Implausibly, the cars were so wide that they couldn't fit through all of the doors of the carbarn. Three weeks after 51 arrived a motorman tried to take it through one of the narrower carbarn doors. Both sides of the car were crushed inward for about 15 feet, and the car was returned to Brill for repairs. Four months later the 51, thoroughly jinxed, crashed into the bumping block at the end of the line in Strafford, causing minor damage, and the following year it slammed into car 42 at the other end of the line at 69th Street Terminal.

By the time Nos. 51-52 arrived, the man who had been most responsible for the interurban's success was no longer president. Thomas Newhall resigned on January 1, 1922, to become a partner in Drexel & Company, one of the largest banking firms in Philadelphia. He was replaced by Vice President and General Manager Julius Adams, who lived in Norristown and had joined the P&W in 1912. As of March 5, 1928, Newhall was out as a director, ending more than two decades of leadership with the P&W. The next year he joined J. P. Morgan & Company as a partner, and in 1938 he became a director of the Pennsylvania Railroad.

Adams was greatly in favor of purchasing lightweight cars, and this was again discussed in 1923. The financial savings must have been enticing, but heavy interurbans continued to carry the day with P&W's conservative management.

Another steel passenger car—No. 60—came from Brill in 1924. It was a modified version of the 50-series cars, but at 30 tons it weighed 18,000 pounds less than the earlier steel cars. It was six feet shorter and more than a foot narrower. This time the seats were finished in "hand buffed brown Spanish leather" and met with immediate acceptance by passengers. Like the other three steel cars, 60 had an extra door on the side and trolley poles. It also had folding steps for street loading so it could be used on the Norristown line. No. 60 cost $28,000 and turned out to be a much better car than Nos. 50-52.

So pleased was P&W that five more cars just like it—61-65—arrived in May, 1927, and another five—66-70—were delivered by Brill in September, 1929. The 14 steel cars permitted much of the original St. Louis fleet to be retired. Two of the old cars were scrapped in 1928 and

THE 60 SERIES

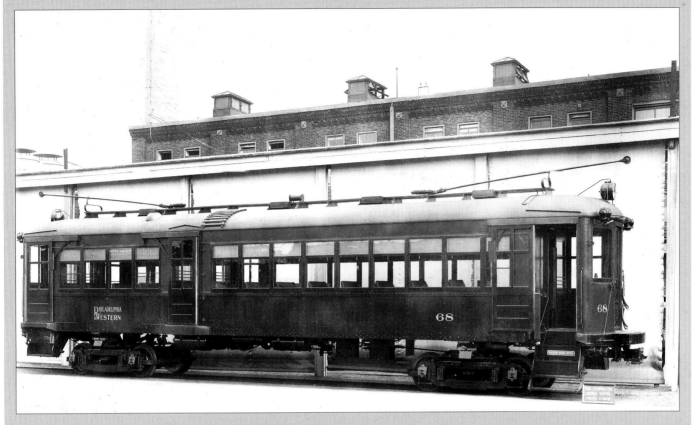

The first of the steel 60-series cars arrived in 1924. It was an immediate success, and P&W ordered five more in 1927 and another five in 1929. *Collection of Andrew W. Maginnis.*

No. 812 on the Norristown bridge. *Photo by Anthony Krisak.*

PROSPERITY AND COMPETITION

A view of the end of a 60-series car. *Collection of Robert J. Lynch.*

Construction view of the 60-series cars at the J. G. Brill plant. *Collection of Bob Foley.*

The interiors of the cars were much more comfortable than the 50-series cars, with leather seats. *Collection of Historical Society of Pennsylvania.*

The varying sizes of the two series of cars are clearly visible in this photo. The 50 cars were wider and higher. *P&W photo. Collection of Bob Foley.*

another—No. 46—was turned into a work car. It was later renumbered 446 and still survives.

LVT ALSO MAKES IMPROVEMENTS

Lehigh Valley Transit, with the Smith company's financial backing, continued to make important improvements. The six additional 800-series interurban cars arrived in July 1913, permitting LVT to run two-car trains. Route realignments further speeded up the line, and by 1914 the running time between Allentown and 69th Street Terminal had been cut to one hour and 58 minutes. Including the ride on the Market Street Elevated, this meant passengers could now get from Allentown to downtown Philadelphia in about half the time required by the old Erdenheim routing. Another important realignment in 1925 reduced the running time to one hour and 55 minutes.

LVT also ran freight trolleys to 69th Street Terminal, and a freight siding and station were constructed adjacent to the P&W carbarn. From there, merchandise was transferred to trucks of the Adams Express Company for final delivery.

Passenger traffic on the LVT continued to grow so fast that three-car trains began in 1914, particularly on weekends. Twelve more interurban cars—Nos. 700-711—were purchased in 1916 from Southern Car Company of High Point, North Carolina. These big cars featured center doors and were designed for both local and express operation. They covered the Erdenheim line as well as running in multiple-unit with 800-series cars in Liberty Bell Limited service. During the 1920s three of the 700-series were converted to extra-fare deluxe chair cars. One more car was added to the Philadelphia Division roster when LVT's private car No. 999 was converted to passenger car 812 in 1921. These 25 big interurban cars performed very well for the LVT. The first to be lost was No. 811, which was destroyed in a fire on the P&W south of County Line Station on September 1, 1929, caused by a short circuit in the car's third-rail equipment.

LVT crews never operated over the P&W, but occasionally P&W crews were required to take LVT trains north of the Norristown borough limits if southbound LVT cars broke down or were seriously delayed. The only known instance of one of P&W's own passenger cars running over LVT trackage occurred on September 18, 1919, when a southbound LVT car had brake trouble and couldn't maintain its schedule. The P&W car ran north as far as Brush Siding near Penn Square, coupled onto the crippled LVT car and ran as a two-car train to 69th Street Terminal.

Only five years after LVT's Norristown connection opened, more than 15 percent of P&W's passengers were riding north of Norristown, either on Liberty Bell Limiteds or transferring at Norristown to LVT local cars. The LVT thus accounted for more than $80,000 of P&W's annual revenue.

Edward B. Smith, whose company had financed the connection between LVT and P&W, died on January 7, 1918. He had been a director of P&W since 1910. The previous year Edward B. Smith & Company had sold its control of LVT to Lehigh Power Securities Corporation, a subsidiary of National Power and Light. Electric Bond and Share Company was engaged to manage the LVT. The color scheme of the cars was gradually changed from green to bright red with a tan roof. The same year that Smith died, Newhall was elected a director of LVT.

DARK CLOUDS ON THE HORIZON

Despite the rapidly increasing ridership on the Norristown branch, the bubble of prosperity was destined to burst. The PRR had tried with its 1915 Paoli electrification to capture some of P&W's passengers and had failed. But a much bigger menace to all interurbans loomed. When autos first began to be popular, electric railways tended to shrug off the possible threat to ridership. One prominent Midwest interurban official declared in 1916 that it was a fad and would wear off.

An LVT train, consisting of a 700-car and an 800-car, raced south at Conshohocken Road Station shortly after the station was built in 1920. *Collection of Railways to Yesterday.*

But it didn't, and as auto ownership rose dramatically, there was tremendous pressure on governments to provide good roads. Nationwide, the 8,000 registered autos in 1900 jumped to 468,000 by 1910 and to more than 8 million by 1920. By 1930 it had reached 23 million, which meant that one family in two owned a car. Henry Ford's mass production techniques dramatically lowered the price of automobiles and increased their availability.

Congress passed the Federal Aid Road Act in 1916, providing 50 percent matching funds for state government highways. Railways and trolleys continued to be used for daily commuting to work, but pleasure and shopping trips were beginning to be made by auto.

In Pennsylvania, the newly formed State Highway Department began purchasing local turnpike companies and paving major highways with concrete. Most roads, however, were unpaved and were often impassable during some seasons. The automobile seemed unstoppable, and transit companies did not know how to fight back. Some established their own bus routes, but this did little good. A full 25 percent of the interurban mileage across the country vanished in the 1920s.

"Those who had faith in them paid dearly," said the definitive book The Electric Interurban Railways in America. "Few industries have risen so rapidly or declined so quickly, and no industry of its size has a worse financial record. The interurbans were a rare example of an industry that never enjoyed a period of prolonged prosperity; accordingly, they played out their life cycle in a shorter period than any other important American industry."

P&W's ridership and revenue had increased every year up through 1924, but then it reversed and went steadily downward. Neither ridership nor income would reach the 1924 level for another two decades, and that was a temporary fluke caused by World War II. The 1924 ridership level of 5 million plummeted to 3.8 million within only five years. P&W's only answer was to substantially increase its fares. On March 24, 1927, the cost of multiple-trip tickets was raised about 10 percent and cash fares were hiked by 1 to 6 cents. Norristown cash fares went up 15 percent. As a result, half a million P&W passengers disappeared in 1927.

When the nation's devastating economic crash came in the autumn of 1929, piling misery on top of the already serious auto competition, it quickly became obvious to the men who controlled P&W's finances that the situation was going to get much worse. But even they had no idea that things would get so bad so quickly that within half a dozen years the railroad would literally be fighting for its life.

A 160-car arrived at Sugartown Road Station, the original end of the Strafford line. Most of the P&W stations had long stairways to reach the trains. *Photo by Bob Foley.*

SERVICE PATTERNS, 1913-1929

The increase in riding that grew heavier after the opening of the Norristown line resulted in the establishment of Strafford express service during peak periods and the operation of two- and three-car trains to Norristown during peak periods and on weekends, with occasional four-car trains. Twenty cars were required for the normal weekday schedule.

Each division continued to operate trains every 20 minutes all day long, with half hourly service on each line after 8:00 P.M. Norristown trains ran express, skipping all stations on the old main line except Bryn Mawr and Villanova; some also stopped at Ardmore Junction. Norristown trains left 69th Street Terminal on the hour and at 20 and 40 minutes after the hour. The running time remained at 26 minutes.

No. 166 is inbound, with Radnor Station in the foreground. *Photo by Edward S. Miller.*

Another ad for the LVT promoting the "Every hour on the Hour" service level. *Collection of Ronald DeGraw.*

Strafford trains during the midday left 69th Street at 10, 30 and 50 minutes after the hour and made all stops, thereby providing departures every 10 minutes for the important stations of Bryn Mawr and Villanova. Bryn Mawr had become the third busiest station on the railroad after 69th Street Terminal and Norristown. During peak periods, additional Strafford express trains ran at 3, 23 and 43 minutes after the hour, skipping West Overbrook, Wynnewood Road, Ardmore Junction and Ardmore Avenue. Express trains made the run to Strafford in 25 minutes, three minutes faster than local trains.

By 1919, there were 266 weekday trains, including those of LVT, carrying 8,800 daily passengers arriving at or leaving from 69th Street Terminal, 625 of whom were LVT riders.

No short-turn trains operated until 1922, when Bryn Mawr rush hour locals began running. Strafford express trains then skipped all stations between 69th Street and Bryn Mawr. The trains were cleverly timed so that passengers traveling between a local station on the lower end of the line and an express station on the upper end of the line never had to wait for more than a few minutes during their transfer at Bryn Mawr, and never had to climb any steps.

Weekend service was every 20 minutes on each branch, with Norristown trains always running express.

Liberty Bell Limited trains left 69th Street Terminal at 57 minutes after the hour and stopped only at Villanova if there were any passengers going to points north of Norristown. The LVT running time was 24 minutes, only two minutes better than P&W's Norristown time. In 1928 the Liberty Bell cars began leaving on the hour, the exact same time as Norristown trains. This was made possible by the adjustment

PROSPERITY AND COMPETITION

of signals in the 69th Street area. LVT cars left precisely on the hour and P&W cars left about 15 seconds later. By the time the Liberty Bell trains reached Villanova, they were scheduled to be two minutes ahead of the following P&W train.

On February 7, 1923, "chair car service" began on two of the Liberty Bell Limited trips each day. Three of the 700-series cars—Nos. 703, 706 and 710—had their seats changed to parlor car chairs or wicker chairs. This extra fare service left Allentown at 8:05 A.M. and 4:05 P.M. and left 69th Street Terminal at 8:57 A.M. and 3:57 P.M. On Wednesday and Saturday nights an additional chair car train left 69th Street Terminal at 12:15 A.M. for theater-goers. Chair cars cost 50 cents extra to ride, later cut to 25 cents. The first southbound trip and the last northbound trip of these special trains ran all the way through to Bethlehem and Easton without the need to change cars. The trains containing the chair cars were billed as "The Philadelphian" southbound and "The Allentonian" northbound.

MITTEN'S REVENGE

A nasty feud between A. Merritt Taylor, president of the Philadelphia & West Chester Traction Company, and Thomas E. Mitten, president of Philadelphia Rapid Transit Company, erupted in 1919, with P&W caught in the middle.

Taylor, who had created a very successful suburban trolley empire, served as Philadelphia's first transportation commissioner beginning in July 1912. During that brief period, he turned out a massive report recommending a long-range plan for transportation construction in the city. It called for a 25-mile rapid transit system including a Center City loop subway, a subway under Broad Street, and elevated lines to Darby, Roxborough, Frankford and Northeast Philadelphia. Philadelphia's "reform" mayor, Rudolph Blankenburg, who had appointed Taylor, succeeded in getting the City Charter changed to include a Department of City Transit, a cabinet position. He named Taylor as its first director in July 1913. Taylor served, without pay, until January 1915.

During these years Taylor clashed frequently with Mitten, who in 1911 was brought in to resuscitate the faltering PRT system. Mitten was extraordinarily successful at his job, but he didn't like rapid transit lines. Although the first subway-elevated in Philadelphia had been built by private capital and was owned by PRT, it had become apparent that any subsequent lines would need government funds because of the rapidly escalating cost of construction. Thus the extension of the Market Street line to Frankford in 1922 and the Broad Street Subway, which opened in 1928, were, indeed, built and owned by the City of Philadelphia.

Mitten believed that his company could generate greater profits by carrying the majority of its passengers on streetcars, rather than transferring them to rapid transit lines which would be owned by the city and which PRT would have to lease. His philosophy was directly opposed to Taylor's, but he couldn't do much to fight Taylor while Taylor still occupied an office in City Hall. Once Blankenburg was no longer mayor and World War I was over, Mitten got his revenge.

Beginning in November 1919, with little warning to passengers, Mitten began turning back many Market Street Elevated trains short of 69th Street Terminal, at 63rd Street Station, where there was a crossover and signal tower. Passengers who made the mistake of boarding a turnback train were dumped onto the open platform at 63rd Street and forced to wait for another train to carry them to 69th Street. It was a great inconvenience and caused many commuters to miss their suburban connections.

At the time, 29,000 weekday passengers were being carried to or from 69th Street Terminal by the Market Street Elevated. So everybody was unhappy except Mitten.

Complaints were lodged with the Pennsylvania Public Service Commission by P&WCT, P&W, the Reading Railway, the Atlantic City Railroad and the Delaware River Ferry Company. Taylor orchestrated the case, and he circulated form letters for angry commuters to send to the commission. It seemed that passengers who attempted to wait at a Center City station for a train going all the way to 69th Street Terminal often found themselves unable to board because the trains were too crowded. But Mitten held firm until the Frankford Elevated opened on November 5, 1922, and was connected to the Market Street line for through service.

Peace reigned for less than five years until April 1927, when Mitten threatened to again curtail service west of 63rd Street. PRT placed newspaper ads claiming that $150,000 a year was wasted in "excess service" to 69th Street which "benefits suburban residents at the expense of Philadelphia car-riders." Mitten also threatened to turn back some eastbound trains at 2nd Street Station. A newspaper article called the case "the product of hate and rivalry between two men."

But the threats were never carried out, and Mitten died in 1929. The suburbanites had won.

POWER FOR THE PEOPLE

A futile P&W scheme for generating more income focused on generating more electricity.

The company's big Beechwood Powerhouse was capable of producing much more electricity than the P&W required, so it was decided to try to sell electricity to homes along the railroad. On April 8, 1913, six subsidiary companies were created, one for each of the municipalities served by the P&W.

Millbourne Electric Light & Power Company was set up to serve residents of Upper Darby Township, Coopertown Electric Light and Power Company to serve Haverford Township, Gladwyne Electric Light and Power Company for Lower Merion Township, Ithan Electric Light & Power Company for Radnor Township, Gulph Electric Light and Power Company for Upper Merion Township and Interborough Electric Light and Power Company for Bridgeport and Norristown.

The officers and directors of the companies were Thomas Newhall, president, Julius L. Adams, vice president, and Gerald Holsman, secretary-treasurer. The three men held the same positions with P&W. All shares of the original stock were issued to these three men and were dated May 29, 1913.

All six companies were consolidated into Interborough Electric Light & Power Company on July 24. There was apparently strong competition at the time among fledgling power companies, and P&W's plan never got off the ground. Interborough was finally dissolved in 1924, never having sold a single kilowatt-hour.

THE ITHAN TRAGEDY

Thomas Newhall was the man most responsible for the fact that the P&W still exists as a viable electric commuter railroad. Without his forward-thinking leadership the Norristown extension may not have been built in 1912, and it is unlikely that the railroad could have survived without the ridership generated by that extension.

Newhall seemingly had everything. He was associated with the largest banking houses in Philadelphia and New York. He was a socially prominent Main Line resident and a descendent of Robert Morris, financier of the American Revolution. His father, Daniel Newhall, was purchasing agent for the Pennsylvania Railroad for 31 years. When the P&W was formed, Newhall was associated with J. L. Blackwell & Company of Baltimore, which had a principal role in the railroad's construction. He became corporate secretary in 1905 of Southeastern Construction Company, the subsidiary formed to build the P&W. Newhall left the Blackwell firm in 1907 to form a new company that bought and sold electric railway securities. He served as a director of the P&W from the time it opened in 1907 until 1928. He became a partner in the banking firm of Edward B. Smith & Company from 1909 and later its president. When that firm took control of P&W in 1910 Newhall became P&W's president, a position he held until he resigned in 1922 to serve as a partner in Drexel & Company, Philadelphia's largest banking firm. He finally resigned as a director of P&W in 1928, and the following year became a partner in J. P. Morgan & Company.

The Ithan Substation in later years. It is still standing. *P&W photo. Collection of Bob Foley.*

The over-achieving Newhall served as a lieutenant commander during World War I and received the Navy Cross. He was chairman of a special committee of the board of directors of Philadelphia Electric Company that supervised construction of the Conowingo Dam on the Susquehanna River. He was for many years a trustee of Bryn Mawr Hospital and of Jefferson Medical College and Hospital. He served as a director of the Pennsylvania Railroad from 1938 to 1944 and was also a director of Baldwin Locomotive Works, General Steel Castings, Midvale Company, Philadelphia & Reading Coal & Iron Company and Sharpe & Dohme, Inc.

With 23 years as an officer or director, he guided the development of the P&W more than any other person. Even after he had ceased to be a director, he took an interest in the little railroad and rode it regularly from his home to his office in Center City. When Dr. Thomas Conway brought a Cincinnati & Lake Erie Railroad car to the P&W in 1930 for testing prior to the design of the bullet cars, Newhall made it a point to ride the car. He and Conway had been acquainted for many years. Conway even routed the C&LE car over the Strafford branch one day just to pick up Newhall at the Ithan Station.

P&W's Strafford line ran along the northern boundary of Newhall's nine-acre estate, called "The Old Place", and he regularly used the Ithan Station, which was right behind his house. The earliest part of the Newhall home was built before the Revolutionary War. The P&W's right-of-way in Ithan and the substation were located on ground that had once belonged to the Newhalls. The P&W's Ithan Substation, adjacent to the Newhall estate, was abandoned after the railroad closed its Beechwood Powerhouse in 1919 and began purchasing electricity. Newhall soon rented the old substation from P&W. The building and a third of an acre were sold by the P&W in January 1926, to Newhall's wife, Honora G. Newhall.

Ithan Substation while in service. A siding barely visible on the right may have led to a quarry. *P&W photo Collection of Bob Foley.*

Newhall converted the building into a recreation and clubroom. He installed a squash court and used part of the building to display his gun collection. Even after Newhall sold his Ithan home in the late 1930s, he continued to keep his gun collection in the Ithan Substation.

On May 12, 1947, at the age of 70 and six months after his wife had died, Newhall drove to the substation and shot himself with a .32-caliber revolver that was part of his collection. Radnor police initially ruled that the shooting was accidental, but a Delaware County coroner's jury later decided that Newhall had died "of a gunshot wound while depressed."

The Ithan Substation, along with the man's legacy, still exists.

CHAPTER SIX

The First Buses

BY 1922 BUSES were a fact of transit life. Competition from a small local bus company and a swarm of privately owned jitneys was beginning to steal away some Philadelphia & Western passengers, so the railroad fought back by creating it own bus subsidiary.

A certificate of incorporation creating Main Line Transfer Company was filed on September 8, 1921, and was approved by the state on April 20, 1922. Two Norristown lawyers served as the officers. Charles T. Larzelere was president and Franklin L. Wright was vice president. Two Ford 10-passenger buses were purchased for $3,495 in kit form and were assembled in the P&W's carbarn, where they were also stored and maintained.

A short loop route was opened on October 1, 1922, connecting the P&W's Bryn Mawr Station with the town center. The route operated via Railroad Avenue, Bryn Mawr Avenue, Lancaster Avenue, Montrose Avenue, County Line Road and Railroad Avenue back to the depot. Trips ran every 20 minutes for most of the day, and the fare was five cents.

The financial results were miserable. The three months of operation in 1922 produced $628 in revenues and a deficit of $1,571. So in June 1923 the fare was increased from five to 10 cents cash or four tickets for 25 cents. Revenue for 1923, the first full year of operation, was $4,340, yielding a net deficit of $3,875. In 1924, 59,000 passengers were carried but the little bus company still lost $3,461. Ridership rose to 63,000 in 1925, with a deficit of $4,721 then dropped to 55,000 in 1926 losing $5,166. Only 200 passengers a day were riding.

COMPETITION FROM MONTGOMERY BUS

Main Line Transfer had been created chiefly because Montgomery Bus Company in 1920 had started a route between Bryn Mawr and the Overbrook area of Philadelphia at 63rd Street and Lancaster Avenue, where buses connected with Philadelphia Rapid Transit Company's Route 10 trolley to City Hall. Montgomery Bus hadn't bothered to get approval from the Pennsylvania Public Service Commission, so the P&W filed a complaint. MB ultimately won permission to operate the route, as well as an extension from Ardmore to Gladwyne. Main Line Transfer unsuccessfully vowed to challenge any further expansion by the upstart and Montgomery Bus soon managed to reach as far west as Garrett Hill and Villanova, further competing with P&W.

Montgomery Bus then sought permission to operate further into the city, connecting directly with the Market Street Elevated at its 63rd Street Station. This would have enabled its passengers to reach Center City much faster than transferring to the Route 10 trolleys. Supporting Montgomery Bus were the Lower Merion Township Board of Commissioners and the Ardmore Chamber of Commerce. The extension was opposed by P&W, the Philadelphia & West Chester Traction, the Pennsylvania Railroad and the Philadelphia Rapid Transit Company. They succeeded in blocking the proposed 63rd Street extension, but Montgomery Bus kept trying.

Left: Main Line Transfer's first buses for the Bryn Mawr Loop were built in 1922. *Collection of Ronald DeGraw.*

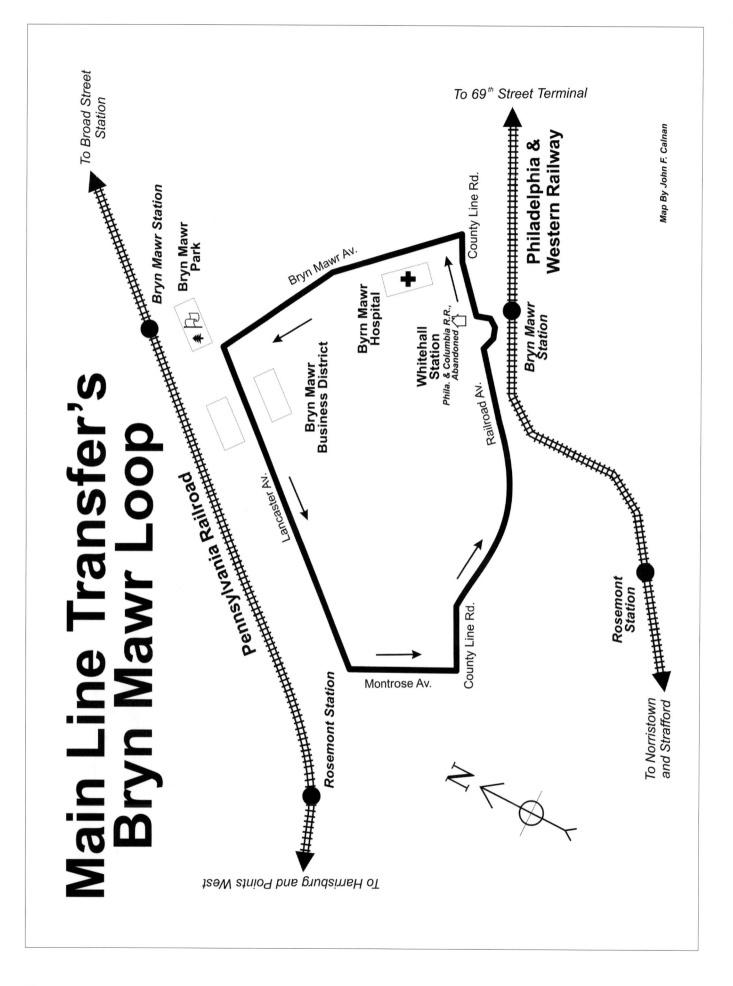

To the consternation of railway managers, Montgomery Bus was carrying 1.8 million passengers a year by 1924, people who otherwise would have ridden the P&W, P&WCT or PRR. These now set out to clip the wings of Montgomery Bus, which wanted to set up a route from Ardmore to 69th Street Terminal to compete with both P&W and P&WCT. The route was instead awarded to P&WCT's bus subsidiary, Aronimink Transportation Company, and began as its Route D on October 4, 1926.

Main Line Transfer requested permission from the Public Service Commission in 1925 to open two other bus routes paralleling the P&W. One would connect Strafford to Bryn Mawr via Conestoga Road and Haverford Road. The other would run from Bryn Mawr via Haverford Road to a point east of Ardmore at Haverford and Argyle Roads, meeting there with Aronimink's Route D. The intention was to purchase new 25-passenger buses to operate this service. Predictably, the routes were opposed by Montgomery Bus, the PRR and Lower Merion Township's commissioners.

The Public Service Commission in February 1926, approved the Bryn Mawr to Argyle Road route but denied the Bryn Mawr to Strafford proposal, the more important of the two. The commission then approved Montgomery Bus Company's application for extending its route westward to Wayne, and an extension to Strafford was approved in June. These additions offered serious competition to the P&W, particularly for local trips.

Main Line Transfer never made any attempt to implement service on the Argyle Road route.

In 1926 three Montgomery County men sought approval from the Public Service Commission to start a bus route paralleling the P&W from King Manor Station through Gulph Mills to Bryn Mawr. Main Line Transfer and Chester Valley Lines easily defeated the proposal.

END OF THE LINE

Main Line Transfer had often borrowed small sums of money from its parent company, usually in amounts of $500 or $1,000. After deficits in each of its first four years, P&W decided Main Line Transfer was a lost cause. The company "temporarily" suspended operation of the Bryn Mawr loop route on March 19, 1927, and sold its two buses.

The corporation officially remained in existence, but dormant. Its tax returns for 1929 showed cash assets of $507.15, which included interest for the year of $6.00 and taxes of $5.00. P&W's first foray into the bus business had not been a smashing success.

The Main Line Transfer name would later be revived in an effort to stay competitive. Almost as small as the fleet number it wore, Main Line bus 2 stands inside the P&W carbarn in 1950. *Collection of John Hoschek and the Motor Bus Society.*

CHAPTER SEVEN

Dr. Conway to the Rescue
1930-1933

THE FRIGHTENING DECLINE of 24 percent of the Philadelphia & Western's ridership during the last five years of the 1920s was greatly worsened by the stock market crash in October 1929. The next year 400,000 more passengers disappeared and profits for 1930 reached only $94,000, less than half of the previous year's earnings.

Even before the Great Depression began, P&W's managers were searching for a solution. Had the P&W reacted as did most of the nation's interurbans, it would have hunkered down, cut service, raised fares, reduced maintenance and spent as little as possible. And like most of those interurbans, P&W would likely have been dead by the time the Depression ended in 1939. When the boom years of World War II arrived, the interurban industry in America was virtually gone.

But not P&W, which took a different route. In mid-1930 the board of directors hired a management consultant to operate the railroad, and they chose the best in the business: Dr. Thomas Conway, Jr.

AN INTERURBAN INNOVATOR

Conway had a remarkable record of transforming down-at-the-mouth electric railways into thriving, profitable enterprises, and the P&W directors were hoping he could perform the same magic in Philadelphia.

A former professor of finance at the University of Pennsylvania's Wharton School, Conway had in 1922 resuscitated the faltering Chicago, Aurora & Elgin Railroad. He sold out in 1926 to utilities magnate Samuel Insull, then moved on to gain control of the Cincinnati, Hamilton & Dayton Railway. He ballooned

Above: Dr. Thomas Conway, a nationally recognized transit expert, was the saviour of the P&W during a troubled period. *Collection of Ronald DeGraw*. **Left:** View of the wind tunnel at the University of Michigan, with Dr. Pawlowski. *P&W photo. Collection of Bob Foley.*

A voting trust certificate from the early 1930s, listing all of the voting trustees. Conway had insisted on the voting trust so that he could acomplish his objectives undisturbed by any stockholder rebellion. *Collection of John R. Nieveen.*

this line into the huge Cincinnati & Lake Erie Railroad, running throughout much of Western Ohio. Within four years, C&LE's gross revenues rose 22 percent and its net earnings were up an incredible 230 percent.

Thus the directors lost little time in hiring Conway "to assist in the management" of the railroad. First they sought his opinion of the P&W's condition and future prospects, which he conveyed—free of charge—in a 13-page letter dated March 12, 1930. Conway blamed several factors for the P&W's rapid ridership decline, including "the shockingly abnormal standard of service which now prevails on the Market Street Subway-Elevated line, which has become progressively worse throughout this period. Such service constitutes a severe handicap to your property; it, without doubt, has driven a large volume of traffic off your lines."

He also cited the private automobile, the Pennsylvania Railroad's free parking at its stations, the serious competition of Montgomery Bus Company along Lancaster Avenue and the institution of reduced fare round-trip tickets on the Reading Railway from Norristown.

Conway observed that the territory served by the P&W had not developed as fast as other nearby areas. "We have in mind particularly the remarkable growth which has occurred during the last decade along the lines of the Philadelphia & West Chester Traction Company, which far outstrips the growth along your system," he wrote. He recommended "a wise revision of your system of fares" to stimulate the development "of dormant territory along your lines."

Substantial economies were possible without affecting service, Conway believed. "In fact, our tentative plan contemplates a substantial improvement in the standard of service for a large proportion of the company's passengers, which in conjunction with the modernization of your fare structure should beget a considerable volume of additional traffic," he told the P&W's board of directors.

Impressed, the directors contracted with the doctor's Philadelphia-based Conway Corporation on June 15, 1930 to implement the improvements. The Conway Corporation was to be paid $12,000 a year, plus the salaries and expenses of Conway and his chief aide, William L. Butler. Conway was named a director and chairman of the board, with Butler becoming vice chairman.

The new plan established five voting trustees. Two were chosen by the P&W's board, two by the Conway Corporation and the fifth by the other four. Such a move guaranteed that Conway would suffer no interference from dissident stockholders and no attempt to take over the company by outsiders. Conway also insisted on the right of the Conway Corporation to purchase 3,000 shares of P&W's common stock at any time over the next 10 years at the then-current price of $3.00 a share.

The board gave Conway carte blanche to put the P&W back on its financial feet. Conway's power was further increased later when P&W president Julius L. Adams died on March 1, 1932. Conway was unanimously elected president on April 20, in addition to being chairman. Butler was named executive vice president, the same position he held at the Cincinnati & Lake Erie.

At this point Conway was firmly established as one of the most preeminent men in the electric railway industry in the United States. He had developed an extremely impressive record of rescuing dying interurban lines. He believed in the future potential of interurban railways. He also headed the group that developed the most successful streetcar in America.

Born in Drexel Hill, Pennsylvania, on August 30, 1882, Conway attended the prestigious Friends' Central School. After graduating from the University of Pennsylvania's Wharton School of Finance and Commerce, one of the most prominent financial colleges in the country, he became an instructor at Wharton in 1905, and continued teaching there as a professor of finance until 1929.

The Philadelphia & West Chester Traction Company's Collingdale branch was built across part of the 105-acre Conway family estate in 1906. Conway deeded land from the estate, which was called "Lansdowne Highlands", to create Delaware County Hospital, and he served as a trustee and board president. The balance of the Conway property became the residential development of Drexel Park beginning in the mid-1920s, and Conway continued to live there. By the mid-1940s he was living at 2045 Spruce Street in Philadelphia's fashionable Rittenhouse Square area.

Ironically, while Conway lived along and commuted on the Philadelphia & West Chester Traction Company's trolley line, that company's president, A. Merritt Taylor, lived on Atlee Road in Wayne and used the West Wayne Station of the Philadelphia & Western to reach his office.

Conway remained a resident of the Philadelphia area, even while running his midwestern interurbans. In 1924 he established the Conway Corporation, and located it in the Fidelity-Philadelphia Building at 123 South Broad Street. It was through this company that he headed the Philadelphia & Western Railway and the Norristown-based Schuylkill Valley Lines bus company.

It was in his school years that Conway became interested in electric railways, when he began writing papers on the interurban industry. He earned his doctorate of philosophy in 1908 with a thesis entitled "The Traffic Problems of Interurban Electric Railroads," and began providing consultant services to electric railways in 1916.

THE CONWAY TOUCH

He first became involved in the actual management of interurbans when he was sent to Chicago to represent the interests of a major group of Philadelphia bondholders of the bankrupt Aurora, Elgin & Chicago Railroad. This group decided to purchase the 61-mile third-rail division of the AE&C from Chicago westward to Elgin, St. Charles, Batavia and Aurora. The new company, named the Chicago, Aurora & Elgin Railroad, took over the routes on July 1, 1922 with Conway as president.

The new company launched a $1 million rehabilitation including new stone ballast, major improvements to the power plant, expanded shop facilities and 20 new steel passenger cars. Conway's assistant Butler was in charge of the design of the new cars. Much of the track was soon rebuilt to high-speed standards, running times were reduced, and more trains were operated. Conway also greatly expanded the railroad's freight service.

In 1925 the CA&E captured third-place in the annual, and very high profile, speed trophy contest sponsored by Electric Traction magazine.

After his quick success with the CA&E, Conway was called upon to address the 1924 annual meeting of the Central Electric Railway Association. He correctly predicted that many interurban lines, foolishly built with little regard for potential ridership, would soon die. He said the rest of the lines would need greatly improved service, new ideas, fast, lightweight cars and good marketing, a philosophy he was able to put into practice at least three times. Conway fiercely believed that well-planned and well-managed interurbans had a bright future.

Only four years after Conway took over, the CA&E's operating revenues had increased by 65 percent, operating expenses increased only 49 percent and net earnings jumped by 154 percent. He had undoubtedly saved the interurban line from abandonment.

Samuel Insull, who controlled the Chicago elevated railways, the Chicago, South Shore & South Bend Railroad, the Chicago, North Shore & Milwaukee Railroad and other electric utilities, gained control of the CA&E in March 1926. Conway departed, but remained a director and a stockholder. The CA&E survived until July 3, 1957, long after most other interurbans had been scrapped.

A NEW CHALLENGE FOR CONWAY

Not one to sit idle, Conway now took charge of the bankrupt Cincinnati & Dayton Traction Company, formerly a part of the big Ohio Electric Railway system. Conway had been sent by the same Philadelphia bondholders in late 1925 to analyse this company. He became president on March 8, 1926, and the firm was renamed the Cincinnati, Hamilton & Dayton Railway. One of the first things Conway did was to purchase 20 new cars. Butler was named vice president and was responsible for the design of the new but not high-performance cars.

Believing the key to the company's future lay in expansion, Conway embarked on an ambitious acquisition program, buying several connecting lines and merging them on January 1, 1930, into a new company called the Cincinnati & Lake Erie Railroad. The aptly named C&LE ran 216 miles from Cincinnati to Toledo, with a 45-mile branch from Springfield to Columbus. C&LE had trackage rights over the Eastern Michigan-Toledo Railway, and the 277-mile run from Cincinnati to Detroit became the longest regularly scheduled passenger run in interurban history.

"Conway... presided over one of the largest, most complex and perhaps most sophisticated interurban networks in America," wrote Jack Keenan, the line's premier historian.

Even before the C&LE was created, Conway and Butler began designing a radically new high-speed, lightweight interurban car for the long route. The Cincinnati Car Company delivered the 20 cars, nicknamed "Red Devils," in 1930. Ten had a luxurious parlor-lounge section. Butler again headed the design group, with assistance from the University of Michigan. The cars were only 44 feet long, contained a large amount of lightweight aluminum and had a top speed of more than 85 miles an hour. New truck design

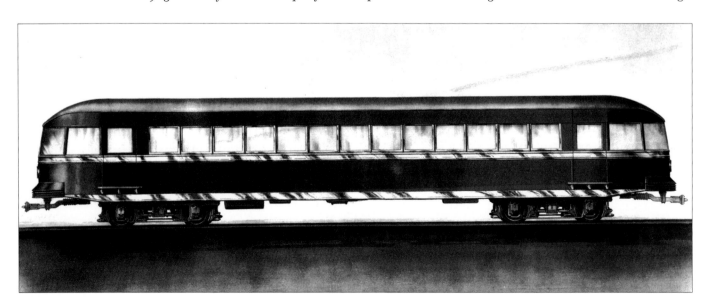

The bullet cars were Conway's crowning achievement, and the things that got the P&W its most favorable press coverage. *Duke-Middleton Collection.*

permitted the cars to travel at high speeds over light rail and still provide a comfortable ride.

The "Red Devils" were the fastest traction cars that had ever been built. Importantly, they led the way toward the design of the famous Philadelphia & Western bullet cars the following year. The Indiana Railroad, another major Midwest interurban, purchased 35 cars similar to the "Red Devils" the following year. Unlike the C&LE cars, the IR cars were capable of multiple-unit operation.

Not adverse to a good publicity stunt, Conway staged a race on July 7, 1930, between a "Red Devil" and an open cockpit biplane, and it was no surprise that the rail car won, attaining 97 miles an hour. The event made the newsreels in movie theaters throughout the country and gained tremendous favorable publicity for the company. The new cars permitted C&LE to rank sixth in Electric Traction magazine's speed survey by 1933. Overall running times were hampered, however, by much street running in towns along the line.

The C&LE was a brave attempt at interurban success, but the Depression and rising auto ownership made this a losing battle. In fact, the interurban industry was doomed. The economic climate and a number of serious collisions on the C&LE caused the line to be completely abandoned by 1939. C&LE buses took over the routes, which were eventually sold to Greyhound.

THE DOCTOR'S NEW STREETCAR

Besides his interurban exploits, Conway was active in the American Electric Railway Association (now called the American Public Transit Association). In 1929 he was appointed to head the organization's Electric Railway Presidents' Conference Committee. This group faced the daunting challenge of designing and producing a radically new streetcar that was lightweight, used less power, was comfortable for passengers, had high acceleration and presented a streamlined appearance. The PCC car, as it became known, was the result of six years of effort by both operators and manufacturers on the committee to bring forth a modern, standardized vehicle that might save the streetcar.

Both the P&W and the C&LE became members of the committee, although neither ever purchased any PCC cars.

With his sterling reputation on the CA&E and the C&LE, Conway seemed a natural choice to spearhead this unique effort. He named as chief engineer for the group Dr. Clarence F. Hirshfeld, whom he had hired from the Detroit Edison Company several years earlier to rebuild the CA&E's antiquated electrical power system. Conway had also sought Hirshfeld's help in solving the vibration problems of P&W's bullet cars in 1932.

The first PCC car was produced in 1936 and the design was an outstanding success. Nearly 5,000 were built for American electric railway companies and another 15,000 for foreign properties.

"The property which stands still, which blunders along with old worn out equipment and operating methods, is doomed to extinction or to the financial graveyard," Conway wrote in 1934. He served as president of the American Transit Association in 1936-1937 and as president of the Transit Research Corporation from 1936 to 1941. During World War II he was a member of the transit advisory committee of the United States Office of Defense Transportation.

A corporate battle saw him ousted from the P&W after a takeover by Philadelphia Suburban Transportation Company in 1946, and in February of the following year Conway was engaged by the Chinese Nationalist Government to plan the rebuilding of transportation in the war-torn city of Shanghai. He remained active in local civic affairs, and in the 1950s served as chairman of the Hospital Council of Philadelphia.

Dr. Thomas Conway died at the age of 79 on January 3, 1962. He had continued to write articles on the transportation industry, and the last one, entitled "Rapid Transit Must Be Improved to Alleviate Traffic Congestion," appeared in a national journal the same month he died.

A BOLD FISCAL APPROACH

Conway's prescription for P&W's financial problems was to start spending money. Fares were reduced beginning November 16, 1930, with the one-way Norristown cash fare cut from 47 to 40 cents. One-way Strafford fares went from 40 to 25 cents, less than they had been since 1918. Half-fare tickets for children were established. Multiple-trip fares were slashed even further the following January, and again in May.

With Depression employment levels plummeting, people counted every penny and avoided unnecessary expenditures, including many transit trips. Conway's plan was to retain as many passengers as possible, even at lower fares, and to keep service and performance levels high.

He believed that while the P&W had been built to very high standards and possessed one of the most impressive interurban rights-of-way in North America, it was actually being operated far below its capabilities. The fastest mostly non-stop Norristown trains averaged only 34 miles per hour. Two-man crews, manual substations, slow cars and the awkward street-loading terminal in Norristown all meant high operating costs.

Furthermore, steam railroads were offering severe competition. The Pennsy had electrified its commuter operation to Norristown on July 20, 1930, cutting the running time by up to 13 minutes. The Philadelphia & Reading, which had changed its name in 1924 to the Reading Company, was electrifying its Norristown branch, which opened on February 5, 1933. Its new schedule shaved 14 minutes from the 50-minute running time. Fighting back, Conway was soon able to advertise that the P&W operated "73 percent more trains each weekday than any other railroad serving Norristown."

Conway quickly saw that the only way to preserve and increase the P&W's traffic to Norristown was to move people faster, as well as cheaper, than the PRR and the Reading. He began to raise the superelevation on P&W's many curves to permit faster operation, with the outside rail as much as eight and a half inches higher than the inside one.

HIGH SPEED CAR DEVELOPMENT

But the main problem lay in the cars themselves. All of them, the early 1907 fleet as well as the more modern 1920s cars, had a top speed of only 45 miles an hour. So the ability to run non-stop for many miles between stations on a superior right-of-way was largely defeated by the inability of the cars to go very fast.

At the Cincinnati & Lake Erie Conway and Butler had pioneered the development of fast, lightweight cars. In September 1930, one of the new "Red Devils,"—No. 127—arrived at Philadelphia for tests. It made numerous test runs on the P&W at up to 85 miles an hour. Conway hoped he could interest LVT in also obtaining new high-speed cars, so the 127 made three round-trips on LVT. On September 28 it ran to Souderton, where it was turned on the carbarn wye. It ran all the way to Allentown on September 29 and went back to Souderton on September 30. The car even made a trip to Strafford that same day. In test service 127 used new Brill trucks, which had shown the need for changes to the truck design and the braking system of the "Red Devils."

Conway believed that the design of the C&LE cars could be improved by streamlining. This was a new concept, and no railway cars had ever been built that utilized streamlining to reduce wind resistance at high speeds, cutting power consumption. Conway engaged Dr. Felix W. Pawlowski, Guggenheim Professor of Aerodynamics at the University of Michigan, on November 18, 1930, to conduct wind tunnel tests. Pawlowski was considered one of the world's leading aeronautics experts and had taught the first college course in aeronautical engineering in America.

Seen here at 69th Street, Cincinnati & Lake Erie car #127 was tested on the P&W from early September through late November of 1930 to evaluate trucks, electrical components and braking systems for possible use in the P&W's order for high speed cars. *Collection of David E. Crawford via Andrew W. Maginnis.*

Using half-inch scale models of cars with interchangeable roofs and ends, Pawlowski tested more than 30 different designs, including that used on the existing C&LE cars. The models were furnished by Brill and the Cincinnati Car Company, builders of the C&LE cars.

Pawlowski's study was sponsored by both the P&W and the C&LE, which hoped to purchase streamlined cars for future service expansion. He concluded that about 70 percent of the power consumed by a non-streamlined C&LE car running at 70 miles an hour was required simply to overcome wind resistance. The results also showed that a streamlined, lightweight car weighing 52,000 pounds could be constructed so that it would use up to 43 percent less power at high speeds.

Pawlowski recommended that the P&W's new cars be designed so that the roof was as low as possible and completely free of clutter, including ventilators, and that the main body of the car was flat on the sides and as short as possible. The front end should be ellipse-shaped, with the roof curving down towards the top of the end windows. The rear end of the car should be parabola-shaped, with the sides curving inward to an elongated point and the roof dipping down towards the point. The windows at both ends should be slanted slightly inward at the top, rather than being perpendicular to the track.

This, Pawlowski thought, was the perfect areodynamic design for a rail car, but it pertained to a single-ended car configuration. The P&W modified the design somewhat, essentially using two of Pawlowski's front ends, because the railroad required double-enders. Thus the new cars were shaped much like the end of a bullet, and so they were tagged "bullet" cars, a name that stuck with them throughout their long life.

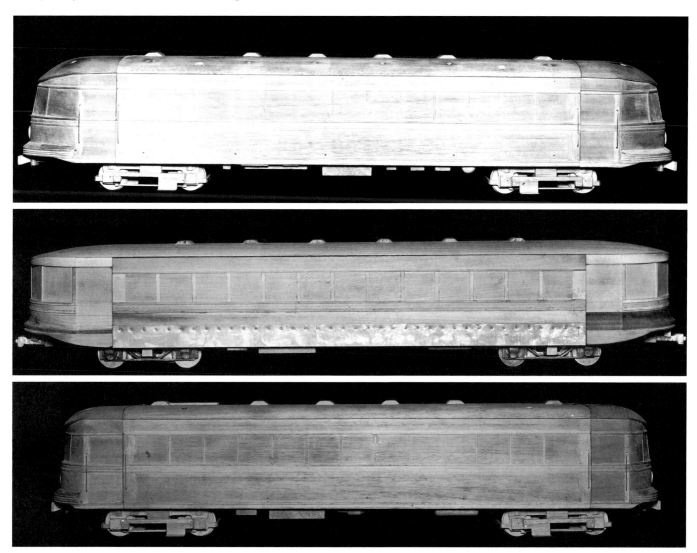

The half-inch models used in the wind tunnel testing had detachable ends. Shown here are a few of the models tested. *P&W photo. Collection of Bob Foley.*

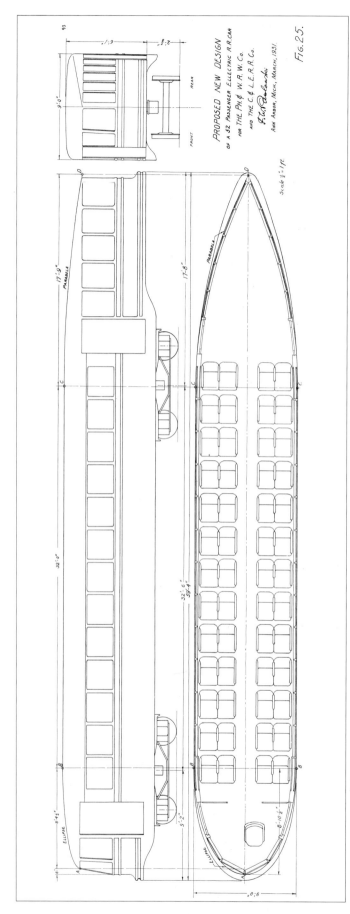

This was Dr. Pawlowski's final recommendation, but it was for a single-end car. P&W modified the design to fit a double-end car. *Collection of Ronald DeGraw.*

Westinghouse Electric and Manufacturing Company was engaged to conduct additional wind tunnel testing on the effect of streamlining interurban cars. Butler, who had been largely responsible for the C&LE "Red Devils", was also in charge of P&W's new car design.

HERE COME THE BULLETS

Brill received an order on June 22, 1931, to build ten of the radically new cars, and the first—No. 200—was completed only two months later. After the beginning of the Depression, Brill had little other business. The prototype car was displayed by Brill at an American Electric Railway Association (AERA) convention in Atlantic City, prior to its delivery to the P&W. Painted pea green with olive green trucks and an AERA insignia in black and gold, it attracted much attention from industry officials and the public because it was prominently displayed on the Boardwalk from September 26 through October 2.

Conway was actively involved with the AERA, and in a coup he persuaded the organization to pay the $500,000 cost of designing the new cars. This was far more than the construction cost of $310,000 for the fleet of 10 cars, which in turn was nearly double that of a conventional streetcar design of the time. Brill had been the low bidder for the bullets at $260,000, a figure that did not include some electrical equipment. Cincinnati Car bid $283,500 and St. Louis Car Company bid $285,390. Most of the cost of the cars—$270,150—was financed through 10-year trust certificates issued by the First Pennsylvania Company. Small brass plaques proclaiming the bank as the owner of the cars remained on the cars until the mid-1960s.

After Atlantic City, the 200 was shipped to the P&W in its green paint scheme for extensive road testing. Field taps, which changed the motor characteristics to provide better speed and acceleration, enabled car 200 to hit 92 miles an hour, which proved to be too fast for the P&W, with its many curves. On one test run, 200 made the 13.5-mile run non-stop from Norristown to 69th Street in just 11 minutes. On October 27 its brakes failed as it was entering 69th Street Terminal and it crashed into the rear of an older car that was unloading passengers. No one was injured, but both cars were damaged. The 200 was sent back to the Brill plant to have its smashed-in nose rebuilt (it returned wearing the red paint scheme).

Conway's new bullets were a 1930s triumphal fusion of power, speed and style. They were the first lightweight,

Before arriving at the P&W, a bullet car--painted pea green--was on display on the Boardwalk at Atlantic City during the American Electric Railway Association's annual conference in 1931. *Collection of Jeffrey Marinoff.*

streamlined, high-speed railway cars in the world. They were also the first to be built almost entirely of aluminum for lighter weight and the first to make extensive use of wind tunnel testing in their design. This saved 7,600 pounds per car.

Soon afterward, streamlined trains and railcars appeared on American and European steam railroads. It's almost never mentioned, but Conway and the P&W had arguably started a world railway revolution.

The sleek new cars—Nos. 200-209—sported Tuscan red bodies with gold leaf lettering outlined in black. The window area was painted a peach color, and the canvas roof was tan. A polished aluminum belt rail and aluminum skirting added to the streamlined appearance. Windows, storm sashes, handrails and most of the cars' hardware were stainless steel.

While the bullet was only one of several cars on display, it received the most attention. It is shown here on the right. *Collection of Jeffrey Marinoff.*

Seven of the cars went into service on the Norristown line on Sunday, November 15, 1931, and thousands of people turned out to ride. They gained nationwide publicity, and even Universal Newsreels ran a short segment shown in theaters throughout the land. "Queer vehicle astounds passengers with 80-mile speeds!" quaintly proclaimed the newsreel as the blur of a bullet car sped by.

The most important thing that the bullets accomplished was to reduce the running time from 69th Street to Norristown from 24 to 16 minutes for limited-stop trains, an average of 51 miles an hour, putting the P&W in hot pursuit of the PRR and Reading electric commuter trains. To further improve the performance of the new cars, Conway boosted the P&W's electrical power from 625 volts direct current to 740 volts.

P&W's terminal-to-terminal speed of 51 miles per hour was the fastest of any interurban line in America. A prestigious interurban speed trophy was awarded annually by Electric Traction magazine and the American Electric Railway Association. It was won for several years by the Chicago, South Shore & South Bend Railroad, whose speeds in 1929 averaged 45 and by 1933, 49 miles an hour. The P&W, however, was ineligible for the award because of its short length.

A report by the Mechanical Committee of the American Railway Association in 1932 stated: "Without exaggeration, the new car is a remarkable advance over other previous types of interurban cars. Riding qualities were uniformly good, acceleration was unusually rapid, braking rates were high but not uncomfortable, noise was limited, operating speeds were high and the general impression of both car and ride was excellent. High speed operation seems to have, aside from the actual saving in time, a certain favorable psychological effect on the passenger...."

The motorman's area of the bullets was clean and modern, with collapsible seats for four more passengers. *P&W photo. Collection of Bob Foley.*

Dr. Thomas Conway (left) chats with a fellow passenger on the inaugural trip of the bullet cars on November 14, 1931. *Collection of Bob Foley.*

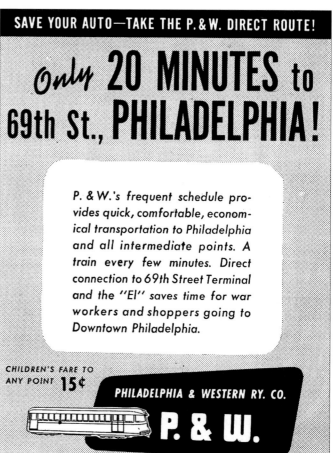

P&W ran this ad in local newspapers in the 1930s to advertise the new bullet cars. *Collection of Ronald DeGraw.*

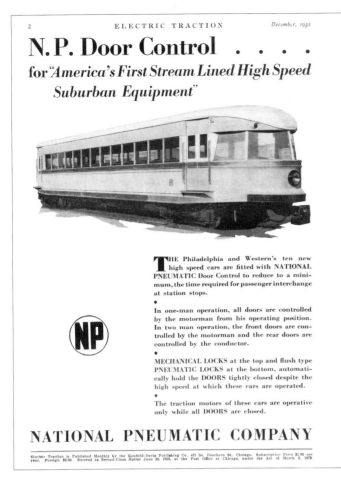

Various manufacturers advertised their roles in the production of the bullet cars. *Collection of Ronald DeGraw.*

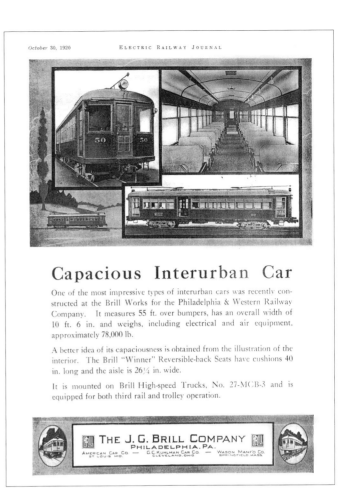

Brill expected to receive many more orders for bullet cars from other interurban companies. The only order they received was for five more of the cars. *Collection of Ronald DeGraw.*

The cars seated 57 passengers, including drop seats for four at each end adjacent to the motorman's seat. These seats were only supposed to be used at the rear end of each car, but they were later removed because passengers also used them in the front ends and distracted motormen. Door control was pneumatic so that the unusual folding doors could be opened and closed as quickly as possible. Passenger dwell time was reduced to eight seconds for the average station.

Designed for multiple-unit operation, the cars came equipped with Tomlinson self-centering couplers that automatically made car, electrical and air connections, and literally required only seconds to couple and uncouple. Trains could easily be made up or broken apart at points along the railroad. Two-car bullet trains were common and a few three-car trains were seen.

As part of its aerodynamic design, the rooflines of the bullets were completely smooth, unusual for rail cars of any sort. In order to provide ventilation to the inside of the car and to the electrical equipment between the ceiling and the roof, the cars featured automatic intake exhaust fans in the ends of the roof, flush with the canvas skin. In the winter they warmed the air before it reached the passenger compartment. Even the underfloor apparatus was hung so as to reduce air resistance

TEETHING TROUBLES

Three days after going into service, the bullets were temporarily withdrawn because of mechanical and electrical problems. They were back on November 28 but they still exhibited "unsatisfactory riding qualities," according to Conway, and P&W refused to pay Brill until nearly a year later. At that point, Brill agreed that P&W could withhold $20,000 of the purchase price and spend it on new trucks for the cars.

"While the bullets clearly represented the 'state of the art' in streamlined carbody and passenger accommodation, they were not state of the art in terms of motor control and brake system technology," Dr. Donald R. Kaplan has written. "Because of their experience with similar propulsion and braking systems on the C&LE high speeds, Conway's engineers

The interiors of the bullet cars were pleasingly modern and comfortable. *Collection of Andrew W. Maginnis.*

A bullet car unloads at 69th Street Terminal. *P&W photo. Collection of Bob Foley.*

opted for proven 1920s technology for the bullets. It is possible that some of the maintenance problems encountered with them through the years might have been alleviated if newer technology had been employed ... even their aluminum bodies, which were intended to (reduce) weight, were a mixed blessing. Because of the emphasis on weight reduction, the carbodies had weak areas and did not stand up well over the years. Significant cracks developed [in later years] which had to be patched with pieces of steel or aluminum."

Overall, however, the cars were an overwhelming success, attracting new riders at lower operating costs. The last of the bullet cars was removed from service 59 years later, each having logged more than five million miles. They endured in regular service longer than almost any other electric railway cars in America.

Nevertheless, the cars "set up a sickening vibration on tangent track" at high speeds, Butler recalled many years later. He said they "didn't vibrate on the curves at high speeds because the centrifugal forces held the wheel flanges up against the outer rail, creating sharp wheel flanges and hollowed out treads and wearing out the outer rail." Experimental trucks were ordered from Standard Steel Car Corporation and the Aluminum Company of America and roller bearings were tried, but the problem remained. P&W finally discovered that grinding the wheels after 15,000 miles of service partially solved the problem.

A few additional glitches occurred but were quickly eliminated. Thermal cracking of the wheels as a result of vigorous service was solved by the development of a special heat-treated wheel. Field taps were removed from the cars after a few years because it was determined they were hard on the traction motors. This reduced the speed of the cars to about 80 miles an hour, but did not affect scheduled running times.

But in virtually every other aspect, the bullets were an unqualified success. During the month of December 1931, ridership increased 1 percent. Operating expenses dropped sharply because the cars consumed much less power and required only one operator.

A NEW TERMINAL AT NORRISTOWN

A major feature of Conway's plan to upgrade the P&W was the replacement of the unsatisfactory Norristown terminus. The street terminal in front of the Court House was replaced by a new building on the southeast corner of Main and Swede Streets. The old William Stahler Drug Company structure, built in 1876, was torn down and a new terminal was constructed adjacent to the P&W's original elevated structure. It had a 23-foot frontage on Main Street and was 100 feet long on Swede Street.

Passengers entering the building at street level could choose between a stairway and an elevator to reach the trains on the second floor. The first floor had a soda fountain, a luncheonette, a newsstand, a cigar stand, parcel checking facilities, a barber shop, and an order desk for a dry cleaning establishment. The kitchen was in the basement. The second floor included a ticket office, restrooms, another newsstand and a large waiting

The new terminal under construction. *P&W photo. Collection of Bob Foley.*

The site of the Norristown Terminal was originally the William Stahler wholesale drug company at Main and Swede Streets. *P&W photo. Collection of Bob Foley.*

For a few days before the new Norristown Terminal was opened, a bullet was posed outside on the Public Square for public inspection. More than 10,000 people walked through it on the first day. An LVT train passes by. *P&W photo. Collection of Bob Foley.*

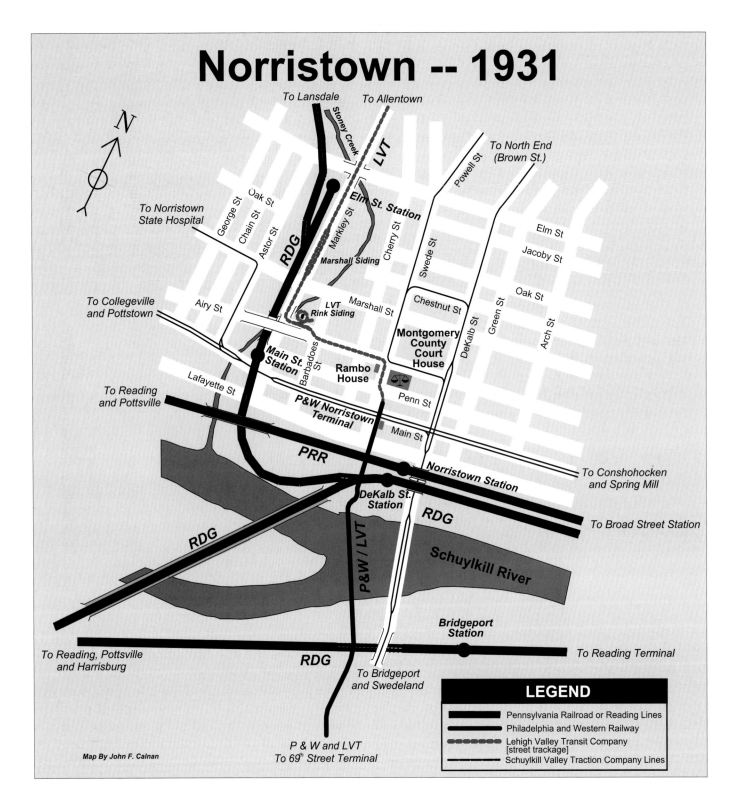

room furnished with dark green leather sofas, club chairs and chandeliers. Passengers then climbed nine steps to reach the outdoor train platform adjacent to the elevated structure.

The train platform was over the Swede Street sidewalk. A pedestrian ramp led down the sloping portion of the elevated structure to Penn Street so that passengers arriving at the P&W did not have to climb any steps.

On the third floor of the terminal building were the company's new offices, which were reached via the elevator or stairs from the passenger platform. The new building cost $205,000, and its opening meant that P&W cars no longer had to run down the ramp to Penn Street and raise a trolley pole for one block of street operation. LVT cars, of course, continued to use the rail ramp.

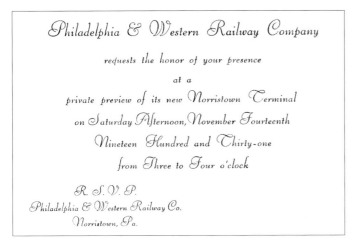

An invitation to the opening of the Norristown Terminal. *Collection of Ronald DeGraw.*

The first floor of the terminal contained a lunch counter in the front and signs of the Zodiac on the ceiling. Passengers could choose between stairs or an elevator to reach the train platform. *P&W photo. Collection of Bob Foley.*

A short flight of steps led up to the train platform. *P&W photo. Collection of Bob Foley.*

The second floor was the waiting room for trains, complete with a ticket office, phone booths, chandeliers and overstuffed club furniture. *P&W photo. Collection of Bob Foley.*

The new terminal opened on November 14, 1931, one day before the bullet cars went into service. No. 207 was temporarily put on display on the sidewalk next to the Public Square, across the street from the new terminal. The car was opened for examination the same day the terminal opened, and 10,000 sightseers wandered through it on that day.

OTHER IMPROVEMENTS

Conway continued to slash costs. The substations at Beechwood and Villanova and the signal tower at Villanova Junction were automated so that men would not have to be paid to operate them 24 hours a day, and the old semaphore block signals were gradually changed to color light signals. Additional signals were installed to permit higher speeds and more frequent service. The manual semaphore passenger signals at stations were changed to automatic signal lights.

Another important part of Conway's grand design involved the rebuilding of the older steel cars to keep up with the bullets, which usually held down the express service. The older 50-series and the 60-series cars were relegated to the slower Strafford trains and Bryn Mawr locals. In January 1931, work began to rebuild the slow 60-series cars into 70-mile-an-hour one-man vehicles by changing the motors from 60 to 100 horsepower, also improving acceleration. The center doors and separate smoking compartments were removed, as were the end doors that made it possible to walk between cars. An improved braking system was installed and the operating controls were moved from the right hand side of each platform to the left. Passengers now boarded at the right front door where the operator collected fares, eliminating the expense of a conductor. The spacing of seats was also modified for more legroom.

As part of their aerodynamic design, the bullets had floors that were eight inches lower than the older cars. All station platforms were lowered by eight inches to accommodate the bullets, and the 60-series cars had their bodies lowered a like amount during their rebuilding. Lower floors were made possible by substituting 28" wheels for the old 30" wheels and lowering the body of the cars by seven inches.

The original plan was for the company's own shops to first rebuild No. 63 as a prototype, then send the other 10 cars to Brill to have the work done. It was later decided that it would be cheaper to do all of the work at the carbarn. It took several years for the company's small shop force to rebuild all 11 cars, although eight of them had their controls moved and other improvements made during 1931 for one-man operation. As they were rebuilt, they were renumbered into the 160-series and were painted the same dark red as the bullet cars.

One-man operation of the 160-series cars began on April 1, 1931, less than a year after Conway had arrived. By this time, enough cars had been modernized so that running times to Strafford could be reduced. Effective November 15, the same day the bullets went into service, the running time for express trains to Strafford was cut from 24 to 19 minutes, and from 28 to 23 minutes for locals.

The Norristown Terminal was originally long enough to accommodate three cars. It was later shortened. *Photo by Ernest A. Mozer.*

For some reason, cars 50-52 were never rebuilt, although they were changed to one-man operation. They remained slow and were used only in Bryn Mawr local service. During the rebuilding program, boards about three inches high were placed at the end of each platform on all the Strafford line stations so that passengers could more easily climb into the cars with higher floors.

The arrival of the bullets permitted the entire original 1907 wood fleet to be retired. Half of them were burned behind the P&W carbarn in 1933. The rest were placed in dead storage, and all were scrapped by 1937.

The Terminal viewed from the ground level, taken in the 1950s. The third-floor, formerly the P&W's offices, by that time was leased to a dance studio. The Terminal was in the heart of Norristown's downtown. *Photo by R. L. Long.*

RIDERSHIP CAMPAIGN LAUNCHED

Conway took other action to improve ridership. A spartan new station, without any waiting room or overhead canopies, was built at Villanova Stadium in 1933, just south of Villanova Station. It was opened only during sporting events at Villanova College.

P&W had its own ticket agents at 69th Street Terminal, Bryn Mawr and Norristown, and Conway moved to get the maximum use out of them by offering all sorts of joint excursion tickets. Round-trip tickets from Norristown to the Delaware Bay began to be sold in 1930 for $1.40, with Wilson Line excursion boats providing passage down the Delaware River. Excursions to the Pocono Mountains via the LVT went for $4.25 a round-trip. Everything was tried; the next few years saw joint tickets for a round-trip on the P&W and a seat in the balcony of the Tower Theatre on 69th Street Boulevard, and for dozens of flower shows, dances, horse shows, golf matches, rodeos, sporting events, circuses and seashore trips.

Round-trip excursion tickets to South Jersey seashore points were sold for as little as $1.30, which included travel on the P&W, the subway-elevated, the Delaware River ferries and railroad trains from Camden. Children's fares were only 75 cents. Passengers using these tickets were entitled to purchase lunch and dinner at the Devonshire Hotel in Atlantic City for $1.25, including use of the hotel's lobby and bathhouse changing rooms.

Tours of Valley Forge Park remained popular. Day long guided tours via Norristown were only $1.00. P&W's Norristown ticket office also began selling tickets for Greyhound and Short Line buses. Conway arranged for taxis to be available for rail passengers at several stations. Free parking lots for passengers were established at Ardmore Junction, Haverford, Bryn Mawr, Villanova, Ithan and Wayne-St. Davids.

A siding was installed at Bridgeport in 1933, holding two cars. Cars were stored at Bridgeport after the evening rush hour and were used for southbound morning peak trips from Norristown. Operators who lived nearby were assigned to these trips. This arrangement saved a couple of hours of pay time and about 50 car miles daily.

Cut-rate round-trip tickets that sold for a mere dime were good in off-peak hours between Norristown and any station on the line except 69th Street Terminal. An

Schuylkill Valley Lines buses loaded on the street below the terminal. Many P&W passengers transferred to the buses. *Collection of Montgomery County Historical Society.*

The waiting platform at Norristown was utilitarian, with only some benches. *Photos by Harre W. Demoro*

unlimited-ride weekly ticket introduced in July 1931, offered rides from Norristown to 69th Street for less than 14 cents a trip. By the end of 1931 new round-trip children's tickets good anywhere on the railroad were selling for ten cents.

In 1933 LVT reduced its rates, permitting cheaper joint fares to points north of Norristown. This was a desperation move, since joint P&W-LVT traffic decreased more than 40 percent in 1932 alone. LVT modified its cars to permit one-man operation, effective August 1, 1932.

LVT told Conway in 1933 that it wanted to be reimbursed 10 cents a car mile for the mileage that its cars ran over the P&W, and threatened to discontinue operation south of Norristown if P&W refused. Conway balked, citing the 1912 contract with LVT that called for P&W crews to operate LVT trains south of Norristown. The contract, which was valid until 1942, required P&W to pay for only the crew costs and the power consumed by the LVT trains. In return, P&W kept all of the revenues collected for trips south of Norristown. The convenience of not having to transfer at Norristown was important for LVT, and the matter was dropped.

Patronage on LVT's extra-fare chair cars virtually disappeared with the onset of the Depression. LVT wanted to respond to P&W's massive improvements, however, so it renovated four of its 700-series cars and on April 26, 1931, created four "DeLuxe Limited" trains. These trains made only seven intermediate stops on the 55-mile trip and reduced the running time to one hour and forty minutes. Each of the four round-trips included

This photo was allegedly taken by the famous photographer Margaret Bourke White shortly after the bullets arrived. *Duke-Middleton Collection.*

a luxuriously rebuilt 700-series car that featured an observation lounge with individual chairs, a sofa, table lamps and a card table.

Two round-trips of the "DeLuxe Limiteds" were extended to Bethlehem and Easton beginning November 15, 1931, the same day bullet car service began on the P&W. At the same time, $1.00 round-trip excursion fares between Easton and 69th Street Terminal began to be offered.

RATE WAR WITH THE READING

A rate war broke out in 1933 when the Reading created a round-trip shopper's ticket selling for only 50 cents.

With the arrival of the bullet cars, all 22 of the original St. Louis cars were scrapped except #46, which was converted into an "emergency" car. Most had been in dead storage for several years and were ready to be scrapped. #27 sits behind the carbarn. *Photo by Anthony Krisak.*

An advertisement by the J. G. Brill Company in the early 1930s. *Collection of Andrew W. Maginnis.*

Bullet cars were usually stored in front of the carbarn during the off-peak hours. *Photo by Anthony Krisak.*

The PRR quickly followed, and P&W too was forced to slash its fares. P&W sold such tickets for 35 cents and established a new non-stop shopper's train from Norristown at 9:10 A.M. To further rattle the Reading, the P&W implemented more peak hour "limited" trains between 69th Street and Norristown, stopping only at Bryn Mawr and Bridgeport. These were in addition to the regular 20-minute express service.

Conway's numerous efforts succeeded in slowing ridership decline. In 1931, 253,000 passengers

The old Gulph Station was located a tenth of a mile south of the existing station. It was eliminated in the 1950s due to construction of the Schuylkill Expressway. *Photo by E. Everett Edwards.*

disappeared, far fewer than the 400,000 drop the previous year. In 1932 the decline was 237,000, and in 1933 it was down to 192,000. Then it began to increase, and continued to do so for most of the next 15 years.

Unfortunately, revenues did not follow suit. Wages for all employees were cut by 10 percent on March 19, 1933, an increasing trend by firms facing the Depression. In 1934 the company showed a deficit for the first time in its history, and Conway promptly filed for bankruptcy.

SAFE. BUT NOT FOOLPROOF

Along with high speeds, Conway attempted to make the P&W as safe as possible. Train operators were required to telephone the dispatcher at 69th Street Terminal before leaving their initial station immediately before the scheduled departure time. Trains could not leave 69th Street until the dispatcher acknowledged with a bell signal on the departure platform.

The dispatcher's office overlooked the departure track at 69th Street Terminal. When a train left, the dispatcher noted which car number was filling the trip. Overnight, a clerk calculated how many miles each car had operated during the previous day. It was on this mileage basis that cars were scheduled for preventive maintenance.

But the safety measures were not foolproof. Two major accidents with the 200-series cars in 1933 marred P&W's good safety record.

On March 14, car 203 was the first train of the morning leaving Norristown. There were no passengers aboard. Halfway across the bridge, an electrical short caused a

A serious wreck at Penfield Station occurred in 1933. The front vestibule was completely destroyed, but the rest of the car was undamaged. The car was completely rebuilt by P&W shop forces. *P&W photo. Collection of Bob Foley.*

fire to break out. The motorman attempted to reach Bridgeport Station so that firefighters could reach the car, but he had to abandon the blazing car right over the Reading tracks in Bridgeport, where the burning molten metal dropped into railroad freight cars. Only a skeleton of No. 203 remained, although its trucks were salvaged. A new car was ordered from Brill and was delivered the following year. Its cost of $34,000 was partly covered by insurance payments of $23,000.

Car 166, a local from Strafford, had just pulled away from the southbound Penfield Station in the morning rush hour on a cold, rainy December 13, 1933. Behind it was a two-car express train of bullets from Norristown. Rounding the bend into Penfield at about 50 miles an hour, the motorman of the express train slammed on his brakes when he saw a red signal. The train slid on the icy rails and crashed into the rear of 166. The impact caved in the entire front vestibule of No. 209, the lead car in the express train. Miraculously, no one was killed, but 16 passengers were injured and car 209 was out of service for several months while it was rebuilt in P&W's shops.

The other serious 1933 disaster occurred when #203 caught fire on the Norristown bridge. It literally melted away. *Collection of Ronald DeGraw.*

SERVICE PATTERNS, 1930-1933

The Conway improvements, including the new bullet cars, transformed the P&W. Running times to Norristown were slashed by 33 percent, and the number of trains operated dramatically increased.

A trip to Norristown dropped from 24 to 16 minutes on the "limited" trains that made intermediate stops only at Bryn Mawr and Bridgeport. More and more limiteds were instituted so that by 1933 there were 19, operating an average of every 13 minutes during the rush hours. Eleven of them ran southbound in the morning and eight of them northbound in the evening. The regular Norristown express trains operating every 20 minutes up until 7:30 P.M. had running times of 19 minutes.

Between 7:30 P.M. and 2:30 A.M. Norristown service was every 30 minutes. All Norristown trains ran either express or limited until after midnight, when they became locals.

By 1933 there were a total of 151 weekday trains to or from Norristown, 104 trains to or from Strafford and an additional 23 rush hour Bryn Mawr short-turn trippers, a total of 278 daily trains. Two-car trains were common in the peak.

Three-car trains were seldom scheduled on the P&W because most platforms were too short. *P&W photo. Collection of Bob Foley.*

Strafford service maintained the same 20-minute headway as Norristown express service. For most of the day, Strafford trains made all stops. During peak periods, they ran non-stop between 69th Street Terminal and Bryn Mawr. With the rebuilt 160-series cars, the Strafford running time in 1931 had been reduced from 24 to 19 minutes for express trains and from 28 to 23 minutes for local trains.

Weekend service was similar, with each branch operating trains every 20 minutes and all Norristown trains running express.

Lehigh Valley Transit continued its hourly service between 69th Street Terminal and Allentown, with trains every two hours in the evenings. On weekends, the evening service was every hour and on Saturday nights an additional train left 69th Street Terminal at 12:15 A.M. "to accommodate theatre parties." LVT trains left 69th Street Terminal on the hour.

Beginning April 26, 1931, four of the hourly LVT round-trips became "DeLuxe Limiteds". One car on each train was a rebuilt 700-series with a luxurious parlor car area at no extra fare. Nos. 702, 703, 704 and 710 were converted for this service, which left each terminal at 8:00 A.M., 10:00 A.M., 2:00 P.M. and 4:00 P.M. They made only seven intermediate stops between Allentown and 69th Street Terminal, and their running time of one hour and 40 minutes was the fastest ever made by Liberty Bell Limiteds up until then. The other regular Liberty Bell trains

A postcard advertising the "DeLuxe Limited Service." *Collection of Ronald DeGraw.*

continued to need two hours southbound and one hour and 58 minutes northbound. The extra-fare chair car service that had begun in 1923 was eliminated with the advent of the new trains.

On the P&W, the "DeLuxe Limiteds" made no stops. Their running time was cut to 22 minutes southbound between Norristown and 69th Street Terminal and only 20 minutes northbound, five minutes faster than the other LVT trains.

Changes in the running times of the "DeLuxe Limiteds" also forced a revision in the meeting points between P&W and LVT crews. Some crew changeovers were moved to the P&W's end of double-track just south of Bridgeport Station. This was the first time LVT crews had operated over a portion of the P&W. Crew changes for the rest of the trains remained at Marshall Siding on Markley Street in Norristown.

All of the "DeLuxe Limiteds" were extended to Bethlehem and Easton beginning November 15, 1931, and a one-day round-trip fare between Easton and 69th Street Terminal of only $1.00 was created.

The "DeLuxe Limiteds" did not last long. On August 1, 1932, when the LVT established one-man operation and abolished conductors, the special trains disappeared, replaced by the older 800-series cars.

TICKETS, PLEASE!

By the early 1920s two-thirds of all the P&W passengers were using tickets, and there was a bewildering variety of them. Dozens of different one-way tickets were available. There were separate tickets for trips from 69th Street Terminal to every station on the line, and there were even tickets for trips between two intermediate stations. There were children's tickets and school tickets and several types of round-trip tickets. Some tickets were date-stamped on the back and had to be used on the day they were purchased.

In addition, there were several types of multiple-trip tickets, including 10-trips, 20-trips, 60-trips, family monthlies and others. Multiple-trip tickets were punched by motormen each time they were presented and lifted when they expired. Special tickets were printed for each employee, like miniature business cards, bearing his name. There were even separate tickets for the families of employees. There were four-part round-trip tickets for trips from points on the P&W to points on the LVT, with each motorman or conductor collecting his proper portion.

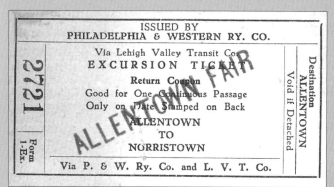

(A selection of P&W tickets. *Collection of Howard L. E. Price.*

Motorman George Pointon poses with #208 in front of the carbarn. *Photo by E. Everett Edwards.*

There were ticket offices at the busiest stations, such as 69th Street Terminal, Bryn Mawr, Strafford and Norristown. At several other locations nearby stores sold P&W tickets and received commissions. Conway's changes to the fare structure simplified the number of different tickets somewhat, but not much.

At the end of every day operators filled out waybills showing how many of every type ticket they had collected during the day. Cash and currency received had to be sorted and listed by quantity. Waybills took 20 to 30 minutes of hard work to fill out.

Motormen documented each fare as it was collected on an overhead Ohmer fare register. The system must have been an accountant's nightmare, but all the waybills were dutifully reconciled each night and compared with the Ohmer register records. Each morning a note was posted in the dispatcher's window showing motormen whose accounts didn't reconcile properly. Motormen who showed chronic shortages of more than a dollar or so didn't last.

P&W LEADS IN STREAMLINING

Conways's bullet cars were the immediate forerunner of major streamlining efforts by railroads generally. Interurban companies and car builders studied wind resistance as early as 1905, when the dynamometer car "Louisiana" underwent testing on the Indiana Union Traction Company near Indianapolis. The testing measured side and roof wind resistance as well as head-end and rear-end pressures at speeds of up to 70 miles an hour. The rooflines of the car were smooth and two detachable fronts were tested, one of a parabolic shape.

The wedge shaped parabolic end exhibited less wind resistance, and therefore required less electrical power than the standard rounded front. While the tests provided encouraging information, nothing much was done by the interurban industry to develop this concept.

The Germans were so pleased with their high-speed "Flying Hamburger" that they even issued a postage stamp in its honor. The curved ends of the train were somewhat similar to the P&W bullets. *Collection of Ronald DeGraw.*

But William R. McKeen, superintendent of motive power for the Union Pacific Railroad, followed the "Louisiana's" tests with interest. He developed the strange-looking McKeen motor car, which included a sharp parabolic front end and porthole windows. The gasoline-powered vehicle was designed for use on railroad branch lines, and 150 of them were built by the time the company went out of business in 1920. They did not however travel at high speeds, they tended to break down and were not a great success.

It was perhaps the German airship Zeppelins that led to an interest in streamlining in the 1920s. Soon automobile manufacturers were producing attractive designs that appeared to be streamlined, even though they didn't really reduce wind resistance. But streamlining had yet to reach rail car design until the Philadelphia & Western Railway's bullet cars were designed in 1931.

The Edward G. Budd Company, of Philadelphia, was quick to follow up on the bullet car design for railroad use. In 1932 it produced an unusual rubber-tired railcar in conjunction with the Michelin Tire Company of France. The aluminum body bore a strong resemblance to the P&W bullets, and some of them ran on branch lines of the Reading Company in the Philadelphia area. The Pullman Company responded the following year with its diesel version of a streamliner that it called a "Railplane," but nobody bought it.

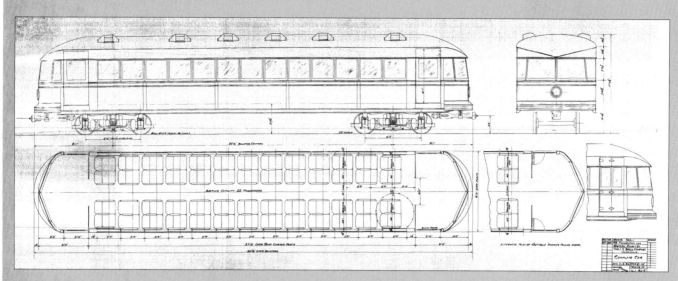

Brill's original design did not have the parabolic ends or folding doors. Collection of Andrew W. Maginnis.

RAILROADS EMBRACE STREAMLINED PASSENGER TRAINS

The "Zephyr" of the Burlington Railroad is usually credited with being the first American railroad streamliner. Built by Budd, the diesel train went into service in 1934 between Chicago and Denver and immediately fired up the imagination of the American public. The Union Pacific's famous bulbous-nosed streamlined diesel "City of Salina" train made its debut in early 1935. From then on, everything on rails had to be streamlined.

A Belgium stamp honored what appeared to be a "dead ringer" for a bullet car. Collection of Ronald DeGraw.

The streamliners were not just attractive, they greatly speeded-up railroad passenger service across the land. Before the advent of streamliners, there were only two long-distance trains scheduled at 60 miles an hour or more between stops. Both were operated by the Reading on its South Jersey seashore service using conventional locomotives. By 1936 there were 644 trains running at these speeds, and by the end of the decade passenger service scheduled at 60 miles an hour or more spanned 56,000 miles of American tracks. The 10 fastest passenger runs in the world were in America.

Brill had hoped to cash in on the streamlined craze, but failed badly. Like so many other manufacturing companies, Brill had been hit hard by the Depression. For most of its existence it had been the largest builder of electric railway cars in the world, and within a few months it had seen its orders for new cars virtually disappear. The company was therefore enthusiastic about constructing the bullet cars for the P&W.

THE "OTHER" BULLETS

It was hard going, but Brill now resolved to convince the nation's hard pressed interurbans to fight for their lives. Of course the Philadelphia company tried to market the car to interurbans across the country. The third-rail Wilkes-Barre & Hazelton Railway, in northern Pennsylvania, was one of the companies approached. The Wilkes-Barre line was interested but couldn't raise the funds. Instead it bought three gasoline railbuses and went out of business in 1933.

Brill approached other railway companies, and even considered a gas-electric adaptation of the bullet design. Finally, one other interurban ordered bullet cars. That contract, for just five cars, came from the Fonda,

Johnstown & Gloversville Railroad in upper New York State. This 33-mile interurban included some street running, so the bullets were modified to include passenger steps and full doors for street loading, along with trolley poles instead of third-rail shoes. Costing $20,000 each, the FJ&G's cars were eight feet shorter than the 55-foot P&W version and had a top speed of 75 miles an hour.

These single-end bullet cars were ordered in July 1931, and entered service on March 1, 1932 carrying fleet numbers 125-129. Painted in an attractive livery of orange and yellow with polished aluminum trim and a black roof, the cars seated 48 passengers and even included a restroom. As on the P&W, the cars were successful in lowering operating costs and reducing running times. A flood in April 1938 weakened the FJ&G's bridge connecting Scotia with Schenectady over the Mohawk River, causing the line to be cut short of its terminal. Without a turnaround loop, the single-end bullets had to be replaced with older double-end equipment. The entire line ceased operation on June 28, 1938. FJ&G had not fully paid for the bullets so they were reclaimed by Brill, which sought a new owner.

Lehigh Valley Transit, then undergoing a major equipment rehabilitation program, examined the FJ&G bullets for possible use on the Liberty Bell Route. They were not what LVT wanted, and the cars were sold by Brill the following year to the Bamberger Railroad which operated a high-speed interurban between Salt Lake City and Ogden, Utah. Here, their paint scheme remained approximately the same and they kept their same numbers. The cars ran for 36 miles through the flatlands of Utah at mile-a-minute speeds until September 7, 1952, when the Bamberger line abandoned passenger service.

After this the bullet cars were sold off for laborers' living quarters. Three cars ultimately survived. No. 127 was acquired in 1971 by Orange Empire Railway Museum in Perris, California, where it is being restored as a Bamberger car. Seats and some electrical equipment were obtained from the P&W bullet cars for No. 127's restoration.

The other four bullet car bodies were sold to Trolley Square Shopping Center in Salt Lake City, then later resold or scrapped. Two bodies remain, one belonging to the Ogden Union Station Museum and the other serving as part of a restaurant.

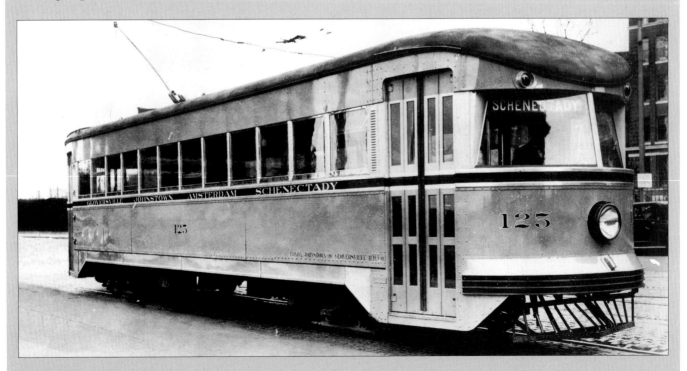

"The other bullets" were five smaller versions made for the Fonda, Johnstown and Gloversville Railroad in New York State. Brill could not find any other buyers for the cars. Collection of Andrew W. Maginnis.

CHAPTER EIGHT

Bankruptcy and War
1934-1942

AS 1934 DAWNED, it was apparent that ridership was again climbing after a decade of decline. That year turned out to be the beginning of an upward trend that would last for 15 years. Ridership for 1934 went up by 22,000 to 2,762,000.

Unfortunately, revenues were not going in the same direction. Thomas Conway had been spending a lot of money, believing that for the railroad to survive, it had to make major improvements that would win back lost riders. In the long term, he was very successful. But in the short run, there were serious financial problems. Severe fare cuts coupled with additional service and major capital improvements brought a net deficit in 1934 for the first time in the railroad's history. The P&W wound up posting a net loss of $42,002 that year.

Conway had anticipated this problem, realizing that improved revenues would eventually follow increased ridership. To postpone the inevitable, Conway had ceased paying dividends to P&W stockholders beginning in 1931. As soon as it became apparent that the P&W was losing money, Conway declared bankruptcy in order to preserve the railroad's assets from impatient creditors. He had seen lenders drive other interurbans out of business.

Above: No. 46 survived as an "emergency" car. *Photo by Ernest A. Mozer.* **Left:** No. 401 was used in snow service. Crewmen shovel out the third-rail shoes of an inbound 160-series car at Ardmore Junction Station. *P&W photo. Collection of Bob Foley.*

On the Cincinnati & Lake Erie, the LVT's 1000-series cars employed much street running in the towns it served. Here a car poses in Springfield, Ohio, in 1930. *Collection of Andrew W. Maginnis.*

Technically, the P&W was unable to pay the interest on bonds due July 1, 1934. The bankruptcy petition was filed with the U.S. District Court on July 3. It argued that the "forced liquidation of the assets" of the railroad would result in "a sacrifice of these assets, to the great detriment of its creditors…and stockholders." Interest on the 1910 bond issue was $131,500 a year, and the bankruptcy would defer such interest payments for at least five years.

"Considering the economic conditions which have prevailed, the traffic of your property compares favorably with that of other high-grade suburban carriers in this region," Conway wrote in a letter to stockholders. "The economic depression has not seriously reduced the rush-hour traffic; on the other hand, the reduction in off-peak riding…has greatly reduced the revenues of your Company."

Conway said the earnings of the company must be plowed back into maintaining the property at a high level. He said the P&W once ran at a top speed of 45 miles an hour and now ran at over 80 miles an hour, which required a much higher standard of track maintenance.

He now hired the consulting firm of Day & Zimmerman Inc. of Philadelphia to examine the P&W's finances and physical plant and to say how much should be spent "to meet present competitive conditions." D&Z's study, submitted October 22, examined the financial woes of the P&W and its recent accomplishments. In five years, the average fare had declined from 19.3 cents to 14 cents. Norristown and Bridgeport passengers accounted for 33 percent of the line's business and 50 percent of its revenues. The stations between County Line and King Manor were producing very few passengers. The P&W was carrying more passengers out of Norristown than its chief competitor, the Reading.

"The cars and stations are clean and well kept, and service is planned to provide a seat per passenger," said the report. "We believe the property is efficiently and economically operated." The report recommended that additional money be spent for track maintenance and that the signal system be improved. Much of this consisted of two-position semaphore signals that gave no preliminary warning to a motorman that he was approaching a red signal. In addition, dwarf signals were recommended to protect short-turn points such as Bryn Mawr.

Signals apparently were not high on Conway's radar screen. His Cincinnati & Lake Erie Railroad was largely a single-track line with passing sidings and no signals. Crews depended on timetabled passing points or dispatcher's orders. This worked well only in theory. In

128 CHAPTER EIGHT

The 700-series cars also remained in service on the Allentown route, but were repainted in the new cream and red color scheme. *Photo by Ernest A. Mozer.*

actual practice, the high-speed operations of the line's "Red Devils" were causing an increasing number of head-on collisions. Conway was never able to afford signals on the C&LE, but he now followed the P&W consultant's recommendations. Semaphores were eliminated during the late 1930s, replaced by a three-indication color light system installed by the P&W's own forces under the direction of its electrical superintendent, William D. Gable.

Lehigh Valley's through service to 69th Street was becoming increasingly irrelevant to the P&W's fortunes. Interline revenue gleaned from Liberty Bell Limited trains on the P&W had dropped from 13.2 percent of the P&W's total revenue in 1926 to only 8.4 percent in 1934. The average revenue from each interline passenger had dropped from 39 cents to 27.4 cents. P&W was earning only about $34,000 annually by hosting LVT trains. Traffic counts showed that the average ridership on LVT's hourly trains over the P&W had dropped to only 13 in the midday and 19 in the peak hours, and some of these passengers were merely traveling between 69th Street Terminal and Norristown.

STRAFFORD BRANCH IMPROVEMENTS

There were some bright spots. In 1934 it was costing the P&W only 5.2 cents per car mile to run its trains, compared to 9.4 cents five years earlier. Conway had achieved this largely through one-man operation, greater speeds and reduced power costs.

The doctor used the bankruptcy protection, backed by the Day & Zimmerman report, to pour more than $1 million into upgrading the P&W's track, roadbed, signals, substations and passenger stations. By the time the tremendous rush of passengers came with World War II the P&W was in excellent physical condition.

With a maximum of 20-minute service to Strafford, even in peak periods, it did not seem necessary to maintain double-track on the entire branch. To save money Conway early in 1934 removed the outbound track between Wayne-St. Davids Station and Lancaster Avenue. One of the two tracks at Strafford Station was also eliminated.

Improvements continued. The outbound station platform at Sugartown Road Station, which was now single-track, was moved to the east side of Lancaster Avenue and a new station was established on July 8, 1934, at a cost of only $450. Another new station was opened at South Devon Avenue two weeks later, using the redundant platform from West Wayne Station that was moved several hundred feet west to the new site. The outbound platform at Wayne-St. Davids was moved westward to establish a new station at Maplewood Road on June 17, 1935. Willowburn Station, on the double-track between Villanova and Radnor, opened in 1938. This increased the number of stops on the Strafford Branch west of Villanova from six to 10 and slowed down the Strafford trains.

To enhance the attractiveness of Strafford service, two additional trains were added in peak periods and several Strafford trains were operated with bullet cars for the first time. Beginning on May 31, 1935, 200-series cars filled four inbound A.M. and two outbound P.M. Strafford trips. Now, all 10 bullet cars were required for peak hour service, putting tremendous pressure on the carbarn crews.

WAGES AND FARES INCREASE

By the mid-1930s grumbling P&W motormen threatened to join a union. They were being paid 19 cents an hour less than PRT employees. Of course P&W had traditionally paid its employees less than PRT or P&WCT. P&W raised the wages by five cents an hour in 1937, but the employees were not satisfied. By September most had joined the Brotherhood of Railroad Trainmen, and in December the company signed a contract with the union. Maintenance employees joined the Brotherhood of Railroad Shop Crafts of America, but soon switched to the American Federation of Labor's International Brotherhood of Firemen, Oilers, Helpers, Roundhouse and Railway Shop Laborers.

Ridership continued to climb. It went up by only 47,000 in 1935, but then jumped by another 148,000 in 1936. For the next four years ridership held about steady, and even dipped temporarily. But by 1941 it was above 3.1 million, back to its 1931 level.

With this good news, Conway raised the fares. Norristown one-way trips climbed to 30 cents and Strafford to 25 cents in 1936. By the end of the decade fares went up again by five cents. Weekly tickets good for unlimited use remained very cheap, however. The Norristown weekly was only $1.65, or as little as 14 cents a trip, and the Strafford weekly was $1.25, or about 10 cents a ride. Most people still worked a half-day on Saturdays.

Conway continued to foster various types of excursions and other promotions, and each contributed a few more passengers to the P&W. Even the use of the railroad for hiking was promoted. A little book entitled "A Guide to Hikes Along the Philadelphia Main Line" was published in 1943, and 19 of the 25 recommended routes involved the use of the P&W.

CONWAY'S SUCCESS STORY

After 10 years of Conway management, maintenance costs had dropped by 25 percent, largely due to more efficient operating practices, reduced power bills, the automation of substations and the Villanova Junction signal tower. Annual track maintenance costs dropped from $165,000 to $111,000, even though the right-of-way was in much better condition than it had been in 1930. The

Another view on the Norristown line. No. 163 is south at Conshohocken Road. *Photo by Bruce Bente.*

A bullet approaches Ardmore Junction Station outbound, the first stop for Norristown express trains. *Photo by Anthony Krisak.*

An LVT car has just left the Norristown terminal and is on Swede Street in Norristown en route to Allentown. The P&W terminal's platform roof is visible to the rear of the car. *Photo by Edward S. Miller.*

cost of train operation was slashed by 45 percent, because of one-man operation, higher speeds and the reduction of power costs made possible by the bullet cars. The total number of employees shrank from 155 to 114.

"These very substantial economies were effected under a plan which affords to the company's patrons a greatly improved and much more attractive standard of service," a beaming Conway told his directors. In the six years following the bankruptcy, he had managed to re-ballast half the railroad, replace 6,000 untreated ties with creosoted ones that lasted much longer, install six miles of new rail, replace nearly all of the rail joints, add rail anchors and replace much of the original third-rail.

Conway was particularly pleased that the P&W had managed to retain the bulk of passenger traffic at Norristown, despite improvements made by competitors Reading and PRR. Norristown was now the most important station on the P&W except for 69th Street Terminal.

More than 1,000 new homes were built along the P&W during the 1930s, and every new homeowner was visited by a P&W representative who offered a timetable, fare information and a free ticket. "Many letters expressing astonishment and appreciation of this personal attention have been received," said Conway. Despite this residential boom, much of the land along the P&W from Villanova to both Strafford and Norristown remained sparsely developed.

THE LVT STRUGGLES TO SURVIVE

Most of Lehigh Valley's rail lines managed to survive the Depression, although revenues declined by 68 percent from 1928 to 1938. Part of this was due to a reduction in fares in an attempt to entice lost passengers. The one-way fare from 69th Street Terminal to Allentown was reduced from $1.65 to $1.15, or about two cents a mile. A number of rural rail lines in the Lehigh Valley area were abandoned and replaced by buses, but most city and suburban lines remained. By the mid-1930s LVT was running about the same number of route miles with buses as with rail cars. Hourly service was maintained on the Liberty Bell Route throughout the Depression, although ridership had dropped sharply.

Electric Bond & Share Company, which operated LVT, decided in the late 1930s to undertake an ambitious modernization program. It vowed to retain most of the remaining rail routes, including the Liberty Bell Route, and to acquire a number of second-hand trolleys and interurbans. LVT's newer trolleys were reconditioned, and the company took advantage of second-hand bargains in rolling stock made available by various rail abandonments.

Most of the big 800-series interurbans were removed from passenger service during the 1930s, replaced by the 700-series, with some being converted to freight motors for use on the Philadelphia Division.

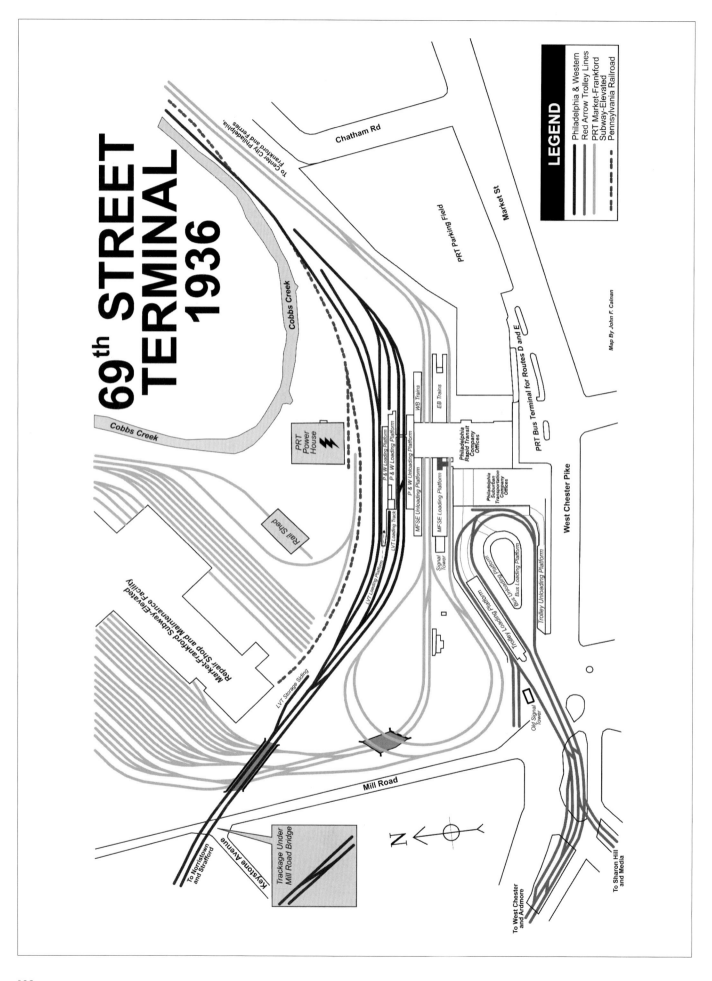

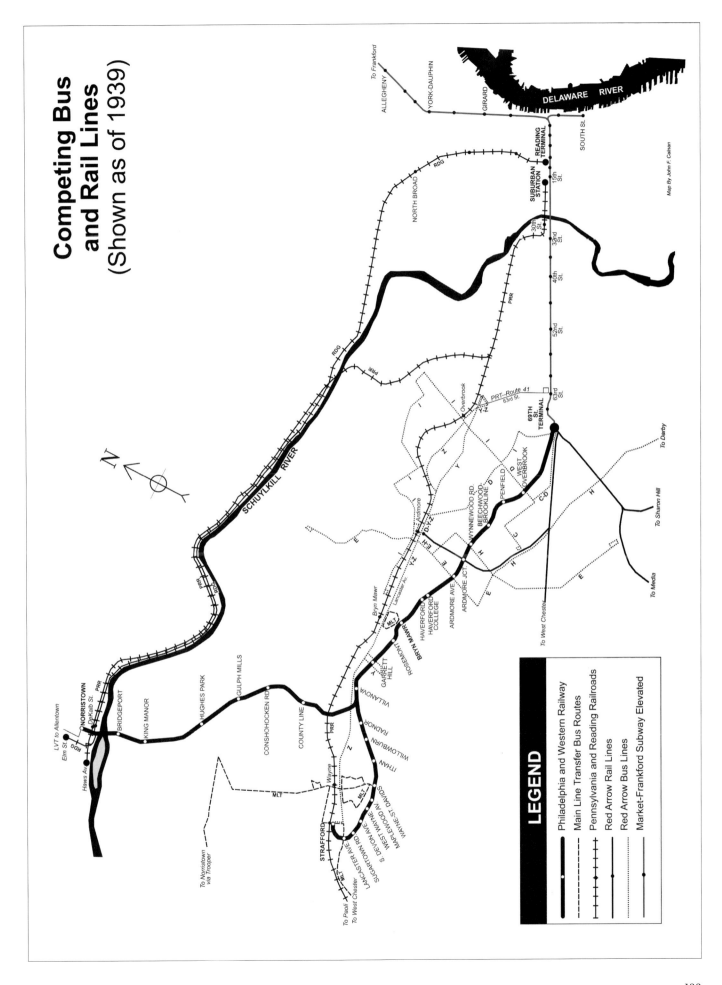

The LVT's loading facilities at 69th Street Terminal were spartan and snug. *Photo by Stephen D. Maguire.*

A long, very narrow loading platform served the LVT cars at 69th Street Terminal. *Photo by David H. Cope.*

A 1000-car approaches the old Gulph Station. *Photo by Lester K. Wismer.*

A 1000-car passes through Villanova Junction northbound, having just passed the southbound LVT train. Notice the smoke marks on the side of the car, which were common due to the number of fires that LVT cars had. Truck fires were frequent when southbound cars passed from the LVT to P&W's higher voltage at Norristown. *Photo by David H. Cope.*

Between trips, the LVT cars were turned on a wye opposite the P&W carbarn. Here one emerges from the south end of the wye. *Photo by Lester K. Wismer.*

Even Conway helped out. The last portion of his Cincinnati & Lake Erie Railroad was abandoned on October 29, 1938, a victim of the Depression and the automobile, and the beautiful "Red Devils" became surplus less than a decade after they were built. Even before the final abandonment, Conway put the car fleet up for sale. The timing was perfect for LVT's modernization program. Because of the reputation of the C&LE cars, it would have been natural for LVT to be interested in them. But Conway must certainly have had a hand in the LVT decision; seventeen of the "Red Devils" were still operable by the time C&LE was abandoned, and LVT bought 11 of them.

The first of these arrived in Allentown on September 21, 1938, and the final one was delivered October 29. LVT immediately went to work on renovating the cars to make them compatible with LVT and P&W service. The cars with Westinghouse electrical equipment became Nos. 1000-1006, and the ones having General Electric equipment became Nos. 1020-1023.

These single-end cars required a left side door in the front of the car to handle southbound loading at the P&W's Norristown and Bryn Mawr stations. Both front doors had traps for street loading or P&W's high platforms. Car exteriors were painted a striking picador cream with a trim of mountain ash scarlet and silver roofs. The spoked pilot at the front of the car was covered by stainless steel, which gave the car a rakish, streamlined appearance. Third-rail pickup shoes were added to the trucks. The cars were turned at 69th Street Terminal using the wye opposite the carbarn.

A loop was built at the stub-end Rink Siding at Airy and Markley Streets just north of the Norristown Terminal in 1938 to turn the new cars if they ran only in Allentown-Norristown service.

The first of the renovated 1000-series cars entered service on the Liberty Bell Route on February 13, 1939, and all were in operation by July. They were an immediate success, reducing running times by 10 minutes and increasing patronage. LVT purchased two more C&LE cars, which became Nos. 1007 and 1008 and entered service in August and September 1939. The remaining 700-series cars and No. 812 were repainted into the scarlet and white color scheme.

One of the new cars did not last long. No. 1004 was destroyed by fire on December 20, 1940, at the P&W's King Manor Station. The fire also took part of the station platform. LVT No. 703 had been destroyed by fire at the same location on November 18, 1935. Numerous other minor fires also occurred. LVT asked P&W to share in compensating passengers on No. 1004 for lost belongings. Conway refused, citing the frequency of the LVT's fires. P&W did, however, take out an insurance policy to cover damage to LVT cars while they were on the P&W.

Meanwhile, LVT sought a replacement for the burned car. The other C&LE cars had already been sold to the Cedar Rapids & Iowa City Ry. (CRANDIC), so LVT turned to the Indiana Railroad for a replacement. Its No. 55 was converted to LVT's 1030 and entered service on the Liberty Bell Route on October 3, 1941. Its body was very similar to the C&LE cars, but its interior was unique. In 1934 IRR had converted this car to a club car, with overstuffed chairs. LVT added to the opulence with monogrammed headrest cloths, plants, cigarette stands and magazines in leather binders. There was no extra charge for riding in No. 1030.

With the low ridership levels of the Depression years, the 1000-series would have been very practical on LVT. But their inability to operate in multiple-unit service turned out to be a severe handicap as ridership boomed during World War. At first, LVT maintained its traditional hourly frequency and ran second and even third sections on busy weekends and holidays. This meant that separate cars operated within minutes of each other on the single-track Liberty Bell Route when traffic was heavy. Fine in theory— dangerous in practice.

Sure enough, No. 1003 ran head-on into a heavy freight motor on a curve at Washington Square just north of Norristown on July 8, 1942. The freight motor rode over top of the lightweight car, crushing the front portion, killing 12 passengers and injuring another 30. A rescuer said, "In the front part of the car, almost down to the middle, men and women were lying on top of each other, screaming and yelling. It was terrible. Blood was everywhere…" LVT's once good safety record was further marred by a rear-end collision only 17 days later and a grade crossing smashup with a truck two months after that, both at Perkasie.

This was too much, and LVT changed its schedule on September 20, 1942. Trains now ran every 30 minutes instead of hourly between Allentown and Norristown on weekdays, with every other train continuing to 69th Street Terminal. On weekends and holidays, trains ran

An LVT is backing from the Terminal to the wye, a move that occurred between every trip. *Collection of Andrew W. Maginnis.*

No.1001 speeds through Ardmore Junction Station in 1941. *Photo by Edward S. Miller.*

An LVT train roars through West Overbrook. *Photo by David H. Cope.*

160 cars seldom ran to Norristown, remaining instead in Strafford and Bryn Mawr service, but it was possible to occasionally catch one heading toward Norristown. *Photo by Bruce Bente.*

No. 812 remained in Liberty Bell service even after the arrival of the 1000-series cars, even though all of the rest of the 800-series were scrapped. *Photo by Ernest A. Mozer.*

A 1000 crosses over the Market Street Elevated yard tracks upon leaving 69th Street Terminal. No. 812 is in midday storage on the "LVT track" in the background. *Photo by Ernest A. Mozer.*

North of Norristown, the LVT covered many wide open spaces. Here a 1000-car races between Sellersville and Telford. *Photo by Lester K. Wismer.*

No. 1003 is in midday storage on the P&W freight track at 69th Street Terminal after the cars had only been in service for a month. The P&W loading track is on the right. *Photo by Ernest A. Mozer.*

This is the P&W, but only three LVT cars are visible. The car in the center has just left its loading track (right) for a trip to Allentown. The car on the left has just arrived at 69th Street; it is preparing to follow the regular service car to turn at the wye. A 700-series car is parked on the LVT storage track. *Collection of Railroad Avenue Enterprises.*

Bullet cars handled snow storms very well. *Collection of Richard Allman.*

No. 812 crosses the Norristown bridge over the Pennsylvania Railroad tracks. *Photo by R. O. Johnstone.*

every 30 minutes all the way from Allentown to 69th Street Terminal. Running times were lengthened by an extraordinary 24 minutes as a further safety measure, making the interurban much less competitive with Reading trains. The irony of this was that the fastest cars ever to run on the Liberty Bell Route now maintained the slowest schedules ever operated.

By 1940 the P&W was again in the black, for the first time since 1933. There was a deficit of $348 the following year, but then the jump in ridership assured continued profitability. This was certainly a blessing for the P&W, but it also set it up as a candidate for what today would be called a "hostile takeover". And P&W's big neighbor was set to move in for the kill, as we shall see. Meantime, P&W fares went up about 10 percent on February 15, 1942, and there seemed to be no impact on ridership. The Interstate Commerce Commission stepped in, however, and forced P&W to rescind the increases on May 15, 1943.

COPING WITH THE WAR

The outbreak of war on December 7, 1941, caused a further surge in ridership on transportation systems throughout the nation. Most were soon facing more passengers than they could properly handle. In the depths of the Depression the P&W had been using only 15 cars during peak periods, and there were seats for all. Only six two-car trains were required. Within a year after Pearl Harbor day, 22 of the railway's 24 cars were needed every day. Every Norristown express trip in the rush hours was a two-car train, in addition to "limited" Norristown trains every 20 minutes. Even a few Strafford trains ran with two cars, and Villanova and Bryn Mawr short-turn trips were operated.

Thus the remaining three unrebuilt 60-series cars were quickly reconditioned and speeded up to 70 miles an hour. They became Nos. 168-170. The three 50-series cars were also returned to service, although they were still capable of only 45 miles an hour and were used only in Bryn Mawr local service.

In the two years from 1941 to 1943 ridership skyrocketed from 3.1 million to 5.4 million. Some trains couldn't pick up all the passengers who wanted to board, and total income rebounded to the 1920s levels. Flush with cash and eager for more, P&W increased the number of free parking spaces at its stations.

The P&W also experienced a freak collision as 1943 dawned. Early on the morning of January 15 a motorman was moving a bullet car from overnight storage in the Bridgeport siding. He failed to pay attention and as the car reached the switch on the northbound main line it crashed into the side of another bullet car heading for Norristown. The first car went off the track and tumbled down the embankment toward Merion Street. The second car jumped the rail and bounced along the roadbed for a hundred feet, stopping just before the beginning of the Norristown viaduct. No one was seriously injured, but two cars were temporarily put out of service during a time when every car was desperately needed.

Conway's P&W would have its hands full during the war. And afterwards, as a corporate drama began to play out.

A newspaper photo showing the damage done in the Bridgeport collision. *Collection of Ronald DeGraw.*

SERVICE PATTERNS, 1934-1942

The schedules implemented when the bullet cars arrived in 1931 basically continued throughout the 1930s, except that additional peak hour service was gradually added as ridership began to improve. One minute was added to the Norristown "limited" trains, bringing the time to 17 minutes, and more "limiteds" were added. These trains stopped only at Bryn Mawr, Villanova and Bridgeport, and they were very popular.

Beginning in 1935, bullet cars were used to operate Strafford express trains. Two additional Strafford trips were run in the morning, beyond the regular 20-minute frequency, resulting in an average headway of 13 minutes.

An advertising exhibit touting the P&W's frequency of service and Riverview Beach and seashore excursions. Such excursions gained many riders for the P&W during the 1930s. The location is the P&W's Norristown terminal. *P&W photo. Collection of Bob Foley.*

Indiana Railroad #55, which became LVT No. 1030. *Collection of Harre W. Demoro.*

All of the rush hour Strafford trains operated non-stop between Bryn Mawr and 69th Street Terminal, except for Ardmore Junction. Local stations were handled by Bryn Mawr trains. Trains served Bryn Mawr and Villanova stations an average of every five minutes in rush hours.

In the mid-1930s, only four two-car trains each day were needed for Norristown service in the summer, and six two-car trains the rest of the year. World War II saw every rush hour Norristown train consisting of two cars and a single-car "limited" preceded each Norristown express by about three minutes.

Conway's policy had been to provide a seat for every passenger, but by the early 1940s many passengers were fortunate just to be able to get aboard and find a place to stand. Fifteen cars were enough to provide seats for everybody in the mid-1930s. Half a dozen years later every car that could move was pressed into service, with 22 of the 24-car fleet often running.

HOW FAST?

How fast did the legendary bullet cars really go? The answer is, for most of their lives, as fast as they could.

When first built, Nos. 200-209 were capable of 90 miles an hour. After removal of their field taps in the mid-1930s, their speed was limited to about 80. On most of the railroad there were no speed restrictions. Motormen literally traveled as fast as their cars would go. Norristown express trains, with several miles between some station stops, ran at sustained speeds of well over 70 miles an hour. Sharply super-elevated curves made speed restrictions unnecessary on most of the line. The older 160-series cars, after being rebuilt in the 1930s, could run almost as fast as the bullet cars.

No. 1030 approaches the Norristown Terminal from the street running through Norristown. *Collection of Ronald DeGraw.*

A 1943 employee rulebook listed speed restrictions only at these points:

In addition, there was a 25 mph restriction through the deep cuts around

6 mph:	Through the sharp curve on the bridge near Norristown Terminal.
10 mph:	Through Villanova Junction.
15 mph:	In 69th Street Terminal, through the area of Bryn Mawr Station, on the Norristown bridge, through the switch at the end of double-track at Wayne-St. Davids Station and from Sugartown Road Station to Strafford Station.
25 mph:	Around Hanging Rock cut.
30 mph:	Through the curve at Ithan Station (southbound only).
45 mph:	Approaching the curve at Willowburn (northbound only) and through the curve at Beechwood-Brookline Station (southbound only).

County Line Station during rainstorms because of the possibility of rockslides.

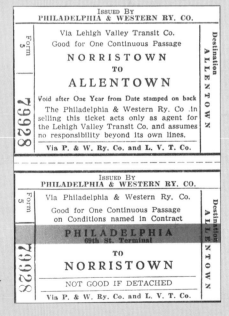

A joint ticket to Allentown issued by the P&W. P&W operators lifted the bottom half of the ticket. *Collection of John R. Nieveen.*

CHAPTER NINE

Buses are Back

THERE WAS ANOTHER light electric railway in Philadelphia & Western territory. Philadelphia & West Chester Traction Company, which served much of eastern Delaware County and had a long trolley line to West Chester, competed with the P&W in a small way. The P&W crossed over top of P&WCT's Ardmore trolley line, which had opened in 1902, at Ardmore Junction Station. The ride from the Ardmore Junction area to 69th Street Terminal was 17 minutes via the trolley but only five minutes on the P&W. But since few people lived near that station, the impact on either company's fortunes was miniscule.

Ardmore, however, was another story. A large town on Lancaster Avenue, it was conveniently served by both the trolley and the Pennsylvania Railroad. It was more than a mile beyond the P&W's Ardmore Junction Station. The quickest way to reach 69th Street Terminal from Ardmore was to take the trolley to Ardmore Junction and transfer to the P&W. But this required two separate fares as well climbing stairs. Most passengers simply boarded a trolley at Ardmore and remained on board all the way to 69th Street.

Competition heated up when P&WCT's bus subsidiary, Aronimink Transportation Company, began Route D between Ardmore and 69th Street Terminal via Argyle and Haverford Roads in 1926. The bus captured some passengers who found it more convenient than walking to the P&W's Penfield or West Overbrook stations. Aronimink's Route C, also begun in 1926, attracted P&W customers at Brookline-Beechwood, Penfield and West Overbrook stations.

Aronimink also operated bus routes past the P&W's Ardmore Avenue and Wynnewood Road stations, although both were low-volume lines that did not serve 69th Street Terminal. Aronimink's routes, combined with the Ardmore trolley, virtually surrounded the P&W east of Haverford Station.

MORE BUSES FOR P&WCT

In December 1935 P&WCT took a step that frightened Conway. Aronimink Transportation secretly negotiated the purchase of Montgomery Bus Company, a concern that had offered stiff competition to the P&W since it began in 1920. Montgomery operated from the Overbrook area on the western edge of Philadelphia along Lancaster Avenue as far west as Strafford, with a branch to Garrett Hill, and connected at Overbrook with Philadelphia Rapid Transit Company bus and trolley lines.

As it was, MBC carried a million passengers a year, all of whom would otherwise have used the P&W, the PRR, the P&WCT or Aronimink. Montgomery had also been hard hit by the Depression, and its ridership was half of what it had been 10 years earlier. But it still ran every 10 minutes along Lancaster Avenue, and people

Left: Signed-up for Paoli, Yellow Coach-built number 12 was actually posed for its "builder's photo." *Collection of John Hoschek and the Motor Bus Society.*

Yellow Coach #203 at Victory Avenue Bus Garage. *Collection of John Hoschek and the Motor Bus Society.*

No. 201 was manufactured by American Car & Foundry. It was a former Aronimink Transportation Company bus. *Collection of John Hoschek and the Motor Bus Society.*

who lived in the towns along the Main Line found it especially useful for short distance trips. The bus route served an area of much greater population density than did the P&W's alignment to the south of Lancaster Avenue.

Conway realized the importance of Montgomery as a competitor, but he had failed to do anything about it. The same month he was elected P&W president in 1930, he resurrected Main Line Transfer's earlier request to run a bus route from Strafford to a point east of Ardmore via Conestoga and Haverford Roads. The Pennsylvania Public Service Commission had once turned down the application; now it was approved. But Conway at the time was busy improving the P&W and he really didn't believe such a bus route could be successful, so he failed to take any action.

Now, Conway did something. He asked the PSC to refuse to allow P&WCT to institute transfers between its bus and trolley routes and the Montgomery Bus route, and to prohibit P&WCT from extending its Lancaster Avenue service directly into 69th Street Terminal. Such actions, he feared, "would result in the diversion of a substantial amount of P&W's traffic to Aronimink."

The doctor then suggested to P&WCT President Merritt H. Taylor that P&W be permitted to purchase Montgomery Bus. Taylor refused. Conway then proposed the two companies jointly purchase and operate Montgomery Bus. Taylor wasn't interested. But Conway finally persuaded Taylor to agree not to operate through service from Lancaster Avenue to 69th Street Terminal or to issue transfers. In return, P&W withdrew its opposition to Aronimink's purchase of Montgomery Bus.

Montgomery Bus disappeared effective July 1, 1936. The Overbrook to Garrett Hill route became Aronimink's Route Y and the Strafford line became Route Z. Aronimink ran service every 30 minutes on each route and purchased new Mack buses. Routes Y and Z soon began carrying more passengers than had Montomgery Bus. Conway's worst fears were coming true, but little did he realize what this was all leading up to.

Up until then, he had been on good terms with P&WCT's management. It was Conway's strong opposition to P&WCT's purchase of Montgomery Bus that dramatically changed the relationship between the two companies and ultimately ended Conway's control of the P&W.

To battle Aronimink's ascendancy, Conway now told his board that the P&W should reestablish the old Bryn Mawr bus loop and begin another one in Wayne. Conway in 1934 had rejected resurrecting the Bryn Mawr route and beginning a Wayne loop because he feared they wouldn't be self-sustaining. Now he wanted them for the P&W's self-protection, at any cost.

BACK AGAIN: MAIN LINE TRANSFER

P&W surveys showed that half of the passengers boarding at its Bryn Mawr Station lived closer to Lancaster Avenue than to the P&W and "would find it more convenient to board an Aronimink bus operating to 69th Street Terminal than to walk to the P&W." The running time of the P&W was obviously much faster than a bus, but some would have found the bus more convenient. The town of Bryn Mawr, on Lancaster Avenue, was half a mile from the P&W station. At 383,000 passengers a year, the Bryn Mawr P&W traffic was worth protecting.

So Conway brought back P&W's bus subsidiary, Main Line Transfer Company, which had unsuccessfully operated the 1.5-mile Bryn Mawr loop route from 1922 to 1927. Conway became president and Clinton D. Smith, the P&W's general manager, was vice president.

The Bryn Mawr loop began on March 29, 1936, running every 10 minutes from 7:00 A.M. until 7:00 P.M. and every 15 minutes until 11:00 P.M. It required one bus and the fare was five cents. A Yellow Coach bus costing $4,211 was obtained for the route and it became No. 2 (later No. 202).

Two bus routes began on May 26, running from the P&W's Wayne-St. Davids Station to the town of Wayne. From the P&W, one route ran via Conestoga Road, Bloomingdale Avenue, Lancaster Avenue, Louella Avenue, Pembroke Avenue and South Wayne Avenue back to the station. It was called the Bloomingdale Loop Line. It, too, was 1.5 miles long. The other route ran via South Wayne Avenue and North Wayne Avenue to a point north of the PRR station, using Beech Tree Lane, Oak Lane and Walnut Avenue to turn around. It was called the North Side Line and was two miles long. Both had a fare of five cents and together required only one bus. Each route operated every 20 minutes, providing a combined frequency of every 10 minutes from the town of Wayne to the P&W.

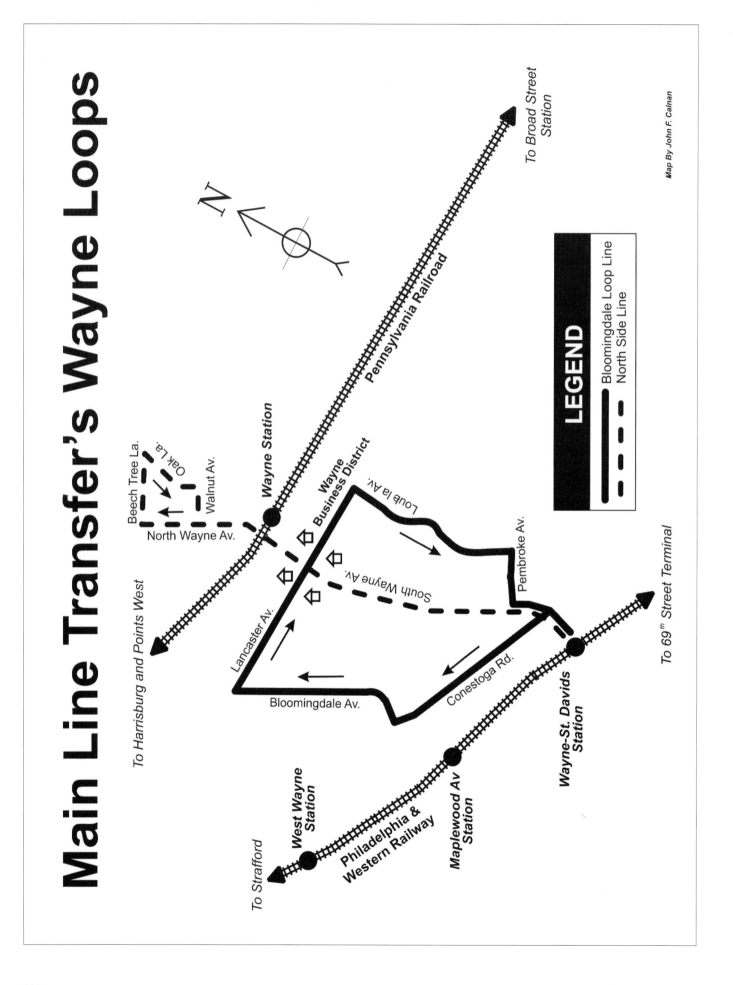

MAIN LINE TRANSFER COMPANY
(Bus Subsidiary of Philadelphia & Western Railway Company)

WAYNE BUS TIME-TABLE

WEEKDAYS
Effective July 26, 1937

NORTH SIDE LINE

From P & W Wayne-St. Davids Station along Summit, Audubon and Wayne Avenues, past P.R.R. Station to Beechtree Lane. On Beechtree Lane to Oak, to Walnut, to Wayne and return over Wayne, Audubon and Summit Avenues to P & W Station.

Bus leaves P & W Station	Bus leaves P.R.R. Station Northbound	Bus leaves P.R.R. Station Southbound	Bus arrives P & W Station
A.M.	A.M.	A.M.	A.M.
7.40	7.43	7.46	7.49
8.17	8.21	8.24	8.27
8.35	8.39	8.42	8.45
8.45	8.49	8.52	8.55
8.55	8.59	9.02	9.05
9.05	9.09	9.12	9.15
9.15	9.19	9.22	9.25
9.25	9.29	9.32	9.35
9.35	9.39	9.42	9.45
9.45	9.49	9.52	9.55
9.55	9.59	10.02	10.05
10.15	10.19	10.22	10.25
10.35	10.39	10.42	10.45
10.55	10.59	11.02	11.05
P.M.	P.M.	P.M.	P.M.
3.15	3.19	3.22	3.25
3.35	3.39	3.42	3.45
3.55	3.59	4.02	4.05
4.05	4.09	4.12	4.15
4.15	4.19	4.22	4.25
4.25	4.29	4.32	4.35
4.35	4.39	4.42	4.45
4.45	4.49	4.52	4.55
4.55	4.59	5.02	5.05
5.05	5.09	5.12	5.15
5.15	5.19	5.22	5.25
5.25	5.29	5.32	5.35
5.45	5.49	5.52	5.55
6.17	6.21	6.24	6.27
6.35	6.39	6.42	6.45
6.55	6.59	7.02	7.05
7.15	7.19	7.22	7.25

See opposite side for Bloomingdale Loop Service
NO SERVICE ON SUNDAYS

MAIN LINE TRANSFER COMPANY
Bus Subsidiary of
PHILADELPHIA & WESTERN RAILWAY CO.

Strafford—Devon—Berwyn—Paoli—
Malvern—West Chester

Effective May 20, 1938

WESTBOUND

P & W Railway Connection Leaves 69th St.	Lv. Strafford	Berwyn	Paoli	Malvern	Sugartown Rd.	Goshenville and General Green	Ar. West Chester
\multicolumn{8}{c}{WEEKDAYS}							
A.M.	A.M.	A.M.	A.M.	A.M.	A.M.	A.M.	A.M.
5.40	6.05	6.12	6.16	6.20	6.28	6.34	6.40
6.50	7.20	7.27	7.32	7.39	7.45	7.51	7.59
8.14	8.40	8.47	8.52	8.59	...	...	...
8.54	9.20	9.27	9.32	9.39	9.45	9.51	9.59
10.34	11.00	11.07	11.12	11.19	...	...	...
	P.M.	P.M.	P.M.	P.M.	P.M.	P.M.	P.M.
11.54	12.20	12.27	12.32	12.39	12.45	12.51	12.59
1.34	2.00	2.07	2.12	2.19	2.23	2.28	2.35
2.54	3.20	3.27	3.32	3.39	3.45	3.51	3.59
4.14	4.40	4.47	4.52	4.59	...	...	...
4.53	5.20	5.27	5.32	5.39	5.45	5.51	5.59
6.14	6.40	6.47	6.52	6.59	7.05	7.11	7.19
S 7.35	S 8.10	S 8.17	S 8.22	S 8.29	S 8.35	S 8.41	S 8.49
9.50	10.20	10.27	10.32	10.39	10.45	10.51	10.59

S—Runs on Saturdays only

SUNDAYS

A.M.	A.M.	A.M.	A.M.	A.M.	A.M.	A.M.	A.M.
8.45	9.20	9.27	9.33	9.39	9.45	9.52	10.00
11.15	11.40	11.47	11.53	11.59	12.05	12.12	12.20
P.M.	P.M.	P.M.	P.M.	P.M.	P.M.	P.M.	P.M.
1.35	2.00	2.07	2.13	2.19	2.25	2.32	2.40
3.15	3.40	3.47	3.53	3.59	4.05	4.12	4.20
5.15	5.40	5.47	5.53	5.59	6.05	6.12	6.20
6.55	7.25	7.32	7.38	7.44	7.50	7.57	8.05

A.M.—Light face type
P.M.—Bold face type

NORRISTOWN—STRAFFORD, Fridays and Saturdays only
Bus leaves Norristown (Main and Swede Sts.) for Port Kennedy, Valley Forge and Strafford at 12.10 P. M.

Sunday schedule will be run on holidays.

(OVER)

A second new bus, also built by Yellow, became No. 3. The color scheme for the buses was the same dark red and tan used by P&W's rail cars. Initially, the buses were stored at local garages in Bryn Mawr and Wayne.

Alas, Main Line Transfer's fiscal performance did nothing to help P&W's bottom line, ending 1936 with a loss of $6,866.

Conway also decided that Main Line Transfer should purchase the rights of Chester Valley Lines's bus route from Strafford to West Chester via Devon, Berwyn, Paoli and Malvern. P&W had a chance to buy this line in 1932 but rejected it because the revenues were low. Now Conway viewed this route, also, as "protective insurance" against a future attempt by Aronimink to expand the Montgomery operation westward from Strafford.

"If modern bus equipment, operated at reasonable intervals, were put in service on the line between Strafford and Malvern, a considerable amount of additional business could be attracted to the P&W," said Conway. "The poor quality of the present bus service is a source of constant complaints to us by the joint patrons of P&W and Chester Valley Lines."

Chester Valley operated nine daily round-trips and was losing money. This route was a logical westward extension for the P&W. Ironically it served all of the same towns between Strafford and West Chester that were on the proposed original P&W rail route announced in 1902.

The West Chester route, operating via Paoli Pike, was purchased on March 1, 1937, for only $8,000 from Short Line, Inc., of Pennsylvania, the owner of Chester Valley Lines. With the franchise came a route from

A full view of bus 12 at the Yellow Coach factory. *Collection of John Hoschek and the Motor Bus Society.*

A larger bus at Bryn Mawr Station. *Collection of John Hoschek and the Motor Bus Society.*

Strafford to Norristown via Valley Forge. Main Line Transfer bought two more 20-passenger Yellow buses for $7,031 to serve the routes, and immediately increased the number of Strafford to Malvern trips by 75 percent. The buses were Nos. 11 and 12.

Main Line Transfer's drivers joined the Brotherhood of Railroad Trainmen in 1940.

The two short Wayne shuttles were discontinued on January 2, 1941, for lack of patronage. The company began running one round-trip daily from Wayne-St. Davids Station to Norristown on January 8, 1941, serving Colonial Village, King of Prussia, Port Kennedy and Betzwood. Two additional round-trips ran from Wayne-St. Davids only as far as Colonial Village. The route was never a success.

On the same date, the West Chester-Strafford route was also connected to the Wayne-St. Davids Station using secondary roads north of Lancaster Avenue. Both of these routes served the town of Wayne, offering some replacement for the abandoned Wayne Loops.

In 1943 a bus garage was purchased for $5,000 on Lancaster Avenue west of Bloomingdale Avenue in Wayne. Prior to that P&W buses were maintained under contract at local garages. Major maintenance work had been performed at the Schuylkill Valley Lines bus garage in Norristown. The Wayne garage was small, and major work on the buses was now done at the P&W carbarn.

No. 12 is parked at the Wayne Station awaiting its trip on the Wayne Loop. *Collection of John Hoschek and the Motor Bus Society.*

A bus at the Ithan Station parking lot. *P&W photo. Collection of Bob Foley.*

BUSES ARE BACK

Main Line Transfer Co. Bus Subsidiary of Philadelphia & Western Railway Company

WAYNE · STRAFFORD · DEVON · BERWYN
PAOLI · MALVERN · MORSTEIN · WEST CHESTER

War Emergency Schedule No. 4 — Effective January 15, 1944

WESTBOUND

EASTERN STANDARD TIME	Week-days A.M.	Week-days A.M. M	Week-days A.M.	Week-days A.M. M	Week-days A.M.	Week-days A.M.	Week-days P.M.	Week-days P.M. M	Mon. to Fri. Inc. P.M.	Saturday P.M.	Week-days P.M. K	Saturday P.M.	Mon. to Fri. Inc. P.M.
Bus Leaves P&W Rwy. Station WAYNE—ST. DAVIDS	...	...	...	7.55	...	...	...	...	...	...	4.05	...	4.53
LANCASTER AVE. WAYNE	...	...	...	7.57	...	...	...	...	...	...	4.07	...	4.55
P&W Rwy. Connection Leaves 69th St. for Strafford	5.42	6.03	...	7.43	8.53	10.53	12.13	1.53	2.33	2.53	3.53	4.13	4.34
Bus Leaves P&W Rwy. Station STRAFFORD	B6.03	B6.35	...	8.05	9.20	11.20	12.50	2.20	3.00	3.20	4.20	4.45	5.00
BERWYN	6.10	6.42	...	8.12	9.27	11.27	12.57	2.27	3.07	3.27	4.27	4.52	5.07
PAOLI	6.14	6.47	8.00	8.18	9.32	11.32	1.02	2.33	3.13	3.33	4.33	4.58	5.13
MALVERN	6.19	6.55	8.07	8.25	9.39	11.39	1.09	2.40	3.19	3.39	4.40	5.05	5.20
MORSTEIN	...	7.05	...	8.35	...	...	...	2.50	...	...	...	...	...
GOSHENVILLE and GENERAL GREEN	6.28	...	8.18	...	9.51	11.51	1.21	...	3.30	3.50	4.51	5.15	5.31
Arrive Short Line Terminal WEST CHESTER	6.37	7.20	8.27	8.50	10.00	NOON 12.00	1.30	3.05	3.39	3.59	5.00	5.25	5.40

EASTERN STANDARD TIME	Week-days P.M. M	Saturday P.M.	Mon. to Fri. Inc. P.M.	Week-days P.M.	Saturday P.M.	Mon. to Fri. Inc. P.M.	Saturday P.M.	SUNDAY A.M.	SUNDAY A.M.	SUNDAY P.M.	SUNDAY P.M.	SUNDAY P.M.
P&W Rwy. Connection Leaves 69th St. for Strafford	5.25	6.13	6.33	7.53	...	9.55	10.08	9.45	11.33	1.33	3.13	5.13
Bus Leaves P&W Rwy. Station STRAFFORD	5.50	6.40	7.00	8.20	...	10.20	10.45	10.30	NOON 12.00	2.00	3.40	5.40
BERWYN	5.57	6.47	7.07	8.27	...	10.27	10.52	10.37	12.07	2.07	3.47	5.47
PAOLI	6.03	6.53	7.13	8.32	9.35	10.32	10.58	10.43	12.13	2.13	3.53	5.53
MALVERN	6.10	7.01	7.19	8.40	9.40	10.39	11.04	10.49	12.19	2.19	3.59	5.59
MORSTEIN	6.20	...	...	...	...	...	...	...	...	...	...	...
GOSHENVILLE and GENERAL GREEN	...	7.12	7.30	8.50	9.50	10.48	11.14	10.58	12.28	2.28	4.08	6.08
Arrive Short Line Terminal WEST CHESTER	6.35	7.23	7.39	9.00	10.00	10.59	11.24	11.09	12.39	2.39	4.19	6.19

B—Leaves from Lancaster Ave. Station Strafford.
K—Leaves Norristown at 3:20 PM. Via Jeffersonville and Port Kennedy Thursday, Friday and Saturday Only.
M—Runs Via Morstein. Does not pass Rush Hospital.   A.M.—Light Face Type.   P.M.—Bold Face Type.
The Sunday Schedule Will Be Operated Thanksgiving, Christmas and New Year's Day.
TIMETABLE SUBJECT TO CHANGE WITHOUT NOTICE.

1/8/44

WARTIME BUS SERVICE REVISIONS

The Bryn Mawr Loop routing was changed slightly several times, and was temporarily suspended when the U.S. Office of Defense Transportation ordered a 20 percent reduction in the amount of bus mileage operated throughout the country. Gasoline and tires were severely rationed, and automobile factories were devoted to the war effort. The use of public transportation jumped rapidly largely due to an acute shortage of gasoline and the ODT finally rationed the use of bus fuel effective May 24, 1943. In addition to temporarily eliminating the Bryn Mawr shuttle, Main Line Transfer was forced to curtail much of its Sunday service to West Chester and most of the Norristown bus route. ODT partially rescinded its order reducing bus fuel in August 1943, and all of the Main Line Transfer service was restored.

ODT's mileage reduction order must have provided Conway with a grin of satisfaction. That's because it temporarily ordered the complete suspension of all bus service operated by Aronimink's Routes Y and Z on Lancaster Avenue, since alternative rail service was offered by the P&W and the PRR. However, service was restored on September 20.

An alternate routing between Strafford and West Chester via Morstein and Green Hill began June 21, 1943. The franchise for the route was purchased for $1,881 from Pennsylvania Greyhound Lines, which operated it after passenger service had been abandoned a few years earlier on the Pennsylvania Railroad's Frazer to West Chester branch. Between the Paoli Pike and the Morstein routings, Main Line Transfer operated 16 round-trips daily from Strafford to West Chester. The Paoli Pike routing continued to offer the greater number of trips.

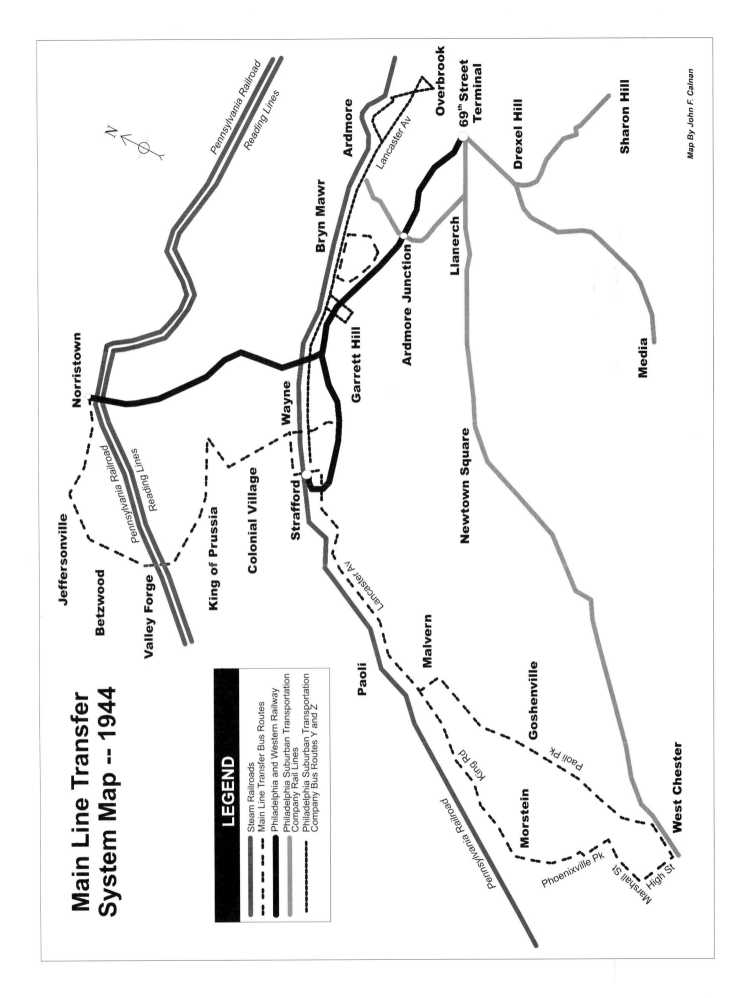

Main Line Transfer did an especially brisk business for a week every year when the Devon Horse Show generated hundreds of passengers, transferring from the P&W at Strafford for the short ride to the Devon fairgrounds. A special round-trip excursion rate of $1.25 from 69th Street Terminal included the fares on the P&W and MLT plus admission to the show.

P&WCT and its successor, Philadelphia Suburban Transportation Company, kept a very close watch on every move taken by Main Line Transfer. Memos flew back and forth between Taylor and his staff on every action taken by the competition, and Taylor even ordered his staff to conduct passenger counts several times. Taylor was determined to foil any sneaky tactic that might harm his company's interests.

MLT's ridership shot upward during World War II, and, like transit companies everywhere, it was desperate for vehicles. In 1943 it even purchased a used school bus for $4,100, bringing the roster to five vehicles. Main Line Transfer broke even for the first time in 1941, then began to show very small profits. Annual revenues rose to $50,000 by 1943.

NORRISTOWN BUS OPERATIONS

Main Line Transfer was not the only bus system connecting to the P&W that Conway was involved with. The local trolley system in Norristown, dating back to 1893, was owned by Schuylkill Valley Traction Company. In addition to lines serving Norristown, the system reached far-flung destinations. To the east, it connected with the Philadelphia Rapid Transit Company at Chestnut Hill and with the Reading's trains at Roxborough and Manayunk. To the west, it ran to Pottstown and Boyertown, where a change of cars could take a passenger all the way to Reading. For much of its life, it was operated under lease by Reading Transit & Light Company, but Reading Transit returned it to Schuylkill Valley Traction in the mid 1920s and the interurban portions of the system began to be abandoned.

By the time Conway arrived at the P&W it was apparent that the remaining trolley lines in Norristown were doomed. Conway was fearful that the Schuylkill Valley franchises would be purchased by the Reading's bus subsidiary, Reading Transportation Company, and that the local Norristown network would be designed to coordinate with Reading commuter trains, P&W's chief competitor. Reading Transportation Company buses already paralleled much of the Reading railroad from Philadelphia to Reading and beyond.

No. 202 was parked at Red Arrow's new Victory Avenue Bus Garage in 1951. *Collection of John Hoschek and the Motor Bus Society.*

So the Conway Corporation created Schuylkill Valley Lines, Inc., on June 2, 1933, and bought the old trolley franchises. The cars ceased running on September 9, 1933, and the next day Schuylkill Valley Lines buses began plying the streets. SVL built a bus garage at 1000 East Main Street in Norristown and shared the general offices of the Philadelphia & Western in the new Norristown terminal building at Main and Swede Streets. It even shared officers. Clinton D. Smith, who was general manager of the P&W, became vice president and general manager of Schuylkill Valley Lines. Conway served as chairman and William L. Butler as executive vice president. A Norristown attorney, Norris D. Wright, was president.

Schuylkill Valley Lines had no official corporate connection with the P&W. The Conway Corporation owned 2,120 of the company's 2,860 shares of common stock.

After one year under Conway's management, the buses were carrying 2.6 million passengers a year, half a million more than the trolleys had carried. It became an important feeder system to the P&W at Norristown, and most of its bus routes terminated at Main and Swede Streets.

Conway used the same tactics with the bus system that he had used to promote the P&W. He modified the fare structure and put forth a tremendous effort to develop excursion business, creating an extensive list of venues. The most popular tourist trip was to Valley Forge Park, and Schuylkill Valley Lines sold round-trip excursions from any point on the P&W to the park for $1.00 and from Norristown for 65 cents. During the summer of 1938, 340 bus trips with 7,000 excursionists were operated. Most of the trips lasted all day and included lunch and a tour guide.

Reduced fare "bus-movie" tickets for the Tower Theatre at 69th Street proved very popular, and helped to fill both buses and the movie theater during the Depression. "Exploring by Motorbus" was a monthly newsletter issued jointly by SVL and P&W, advertising day-trips to as far away as Annapolis, Maryland. A popular route for many years was the Sunday-only service to Graterford Prison, designed for relatives to visit inmates.

The bus system grew to more than 100 route miles, serving as far as Conshohocken, Valley Forge, Phoenixville, Trappe, and all the way up the Perkiomen Creek to East Greenville at the Lehigh County boundary, as well as several local lines in Norristown and Bridgeport.

Conway's policy was to replace buses every five years when possible, and virtually every year the company bought a few new or used buses. It reached a high of 56 buses and $722,000 in revenues in 1951. The company showed a profit every year until 1954. Conway sold the company in 1956.

The system continued operating under the name of Schuylkill Valley Lines until it was purchased by the Southeastern Pennsylvania Transportation Authority on March 1, 1976. Its buses remain an important feeder to the P&W trains at Norristown.

Another bus system in the area that connected with Schuylkill Valley Lines was Auch Interborough Transit Co. It ran east of Norristown and north of the Schuylkill River. Since 1932 it had been running a route that linked Conshohocken with the P&W's Conshohocken Road Station every hour. Joint timetables showed trips from 69th Street Terminal to Conshohocken, and the route continued to run for four decades.

CHAPTER TEN

Moving the Freight

THE STEAM RAILWAY CHARTER under which the Philadelphia & Western was created in 1902 required the operation of freight as well as passenger service. This was intentional since the line was supposed to be the eastern link in a much larger steam railroad network.

Even when that didn't work out, the P&W still had hopes of profiting from freight. A connection with the Pennsylvania Railroad at 69th Street Terminal was included as part of the original line, and three more PRR links were opened within a few years.

Steam locomotives for freight service were originally envisioned, but by 1905 it had been decided to use electricity instead. The initial order of coaches from the St. Louis Car Company included two "express cars" designed for freight service. The 50-foot wooden cars were powerful enough to haul several railroad freight cars. The bi-directional cars had two sliding doors on each side and were originally equipped with small snowplows.

The order of 22 passenger cars, one work car and the two freight motors was set for delivery in the fall of 1905, but the P&W wasn't ready to open. Financial problems had delayed construction. The 22 passenger cars were never delivered, and instead were sold to other properties. The three non-passenger cars were accepted, however. The two freight motors, Nos. 23 and 24, were immediately renumbered to 101 and 102, and still later to 1 and 2, and finally 401 and 402.

A myriad of color schemes were tried out on the two freight motors. They were originally painted dark green then changed in the 1930s to dark red. Later the livery was gray, then changed to dark red around 1955, and finally to yellow in 1961. They were painted orange before being retired in the early 1990s.

But the freight business never prospered, which was a disappointment to P&W's early management. As things turned out, the connecting Lehigh Valley Transit made better use of the P&W for freight than the P&W itself did.

COAL TRAFFIC

The P&W generated its own electricity at a large powerhouse at Beechwood from 1907 until 1919, when it began to purchase power commercially. The original connection with the PRR at 69th Street Terminal was a necessity to enable hopper cars of coal to be delivered to Beechwood. The freight motors hauled hopper cars several times a week to the powerhouse.

Above: P&W motorman James Rothrock poses in front of #402, with a boxcar attached. *Photo by George Pointon.* **Left:** Formerly #700 on the C&LE, this Differential dump car was used for ballast work on the P&W. *Photo by Aaron Fryer.*

No. 402 pushes gondola car #404 northbound at County Line Station. *Photo by James P. Shuman.*

The principal freight motor was originally numbered 2, later becoming #402. It arrived in 1905 from St. Louis Car Company. *P&W photo. Collection of Bob Foley.*

The LVT freight station was built adjacent to the P&W carbarn. *Collection of Bob Foley.*

A siding on the northbound track of the P&W led into the powerhouse. The empty cars were originally crossed over to the southbound track for return to the Pennsy by using the third track that had been installed for turnback movements at Beechwood Park Station. This track was removed two years after the unsuccessful park closed in 1909, and a crossover was constructed just north of the powerhouse. Of course coal destined to the powerhouse didn't really count as freight because it was strictly for company use.

In 1911 P&W sought bids from Baldwin Locomotive Works and St. Louis Car Company for an electric locomotive, but never pursued the idea.

LVT FREIGHT OPERATIONS

P&W's annual freight revenues seldom exceeded $3,000, and half of that was from Lehigh Valley Transit Company's through freight cars. From the beginning of Liberty Bell Limited passenger service into 69th Street Terminal over the P&W tracks on December 12, 1912, LVT also operated freight service. Beginning in 1908 LVT ran door-to-door freight over its Philadelphia Division, with the wagons of Adams Express Company meeting the trolleys in several towns. In 1910 LVT freight began to be transferred at Erdenheim to the wide-gauge cars of the Philadelphia Rapid Transit Company for shipment to the Philadelphia trolley freight terminal at Front and Market Streets. PRT ran freight cars to numerous points on its far-flung system, and the Erdenheim connection was an important one. Most of the larger towns along the Liberty Bell Route had freight stations and many had separate sidings for the freight cars.

LVT built a freight station on the south side of the P&W carbarn just outside 69th Street Terminal and quickly did a bustling business. A new track was built adjacent to the south side of the barn, called Track 0 (pronounced "ought track"). The location was referred to as 72nd Street, although such a street never actually existed. Adams Express moved the freight to its ultimate destination, usually into Philadelphia. Adams had contracts with many large Eastern steam railroads.

MOVING THE FREIGHT

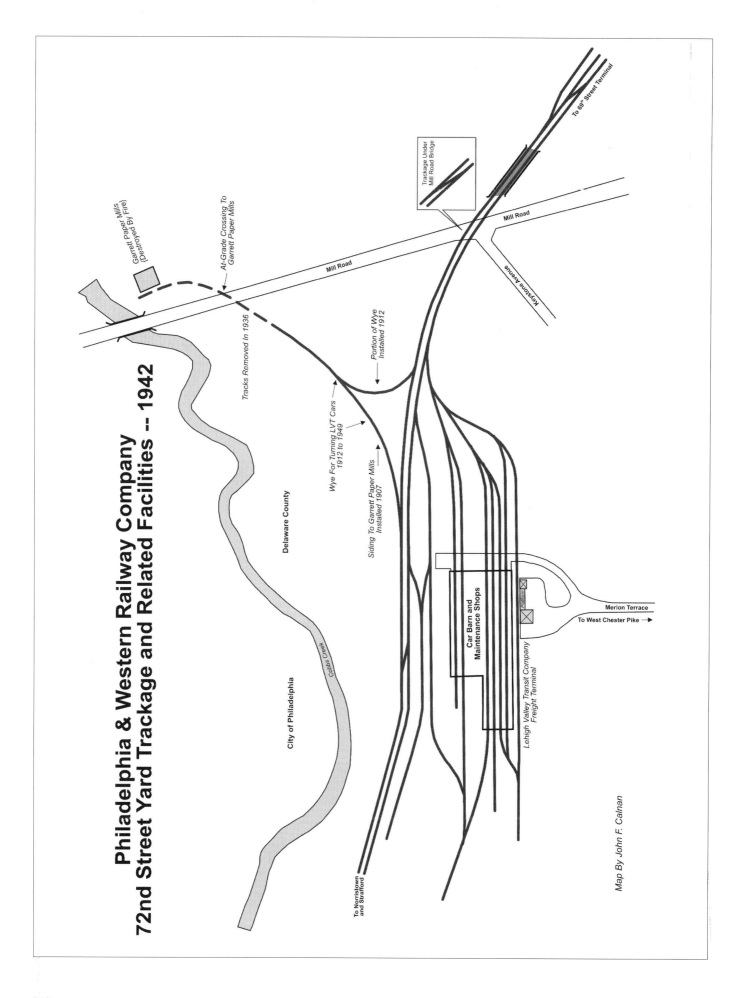

The high-sided gondola dump car was an original piece of work equipment for the P&W. Its original number was 403. *PST Collection.*

In Novenber 1935, LVT freight motors C-14 and C-15 are southbound at Bryn Mawr enroute to the 72nd freight station. *PA Dept. of Highways photo by C. Gorman. Andrew W. Maginnis/Bob Foley Collection.*

The operation of freight cars to the 72nd Street freight station instead of via the time-consuming connection at Erdenheim helped the freight business to grow rapidly. LVT ordered three big freight motors from Jewett Car Company in 1913 and scheduled three daily freight trains. By 1916 it owned 11 freight motors. Between 1934 and 1940 five of the 800-series passenger cars were also converted to high-speed freight motors to help meet the demand.

Shortly after the inauguration of LVT freight service over the P&W, its car C-4 derailed at Bryn Mawr. P&W sent its little derrick car to the rescue, but it couldn't budge the heavy freight car. LVT then dispatched its own crane from its Souderton carbarn. On arrival at Norristown it was realized that the car had no third-rail shoes! This dilemma was soon solved by having a P&W work car tow the crane to Bryn Mawr so that the errant freight motor could be rerailed.

In 1940 LVT bought 14 Mack trucks for operation within Allentown, Bethlehem and Easton. The sides of the trucks proclaimed: "Trolley Freight For Fast Service", the same legend that appeared on the side of the freight motors. The trucking business was sold in 1943 to Modern Transfer Company of Allentown.

AN UNBEATABLE SERVICE

The LVT freight trolleys carried shipments of all sizes, including full carload. Trucks called at homes or offices to pick up shipments then transferred them to the freight trolleys for speedy delivery to the other end of the line. It was an unbeatable service that was fast, inexpensive and popular. Merchants along the Liberty Bell Route who ordered goods from Philadelphia could receive them early the next day via trolley freight.

Produce shipped from Lehigh County and Bucks County farms along the interurban route arrived in Philadelphia's wholesale food district at 3:00 A.M. the next day. Rates for shipping goods from Allentown to Philadelphia ranged between 16 cents and 20 cents per 100 pounds. Small packages and perishable goods were carried in the baggage compartments of the regular hourly passenger trains.

Freight tariffs were even established for through service between Allentown and Baltimore, Maryland, via Adams Express and the Baltimore & Philadelphia Steamboat Company.

LVT freight usually ran as two, three, and even four-car trains. P&W permitted the four-car trains southbound,

An 800-series car, converted to a freight motor, was impressively long. *Photo by Ernest A. Mozer.*

but required that no more than three cars be run northbound because the power consumed on the grades was too great. On occasion, a freight car was operated in a train with two LVT passenger cars and separated at 69th Street Terminal.

A most serious accident involved a LVT freight motor. No. C-14 was running southbound on the single-track line at Washington Square north of Norristown on July 8, 1942, when it crashed at high speed head-on into car 1003. Eleven passengers were killed and 30 injured as the heavy freight car crushed the front of the lightweight passenger car.

Despite such misadventure, LVT's freight service was very successful and three trains a day were usually operated. It is hard, however, to understand why P&W continued to tolerate the inconvenience of freight trains since they produced little revenue for the third-rail line. P&W crews operated the freight trains south of Norristown. LVT kept the freight revenues and paid the P&W only for the crew expense plus car mile costs for power and track usage. The original trackage use rate had been five cents a mile and reached 20 cents by 1948. The power charge by World War II was eight cents a mile.

THE NIGHT FREIGHT

The "night freight" run was particularly popular with P&W crewmen. The eight-hour run for the employees began about 3:30 P.M. with two Strafford passenger trips and a Bryn Mawr trip. Then at 6:35 P.M. the two-man crew took the last northbound freight train of the day, usually two or three cars, to Norristown. The train went into Swede Street, turned left onto Airy Street then backed into the Rink Loop to await the last southbound freight.

At Norristown, a freight siding had been built in 1912 at the Merchants Ice Company at Markley and Marshall Streets. It was abandoned in 1930.

An old skating rink at Markley and Airy Streets was purchased in 1912, where LVT built a freight house and siding. When the single-end Cincinnati & Lake Erie passenger cars were purchased for Liberty Bell Limited service in 1938, the Rink siding was slightly relocated and a loop was built around the freight station. This permitted single-end LVT cars to turn around at Norristown, if necessary. The loop was so tight, however, that multiple-car trains could not use it. So the night freight had to be uncoupled and taken into the loop one car at a time. When the southbound freight arrived, the

An LVT freight train in front of the P&W carbarn. *Photo by David H. Cope.*

P&W's hopper car was built by Mt. Vernon Car Company. It was used chiefly for ballasting the railroad. *Collection of Bob Foley.*

Another former 800-series passenger car, converted during the 1940s. *Collection by Andrew W. Maginnis.*

The siding leading into the Garrett Paper Mill (shown after a fire) crossed Mill Road (Victory Avenue) at grade. *P&W photo. Collection of Bob Foley.*

P&W's primitive derrick car #101 was later replaced by crane car #407. Note the Fox trucks. *Collection of Bob Foley.*

MOVING THE FREIGHT

The siding serving the Bryn Mawr Ice Company did not last long. *Collection of Robert Goshorn and the Tredyffrin-Easttown History Club.*

northbound train had to be brought back to the main line and reassembled. It was a cumbersome and time-consuming operation.

Time, however, was something the P&W crew had plenty of. The last southbound freight was held at Allentown until it was filled and ready to move. It arrived at Norristown after 7:00 P.M., sometimes as late as midnight. The waiting P&W crew took a nap in the Rink freight house and was sometimes even able to put in a claim for overtime. The "night freight" was truly the cushiest job on the P&W.

Freight was a lucrative business for the LVT, and it lasted until the abandonment of passenger service on September 6, 1951. Even after LVT passenger cars were cut back to Norristown in 1949 and ceased running over the P&W, the freight trolleys continued operating to the 72nd Street freight station. Finally, it was torn down in 1954.

P&W FREIGHT OPERATIONS

P&W's own freight consisted mostly of sand, stone, coal and oil. In the early years it amounted to an average of three freight cars a day interchanged with the PRR. A newspaper article that appeared when the P&W opened for business in 1907 claimed that the interurban "intends going into the freight-carrying business on a large scale." Trolley companies in Pennsylvania were forbidden to carry freight until passage of the "Trolley Freight Bill" by the state legislature in 1908. The P&W, operating under a steam railroad charter, was not restricted.

When the P&W was originally built, a connection from 69th Street Terminal to the Pennsylvania Railroad's Cardington branch in Millbourne aided in delivering construction supplies.

At the same time that the Strafford line was extended half a mile in 1911, a freight connection with the Pennsy was constructed just west of the PRR's Strafford Station. Two more links with the PRR were made when the Norristown extension was opened the following year.

The first of these was immediately south of where the P&W crossed under the PRR's Trenton Cut-Off. Here, a spur track swung eastward off of the P&W's northbound main track and traced almost a half circle before it met up with the PRR's Swedeland branch. The Swedeland connection was installed largely because P&W found it could obtain a cheap rate for the slag ballast needed for track maintenance. This connection was abandoned in the 1930s.

The second link opened in 1912, and left the P&W's main line just south of the Swedeland connection and ran westward to serve the Lukens & Yerkes Quarry. Crossing Yerkes Road at grade, the spur continued through the quarry's rock breaker, finally joining the PRR's Trenton Cut-Off at the Henderson freight station. This siding remained in service until the early 1950s.

The last siding to see active use served Merion Golf Club at Ardmore Avenue Station. *Collection of Bob Foley.*

Despite having four PRR connections, P&W's freight business remained sparse.

A siding opposite the P&W carbarn was built in 1907 to serve the Garrett Paper Mill, which had long predated the railroad. To reach the mill, the siding crossed Mill Road (now Victory Avenue) at grade. When LVT began running its trains to 69th Street Terminal in 1912, an additional leg was added to the Garrett siding to form a wye on which to turn the single-end cars. The end of the siding across Mill Road was scrapped in 1936, but the rest of the wye remained until 1949.

In 1911 a siding with a coal trestle was built to serve the J. S. Lowry & Sons Coal Company south of Ardmore Junction. It produced some sand and coal shipments, but it was awkward to serve. Empty cars had to be hauled all the way north to Bryn Mawr before they could be crossed over and returned to the PRR at the 69th Street connection.

There was a siding at Ardmore Avenue for receipt of sand and fertilizer to the Merion Golf Club, also built in 1911. Another at Buck Lane in Haverford brought tank cars to Pure Oil Company, and a freight siding existed for a few years into the Bryn Mawr Ice Plant just north of Bryn Mawr Station. A siding on the Strafford branch served a quarry in Wayne, which was abandoned by the 1920s.

The only siding on the Norristown branch, other than the Swedeland connection with the PRR, served the Lukens & Yerkes Quarry. P&W's own hopper car, No. 422, was filled with ballast stone at this quarry for use on the railroad. This siding's connection with the PRR was seldom used.

By World War II the annual number of freight carloads had dropped to less than 50, most of which were for McGinn's. Sand carried to Merion Golf Club at Ardmore Avenue never exceeded more than five carloads a year.

FREIGHT IS GRADUALLY PHASED OUT

With little freight to handle, No. 401 came to be used chiefly as a maintenance line car, leaving motor 402 to handle most of the freight cars. When 402 was destroyed by fire in 1943, the P&W sought a replacement. Conway's Cincinnati & Lake Erie Railroad had trackage rights over the Eastern Michigan Railway until that line was abandoned in 1932, and he may have been familiar with its freight equipment. At any rate, a steel Eastern Michigan car—No. 2010, built in the 1920s—was sold to the P&W, which renumbered it second 402. P&W used the car for moving freight and as a work car, hauling flat cars and other non-motorized work equipment. On the Eastern Michigan, the car was single-ended. P&W turned it into a double-end car, and each end was slightly different.

P&W's second-hand flat cars assisted in removing junk. *P&W photo. Collection of Bob Foley.*

When #402 burned in 1942, it was replaced by #2010 from Eastern Michigan Railways. *Photo by Ernest A. Mozer.*

Work motor 401 and "pickle car" 406 (2nd): are ready to venture onto the mainline and battle the elements on a cold February 3, 1961. The "pickle car" carries calcium chloride which is dispensed onto the third rail to prevent ice accumulation. *Photo by Andrew W. Maginnis.*

An early version of the "pickle car". *Collection of Bob Foley.*

MOVING THE FREIGHT

Clearly, it was getting very costly for the P&W to handle freight cars. A typical freight trip with a coal car to McGinn's in the 1950s called for No. 402 to leave the carbarn yard at 9:55 A.M., leave the PRR freight connection with a loaded hopper car at 10.09, arrive at McGinn's siding at 10.18, leave McGinn's with an empty car at 11:04, leave Bryn Mawr southbound at 11:14, drop the empty on the PRR siding and arrive back at the carbarn at 11:38. All this for only a few dollars of revenue! And such a trip required three crewmen, including a motorman, a conductor and a brakeman.

The Strafford connection with the Pennsylvania Railroad was out of service by the early 1920s and the Swedeland link by the early 1930s. The Hughes Park quarry siding and the McGinn's siding at Ardmore Junction were abandoned in 1952. Merion Golf Club at Ardmore Avenue was the last active freight customer, lasting until the early 1960s.

P&W continued to use the PRR connection at 69th Street Terminal for the delivery of car wheels, rail, ties and ballast. It was finally closed in 1974.

NEWSPAPER AND EXPRESS SERVICE

P&W and the LVT also handled newspapers and packages. The P&W ceased carrying small packages and copies of the Philadelphia Evening Bulletin on September 23, 1949. The Norristown Times-Herald was still using P&W cars to deliver its papers to Bryn Mawr and 69th Street Terminal as late as the mid-1960s. The newspapers were placed on the front platforms of passenger cars and were handled by motormen.

LVT since 1937 had charged 50 cents for a hundred pounds of newspapers between 69th Street Terminal and any point along the Liberty Bell Route. P&W received a portion of that revenue. Hundreds of copies of the Evening Bulletin were carried each day to towns along the LVT. The P&W charged only 20 cents per hundred pounds of newspapers carried on its own cars. P&W's annual revenue from carrying newspapers had been as high as $700, but by the 1940s seldom amounted to more than $75. P&W's receipts from small packages carried on the front platforms of LVT cars was less than $50 a year. Some wondered why the P&W bothered.

LVT freight motor C-7 was one of three like cars built by Jewett in 1913. Along with five converted passenger cars, they held down freight runs over the P&W in the last years. *Photo by Ernest A. Mozer.*

THE FIRST FREIGHT CONNECTION

Despite the serious feuding between the P&W and the Pennsylvania Railroad in the early years, a branch of the PRR aided in construction of the electric line and permitted the interchange of freight cars.

The Cardington Branch of the PRR opened in 1900 to serve several mills in the eastern part of Upper Darby Township. The two-mile branch never carried passenger trains. The end of the line was originally at Millbourne Flour Mills, located on the north side of Market Street adjacent to Cobbs Creek just west of the Philadelphia city limits at 63rd Street.

When 69th Street Terminal was planned, the Cardington Branch was extended a short distance westward to connect with the P&W. The extension was built by the PRR on land owned by the P&W. Both railroads were of the same track gauge. Through operation was not possible with the Market Street Elevated or the Philadelphia & West Chester because of their wide gauges. The extension brought the length of the PRR branch to 2.3 miles. Shipments of construction material via the PRR helped build the terminal and the P&W. Freight cars were interchanged with the P&W. The line also brought in occasional shipments of rail, ballast and ties for maintenance of the P&W. About 1,000 feet of track at the line's junction with the P&W was equipped with third-rail, including a siding. The trackage was arranged so that a PRR locomotive could drop off a freight car in the third-rail siding; and a P&W freight motor would then pick it up.

Philadelphia Rapid Transit Company built a powerhouse adjacent to the P&W terminal that provided electricity for the entire 69th Street Terminal complex. The Cardington branch brought regular shipments of coal to the PRT powerhouse.

The large Millbourne Flour Mills, which had been operated by the Sellers family for more than 150 years, went bankrupt and was sold to Shane Brothers. The mill continued to operate for another 17 years, and was then torn down. Sears, Roebuck & Company opened a department store on the site in 1926.

P&W President Thomas Newhall proposed to his board of directors in 1913 that P&W electrify a portion of the Cardington branch as far as East Lansdowne, then lay a half-mile of new track to reach the town of Lansdowne. Lacking enthusiasm from the board, the idea was dropped.

All shipments of new P&W and LVT rail cars were delivered over the Cardington branch, as were the two Liberty Liners that arrived in 1963. The branch was abandoned after damage from a storm in the summer of 1974.

A siding served Pure Oil Company near Haverford. *Collection of Bob Foley.*

Another siding served a coal company between Ardmore Junction and Wynnewood Road. *Collection of Bob Foley.*

MOVING THE FREIGHT

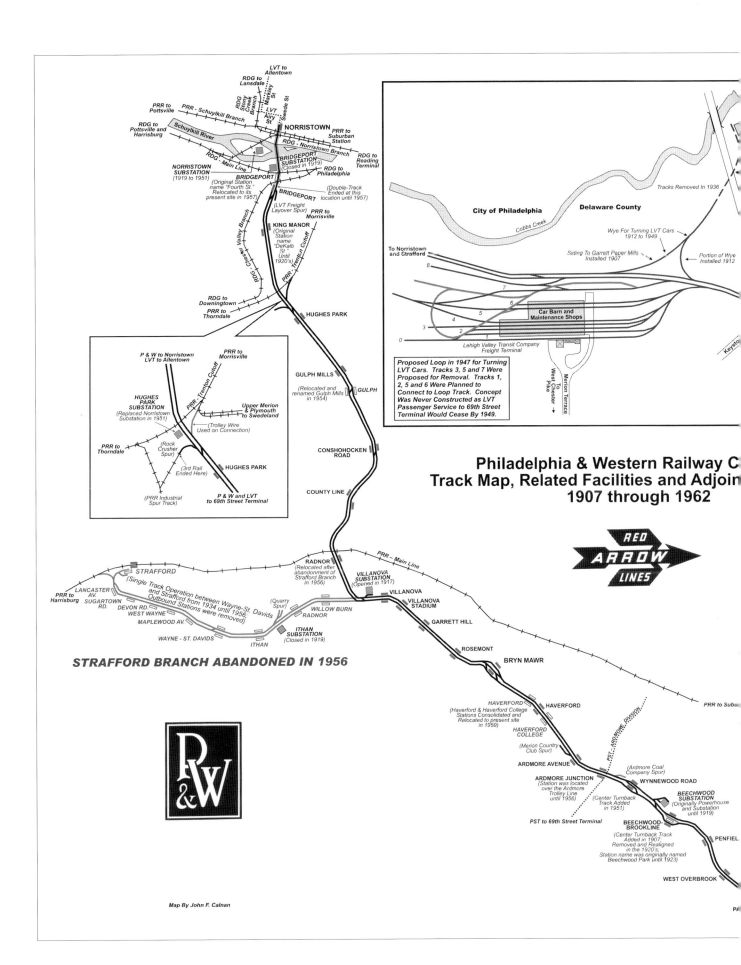

CONWAY VS. TAYLOR

Conway was cautious too and was not anxious to remove his company from the protection of bankruptcy too soon. The reason for the 1934 bankruptcy was that it couldn't make the interest payments on its 1910 first mortgage bonds, and this was still true. Conway was faced with a choice. The P&W could come out of bankruptcy and make its bond payments, or it could stay in receivership and use its earnings to keep the railroad in first-class physical condition. There wasn't enough money to do both.

The doctor knew the answer. If the P&W failed to keep its cars and right-of-way in top shape, maintenance and operating costs would go up. Bad track and cars that broke down would have slowed schedule speeds, making the company less competitive with the Pennsylvania and the Reading railroads. Conway had rebuilt the P&W based on high speeds and superb reliability, and ridership had responded.

Thanks to Conway, the P&W had entered the war as one of the best-maintained electric railways in the country, ready to take on the challenge of swelling ridership caused by severe gasoline rationing and the lack of new automobiles and tires. Bankruptcy was not a pressing issue—or was it?

It was the P&W's strong physical condition that prompted Red Arrow to begin secretly purchasing P&W stock and bonds in 1939, paying the bargain rate of only 20 percent of the face value of the bonds. And it was Red Arrow's involvement that delayed the termination of P&W's bankruptcy.

By early 1942 Conway realized what Taylor was doing, and he tried to put a stop to it.

Switching strategy, Conway filed a reorganization plan on March 2, 1942, with the United States Court for the Eastern District of Pennsylvania. Judge William H. Kirkpatrick referred the plan to the Pennsylvania Public Utility Commission and the U.S. Securities and Exchange Commission for review. The PUC, which had replaced the Public Service Commission, approved the plan on June 3, but the SEC—influenced by Taylor—recommended against it. Despite the SEC, the court gave its approval on July 29, 1943. The majority of the P&W bondholders approved the plan and it looked as if Conway would succeed in retaining control.

Suddenly, during the summer of 1943, Red Arrow bought another $650,000 in P&W bonds at 40 percent of face value. It now owned $800,000—or 30 percent—of P&W's bonds, making it the largest bondholder. Red Arrow now told the court it had a better reorganization plan than Conway's, which it was permitted to file on January 14, 1944, pending a PUC hearing.

RED ARROW'S REORGANIZATION PLAN

Taylor convinced the SEC and the court that P&W's board of directors should include three Red Arrow representatives. This occurred on January 10, 1944. Winning seats on the board were Taylor, John R. McCain, Red Arrow's first vice president, and Charles B. Roberts III, a Red Arrow director and vice president of the Pennsylvania Company for Insurances on Lives and Granting Annuities. This was the same firm that had sold Red Arrow the discounted P&W bonds the previous summer.

William L. Butler, realizing that he and Conway were losing control, resigned as executive vice president in October.

The newest reorganization plan called for Red Arrow to acquire all of the stock and most of the bonds. Red Arrow wanted to reduce the amount of outstanding bonds, using P&W's cash assets to pay off the bondholders. Conway was furious, and he fought hard. The doctor argued that Red Arrow's plan to use P&W's entire cash reserve of $317,000 to reduce the funded debt would seriously harm the future operation of the P&W. He said that the P&W "should be in a position to make renewals and replacements as may be required in

No. 163 has been freshly painted and lettered. The location of the additional side door is clearly visible. *Collection of Bob Foley.*

CHAPTER ELEVEN

The Takeover
1943-1953

THE WAR YEARS once again made the P&W profitable, but they also spelled the end of its independence. And Dr. Thomas Conway, Jr., was not amused.

Neighboring Philadelphia & West Chester Traction Company, which had been expanding rapidly since the 1920s, had weathered the Depression with a fortitude shared by few other transit systems. It had suffered only two years of small deficits, a record virtually unmatched in North America. It had endured by fare reductions, the purchase of new high-speed economies, opening of a revenue-producing terminal building and the purchase of smaller bus companies.

While the P&W took many similar steps, P&WCT had entered the Depression in a much stronger financial position and with a solid ridership base. The many bus routes were a very important part of the company's success.

In 1936, P&WCT changed its name to the Philadelphia Suburban Transportation Company and adopted the nickname of Red Arrow Lines. Its bus subsidiary, Aronimink Transportation Company, was merged into the parent company in 1942.

Red Arrow, with its vast bus network, virtually surrounded the lower half of the P&W by the time the war arrived. Nine of its bus or rail routes crisscrossed the territory served by P&W trains and Main Line Transfer buses. PST controlled all of the transit service in Eastern Delaware County and the Main Line, with the exception of the P&W. Only the Pennsylvania Railroad's Paoli and Media-West Chester trains competed with Red Arrow's growing network.

From a geographic standpoint, acquiring the P&W made a lot of sense for Red Arrow. Its president, Merritt H. Taylor, began to believe as early as the mid-1930s that this was the right step. P&W's opposition to Red Arrow's purchase of Montgomery Bus Company had only heightened Taylor's awareness of the P&W's stragetic importance. Taylor was fiscally cautious, however, and he considered taking such a big expansion step during the Depression and while the P&W was losing money too risky.

Taylor's interest was reawakened as soon as the P&W began making money again.

Above: P&W's carbarn, just outside 69th Street Terminal, did not change physically since it opened in 1907. The LVT's freight house sits on the left. *Collection of Andrew W. Maginnis.* **Left:** A popular—and easy—photograph was available from the Bryn Mawr pedestrian bridge. *Collection of Bob Foley.*

THE TAKEOVER

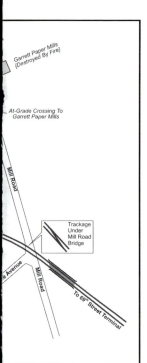

Bullet #204 at speed apporaching Bryn Mawr station. *Photo by Richard Lukin.*

CHAPTER ELEVEN

the future without taking a chance on its ability to raise the necessary funds when the time comes to make the replacements." Conway also asked the PUC to block Red Arrow from acquiring more than five percent of its stock.

Red Arrow claimed that the coordination of schedules and fares would "remove arbitrary barriers to service" for passengers. Taylor stressed that there would be economies in the cost of operations and overhead by combining the companies, but Conway showed that Red Arrow's cost per car mile was 31 cents compared to only 24 cents for the P&W. Red Arrow had announced its intention to extend both of its competing Lancaster Avenue bus routes directly to 69th Street Terminal, and Conway argued such a move would have "disastrous results" for the P&W.

Conway won the initial round, and on June 6, 1944, the PUC rejected the Red Arrow reorganization plan. Its principal objection was that "the proposed distribution of $317,000 in (P&W) cash would be adverse to the public interest."

"Now, in the midst of the war crisis, is not the time to siphon funds out of P&W's treasury, particularly since the distribution of such funds to creditors is not essential to a reorganization of P&W," said the PUC decision. "All funds not absolutely needed for current operation should be conserved until after the war, when it will be clearer how much of the funds will be required to be expended for the public good."

Heartened, P&W went back to court to seek confirmation of its original reorganization plan, but the court delayed a final decision pending Red Arrow's appeal for a rehearing before the PUC.

Taylor got his rehearing. "It is clear that P&W's future lies in its operating unification with Red Arrow," he declared. "Such unity cannot be disadvantageous but on the contrary only beneficial to the transportation public." Conway countered that Red Arrow was attempting "to carry out its plan of buying the P&W property largely with P&W's own money."

The Red Arrow chief's arguments convinced the PUC to reverse its decision. It ruled in favor of PST on December 19. The legal maneuverings and the charges by each side raged through the court and the PUC for another year.

BONDHOLDERS GROW IMPATIENT

Watching the railroad's profits increase each year during the war, many P&W bondholders were becoming anxious to be paid. A bondholders committee was formed in early 1945 and by mid-year had persuaded the court to pay out $75 in interest on each of the bonds. In October the situation became more complicated when the committee filed a suit before Judge Kirkpatrick accusing Conway and six other officers and directors of the P&W of purchasing "hundreds of thousands of dollars worth" of discounted bonds and later selling them "at substantial profit." The court agreed, and the officers and directors were ordered to repay $38,076 to the company.

Red Arrow president Merritt H. Taylor (right) is presented a "Veterans Plaque" by Francis Sharr in November, 1945. *Photo by Lou Larkin, Hagley Museum.*

A bullet car heads southbound toward Gulph Mills. *Photo by Aaron Fryer.*

By the fall of 1945 the court finally approved the reorganization plan set forth by the P&W, with some amendments. Holders of each of the old $1,000 bonds would receive $100 in cash, $300 of the new bond issue and four shares of common stock in the reorganized company.

The new name adopted for the reorganized company was the Philadelphia & Western Railroad Company (instead of Railway Company). This was the same name that the original company had used from 1902 until 1907. The reorganization became effective on June 17, 1946, and the first stockholders meeting of the reorganized company was held on October 1, 1946.

While Conway had technically managed to retain control of the company throughout the difficult bankruptcy reorganization, he knew that he was in trouble. Many P&W bondholders were displeased with the delay in receiving their interest payments, and they blamed Conway. To the stockholders and bondholders, it appeared that the railroad had been earning profits for all of the war years but was refusing to share any of this money with them. The bankruptcy had dragged on for 12 years, during which there were no stock dividends and only $75 of interest had been paid on each bond.

THE CONWAY YEARS COME TO AN END

In Red Arrow, Conway now fought a losing battle against a goliath with seemingly endless funds. Taylor sent a letter to all P&W stockholders demanding that Red Arrow's officers and directors should also become the officers and directors of the P&W. Meanwhile he continued to purchase additional P&W stock. The stockholders were urged to approve a proxy giving Red Arrow the power to elect seven of P&W's 11 directors, and the response was overwhelming.

For its part, the P&W bondholders committee also sent a proxy request to the stockholders, seeking the reelection to the P&W board of the committee's chairman, John H. Koegler, who was an automobile dealer.

When the board meeting took place on October 4, Conway was beaten.

Red Arrow won seven of the seats and Koegler was reelected. Taylor was elected president of P&W and McCain became executive vice president. Taylor's first action was to announce that the Conway Corporation's management contract with the P&W would soon be canceled. Conway was out of a job. He and two of his allies remained on the board, but they no longer had any influence. The doctor was 64 years old and had spent the past 24 years managing interurban railways, including 17 with the P&W.

The vote also marked the end of the last connection with the Edward B. Smith & Company banking firm that had gained control of the P&W in 1910. Edward B. Smith, Jr., the son of the man whose firm was responsible for building the Norristown extension, had served as a director for many years. With the Red Arrow takeover, he lost his place on the board.

Two months later Conway accepted an invitation from the Chinese government to help plan a modern transportation system for Shanghai, where more than two-thirds of the city's transit lines had been destroyed during the war. He left for China in February 1947, and on April 4 Taylor terminated the Conway Corporation's contract. Conway remained a director of P&W for two more years, but attended few board meetings. He finally resigned as a director on April 5, 1949.

Conway continued to write articles on the transportation industry, and the last one, entitled "Rapid Transit Must Be Improved to Alleviate Traffic Congestion," appeared in a national journal the same month that he died. He was 79 when he died on January 3, 1962.

Judge Kirkpatrick's bankruptcy court retained jurisdiction over the P&W until early 1948, and one of the judge's last acts was to order the company to pay a stock dividend using the $38,076 that Conway and the other directors had been ordered to repay. It was the first dividend since 1930.

In March 1948, the PUC bowed to the inevitable and gave Red Arrow official permission to buy "any or all" of P&W's stock. Taylor's success was complete. Red Arrow immediately borrowed $300,000 so it could purchase more P&W shares, and by mid-year Red Arrow owned two-thirds of the stock.

Taylor never regretted his decision to acquire the P&W. Ridership during the war years reached 5.4 million annually, more passengers than it had ever carried. Returning war veterans made the immediate postwar years even busier, with boardings climbing to more than 5.8 million in 1948, or more than 17,000 on the average weekday, the highest ever reached by the P&W. Annual revenues the same year rose to $926,000.

The bullet cars remained the backbone of the fleet throughout their long life. Here one trundles northbound past the Villanova Substation. *Photo by Lester K. Wismer.*

RIDERSHIP AND FARES

The end of World War II marked the beginning of a migration to the suburbs in the Philadelphia area. Rapid development of new housing, particularly in Delaware County, greatly contributed to ridership growth on suburban bus and rail lines. But war's end also marked the gradual elimination of gasoline and tire rationing and the resumption of automobile production, which after 1948 resulted in a sharp decline in transit usage. Within five years P&W's patronage dropped to 4.1 million, but fare increases kept revenues high and profits steady.

Wartime traffic had seen a 25 percent increase in annual rail car mileage, to 1.5 million. Car and property maintenance became more difficult due to a war-induced shortage of employees. Unlike many transportation companies, P&W never hired women to replace the workers who left to join the armed forces.

While war ushered in renewed prosperity to the P&W, it also brought operating challenges when ridership

After Red Arrow took over P&W, joint newspaper ads began appearing. *Collection of Ronald DeGraw.*

nearly doubled. The three old 50-series cars, which hadn't been used for a decade, were pressed into service. Unrebuilt, they still had a top speed of only 45 miles an hour and required both a motorman and conductor. So they were used only on Bryn Mawr

THE TAKEOVER

A bullet car and its principal competition meet at Radnor Station. *Photo by Albert Giantonio.*

A 160 car crosses Lancaster Avenue on its way to Strafford, with the Lancaster Avenue Station on the right. This was the original end of double track. *Photo by Lester K. Wismer.*

trippers, and even then it was difficult to schedule them so that they didn't delay the faster cars. Yet they were needed until 1950.

War-induced inflation forced wages to rise. The Transport Workers Union began representing P&W employees in 1944. Hourly wages for motormen that year were 90 cents, up from 53 cents only 10 years earlier. By 1951 the rate was $1.58.

After acquiring the P&W, Red Arrow moved to simplify fares. P&W and Red Arrow tickets became interchangeable beginning in 1947 and many of the confusing multiple-ride tickets were eliminated. The Strafford line had three fare zones and the Norristown line four. The rates per zone were 10 cents, with a 35-cent fare for a ride to Norristown. The cost of a single-zone ride was increased to 12 cents in February 1951, and to 15 cents six months later. Multiple-zone rides remained at 10 cents per zone and the Norristown fare stayed at 35 cents for another decade. The two fare hikes increased revenue by $85,000 a year.

In a successful attempt to increase off-peak riding, round-trip "shoppers' tickets" from Norristown were sold for 60 cents beginning April 1, 1952.

Despite the fare increases, the combined cost of a trip on the P&W and the elevated line to Center City remained lower than Pennsylvania or Reading trains, and the P&W continued to run more frequent service than the two competing rail lines.

ACCIDENTS AND IMPROVEMENTS

A couple of serious accidents in the early 1950s marred the P&W's good safety record. On April 26, 1951, two cars collided at high speed on a single-track curve just west of Wayne-St. Davids Station on the Strafford line. The two cars telescoped, but miraculously no one was killed. One of the motormen and 12 passengers were injured. Before both cars were repaired, another accident knocked three more out of service. One car was pushing a disabled westbound car between Rosemont and Garrett Hill when a third car crashed into its rear on August 6, 1952. The motorman who caused the accident and 16 passengers were injured.

Two major service improvements occurred on February 9, 1951. A third track and a new station were built at Wynnewood Road, similar to the track arrangement at Bryn Mawr, which permitted the peak operation of short-turn trains every 7 minutes.

Norristown "limited" trains, which had been curtailed during World War II and never restored, again began running in rush hours, making the trip in 17 minutes.

Another major improvement almost happened. P&W by 1951 required 18 cars for its peak turnout. With two cars sidelined for major collision repairs, only 19 were available. The three older 50-series cars were not considered serviceable. Taylor negotiated with the St. Louis Car Company to acquire five new interurban cars, similar to the 14 cars with PCC bodies that St. Louis had built for Red Arrow's trolley lines in 1949. Taylor wanted vehicles with higher speeds than the 160-series cars that had been built in the 1920s. They would have been used as single units for Strafford service.

St. Louis Car proposed cars that would weigh 45,000 pounds each, about 40 percent less than the older P&W cars, and would have trimmed about 12 percent from the Strafford running times. After several months of negotiations, Taylor finally decided the new cars weren't worth the price tag of $75,000 each.

Ironically, at the same time Taylor was investigating faster cars he was also taking steps to slow down the P&W. The electrical power systems of the P&W and Red Arrow were connected at Ardmore Junction, resulting in the P&W's voltage being reduced from 740 volts to 600. This slightly reduced the performance of the P&W cars.

LEHIGH VALLEY TRANSIT WOES

Unlike the P&W, the postwar years were not kind to Lehigh Valley Transit's rail operations. The tremendous wartime traffic virtually ran the wheels off the interurbans, and by the time the war ended the fleet was not in good condition. Motor fires increased, and the sides of many of the cream-colored cars exhibited smoke damage over the area of the trucks.

In 1945, LVT owner National Power & Light Company unsuccessfully tried to sell the company. Red Arrow was approached in July. After looking through the earnings statements of LVT for the past five years, Red Arrow's board of directors turned the offer down.

As ridership fell sharply during the late 1940s, LVT explored ways to save money. With gasoline and tire rationing gone and booming sales of new automobiles, riders melted away from the long-distance rail services. Most of the Liberty Bell Route's half-hour schedules were eliminated in September 1947.

P&W's new management had grown cold about sharing its tracks with the LVT cars. Conway had a blind spot about interurbans and tended to overlook the poor economics of the Liberty Bell trains. He believed that LVT was at least meeting its costs on the P&W, but he didn't delve too deeply into the issue. The no-nonsense Taylor simply viewed the Liberty Bell cars as a nuisance and wanted them off of his railroad.

Taylor knew by 1947 that the P&W was losing money on the Liberty Bell operation. P&W sought increases in the rent that LVT paid for the Norristown ticket office and waiting room, an increased proportion of interline ticket sales and higher rates of compensation for the operation of passenger and freight trains over the P&W. P&W was receiving about $53,000 annually for LVT passengers riding to and from 69th Street Terminal. But the average LVT train was carrying only 15 riders on the P&W.

LVT agreed to pay the P&W a greater percentage of the revenues, and raised its fares accordingly in early 1948, but this further reduced ridership. As revenues dropped, LVT fares went up again in 1950. When LVT decided to save money by terminating its trains at Norristown, there was no objection from the P&W.

So the last LVT passenger car from 69th Street Terminal ran early in the morning of September 25, 1949. After that LVT cars began and ended their runs at the P&W's Norristown Terminal. The single platform was lengthened so that P&W and LVT trains could load at the same time. The transfer involved a walk of only about 100 feet, but was not successful operationally. Philadelphia-bound interurban passenger traffic quickly disappeared, switching to the LVT's new direct bus service between Allentown and Philadelphia or the Reading Company's trains. Within a year, the LVT timetables had even ceased showing the connecting P&W trains. Tickets for joint trips on the P&W and LVT continued to be sold, however.

Actually, LVT operations over the P&W hadn't ended. Freight service remained profitable and three-car LVT freight runs continued to serve the 72nd Street freight station.

LVT BOWS OUT

In May 1950, Lehigh Valley Transit was sold to Allen and Company, which made the electric line a subsidiary of the Cincinnati, Newport and Covington Railway. The LVT was now managed by Allen's American Transportation Enterprises. Two months later the last streetcar ran on the Cincinnati-Northern Kentucky system, and there was no interest in retaining rail service on Lehigh Valley Transit either. Thus LVT formally petitioned the PUC in December 1950 to abandon the 42-mile Liberty Bell Route. When the PUC finally agreed on September 6, 1951, LVT acted with incredible haste to get rid of the interurbans. At 6:00 that day, only hours after the PUC decision, the LVT announced that buses would be substituted the next day. The last Liberty Bell car left Norristown at 1:06 A.M. on September 7. Many passengers who hadn't heard the news waited at Liberty Bell stations the next morning for trains that never came.

By the last day of service only five of the 1000-series cars were still operable, and two of them suffered motor failures while in service that day. All but two of the Liberty Bell cars were sold for scrap. P&W bought the motors and third-rail components as spare parts for the bullet cars.

Conway's Schuylkill Valley Lines sought permission to operate its buses from Norristown to Lansdale, but the PUC awarded the rights to LVT. Within less than two years LVT was running only seven round-trips from Allentown to Norristown (and was gone altogether by 1956). Most remaining passengers were using the LVT bus route that operated in express service directly to Center City Philadelphia.

The three types of equipment lined up in front of the carbarn. *Photo by Aaron Fryer.*

LVT was also replacing its local trolley routes with buses, and the last electric car operated in Allentown on June 8, 1953.

CONWAY'S OLD BUS LINE

Main Line Transfer continued to putter along under Red Arrow control. The single remaining daily round-trip from Wayne to Norristown was discontinued on April 20, 1946, but otherwise the schedules showed few changes. Red Arrow tinkered with the fares several times, eventually making them consistent with its own fare structure. By 1951 the fare was 15 cents for a one-zone ride or 10 cents per zone for multiple-zone trips.

McCain became the president of Main Line Transfer. Taylor was chairman and his son, Merritt H. Taylor, Jr., was vice president and secretary. Main Line Transfer had purchased a sixth bus in 1945, the greatest number it ever owned. When the war ended the fleet was reduced back to four.

Red Arrow had always taken pride in its modern, well-maintained bus fleet. After it took over MLT, Taylor was appalled at the condition of the buses. He called its fleet "inadequate for satisfactory service and performance." So in August 1947, Main Line Transfer purchased two used 1939 36-passenger buses from Red Arrow at $4,638 each and retired two of its older buses.

Red Arrow briefly flirted with expanding Main Line Transfer. In late 1947 it examined the possibility of purchasing Werner Bus Lines, a 16-bus operation headquartered in Phoenixville, Pennsylvania. The company ran a long route from King of Prussia to Pottstown via Phoenixville and Royersford, plus charter buses and local taxi service. The south end of the Werner route was only a mile from the end of Main Line Transfer's Colonial Village line.

LITTLE MLT BUILDS A BIG GARAGE

Red Arrow also needed a new bus garage more conveniently located for its 69th Street Terminal operations. Its bus network had kept on expanding, but its two garages were not well located. The small, unmodernized Ardmore facility was inefficient. Most of the bus routes focused on the main Llanerch bus and

A bullet car speeds across the massive Norristown bridge on its way to 69th Street Terminal. *Photo by Albert Giantonio.*

trolley complex two miles west of 69th Street Terminal. The dispatcher's office was also located there, but Llanerch offered very little bus storage space. A piece of land near 69th Street was leased for midday and overnight bus storage, but they had to be moved to and from Llanerch for servicing, involving considerable deadhead mileage.

To centralize things, Red Arrow planned to construct a new bus garage just outside 69th Street Terminal on Victory Avenue. It chose a large piece of land owned by the P&W where the LVT wye existed on the north side of the tracks opposite the carbarn. Taylor decided it would be financially advantageous to Red Arrow to use the little Main Line Transfer Company to construct the new garage. This was truly a farce, since Main Line Transfer owned only four buses and Red Arrow owned 111.

In the 1930s P&W had leased a portion of the land adjacent to the wye to a swim club. Main Line Transfer went though the charade of purchasing the land from the P&W in 1948, then borrowed money from the P&W to construct a large bus maintenance building and storage yard costing $349,000. The Victory Avenue Garage was opened on June 23, 1950, and was leased to Red Arrow for $5,000 a year. The Ardmore garage was closed and the Llanerch facility was used only for major maintenance work and painting. MLT's small garage in Wayne was sold for $15,000 on July 1, 1950.

Main Line Transfer continued with four bus routes. The Bryn Mawr Loop ran only during peak periods, with its fare remaining at five cents. Red Arrow changed the other routes to connect with the P&W at West Wayne Station instead of at Wayne-St. Davids Station. Only a few trips a day remained on the short route to Wayne, Mount Pleasant and Colonial Village, which included service to Valley Forge Military Academy. Most trips on the two alternate routes to West Chester terminated at the P&W's Strafford Station, and the two that continued to West Wayne carried only two or three passengers a day.

MAIN LINE TRANSFER ABOLISHED

Ridership had dropped severely on Main Line Transfer since the end of World War II. The Bryn Mawr Loop offered two dozen trips on weekdays and Saturdays, each carrying fewer than five riders. Two weekday round-trips remained on the Colonial Village route, and they only ran as far north as Mount Pleasant; only on Saturdays did a trip actually still run as far as Colonial Village.

This was not good for the bus subsidiary's balance sheet. After small profits during the war, deficits were racked up for every year of Red Arrow's control. The losses by 1951, the last full year of operation, reached $7,720. Total revenues for that year were $43,000. Since MLT had begun operations in 1936, P&W had subsidized it by $50,000.

After completion of the Victory Avenue Garage, Taylor no longer saw a need to keep Main Line Transfer as a separate company. MLT ended operations on September 5, 1952, and its routes were abandoned, transferred to Red Arrow or sold. The corporate shell lasted until the end of 1953. Only a dozen loyal riders protested. The Bryn Mawr Loop and the Colonial Village route, with few passengers, were simply eliminated. Red Arrow extended its Route Z from Strafford to Paoli via Lancaster Avenue. The Route Z trips ran every 30 minutes seven days a week, much better service than Main Line Transfer had offered. The only direct Route Z connections with P&W trains were at the Villanova and Lancaster Avenue stations.

The rights for the two routes between Paoli and West Chester, which Red Arrow didn't want, were sold to Short Line of Pennsylvania, Inc. This was ironic since Main Line Transfer had originally purchased the Paoli Pike route from Short Line in 1937. Short Line immediately increased the service by nearly 50 percent.

A new Red Arrow loop route operating to West Wayne Station, the town of Wayne, Mt. Pleasant and the Strafford Station was established, but service was soon down to one trip in each rush hour.

The four buses remaining in service by 1952, now between 13 and 16 years old, were sold. Two were the 20-passenger Yellow Coach vehicles Main Line Transfer had purchased new in 1936 and 1937 and the others were former Red Arrow buses. None was deemed worthy of being added to the Red Arrow bus fleet.

Another subsidiary, the Philadelphia & Western Home Owners' Association, became briefly profitable after the takeover of the P&W by Red Arrow. The company still owned numerous tracts of land along the railroad, and most were sold between 1948 and 1952. Red Arrow liquidated everything it could sell. The only major expenditure of the Home Owners' Association occurred in 1951, when it spent $17,000 to expand the Ardmore Junction Station parking lot.

END OF THE SIX-DAY WORK WEEK

The end of World War II brought an improved economy, rising wages and the elimination of the six-day workweek. Many had traditionally worked a half-day on Saturdays, which was a tremendous boost for transportation companies. This bonanza began to disappear in the late 1940s. P&W employees had to have a five-day workweek too, and this was introduced on May 3, 1952, while the guaranteed pay per week was reduced from 44 to 40 hours, with no reduction in wages.

Taylor's goal had always been to corporately merge the P&W into Red Arrow, and he continued to move steadily in this direction. P&W management was firmly in Taylor's control. Only two P&W management people succeeded in rising to important positions with Red Arrow. Arnold W. Frueh, who joined P&W in 1941 and was assistant secretary and scheduler, eventually became executive vice president of Red Arrow. Edna V. Gane, who had joined the P&W in 1916, served as Taylor's executive secretary.

P&W's offices in the Norristown Terminal building were closed in 1948 and all operations were consolidated with Red Arrow at 69th Street Terminal.

In fact, Taylor's desire was to close the entire Norristown Terminal building and sell it. He wanted to replace it with a smaller, more modern street-level structure that would be cheaper to operate. To accomplish this, P&W in early 1953 proposed to build a new station at the end of the elevated structure at Penn and Swede Streets, a block north of the existing terminal and at the very end of the overhead rail viaduct. This was the same spot where P&W had unsuccessfully attempted to build a station when the line opened in 1912. Inevitably, there was a new storm of protest.

After the LVT was abandoned, Norristown businessmen and borough officials looked forward to the demolition of what the Norristown Times Herald called "the useless and unsightly bridge" over the town's main street and the elevated structure adjacent to the town square and the courthouse. The P&W proposal for a new station meant the bridge and elevated structure

The P&W's portion of 69th Street Terminal was built as a "temporary" station in 1907. It was still going strong 50 years later. *Collection of Bob Foley.*

THE TAKEOVER

would remain permanently. It took Norristown's councilmen less than a month to veto the idea.

In May 1953, P&W permanently closed its 69th Street and Norristown ticket offices. To serve riders, Schulte's Cigar Store on the first floor of the Norristown Terminal was paid a commission to sell P&W tickets. A year later the bridge over Main Street was torn down and the terminal underwent a major renovation. An escalator was installed but the size of the second floor waiting room was greatly diminished and a single wooden bench replaced the overstuffed sofas and club chairs. The vacated space was leased to a dance studio.

Two other important changes occurred on the Norristown branch at the same time. A new substation was opened in 1952 north of Hughes Park Station, replacing the leased facility in Norristown, and Gulph Mills Station was relocated. The original station, built when the line opened in 1912, was at the Gulph Road underpass of the P&W. Its location was moved a few hundred feet further north because of the construction of the Schuylkill Expressway and so that a large parking lot could be constructed. The new station opened on January 21, 1954.

FINALLY, A MERGER

As Red Arrow purchased more and more P&W stock and bonds, the full merger of the two concerns came closer. One major impediment remained. P&W had been created in 1902 as a railroad. It was still operating under its original steam railroad charter and this made it legally difficult to merge with Red Arrow, which had been created under a street railway charter. To solve this, Taylor persuaded the Pennsylvania State Legislature to enact a new law in June 1951 that made it legal for a railroad company to merge with a street railway company.

On May 13, 1952, a new company was created called the Philadelphia & Western Street Railway Company. Taylor became chairman and McCain president. After PUC approval and an exchange of stock, the P&W was officially merged into the P&W Street Railway Company on December 31. At that point, Red Arrow owned 75 percent of P&W's stock.

Now came the final step. Red Arrow continued to buy P&W stock, and by the end of 1953 owned 92 percent. The formal merger of the Philadelphia & Western Street Railway Company into Red Arrow became effective on January 1, 1954.

McCain told newspapers that the merger would result in "a sound, integrated transportation system to efficiently serve the western suburban area of Philadelphia." It did. The fare structure on P&W was simplified, and transfers between P&W trains and Red Arrow's buses and trolleys were offered. The service level on the P&W remained high, and the line always seemed to receive priority treatment in vehicle cleanliness and right-of-way maintenance.

The old P&W became the Norristown Division of Red Arrow, but most passengers were never aware of the change. P&W motormen worked under a separate seniority list that assured the continuation of a knowledgeable, dedicated, on-time service that would have even satisfied Thomas Newhall and Thomas Conway.

The P&W did well under Red Arrow's management. While the Strafford branch west of Villanova Junction was abandoned in 1956 because of low ridership, the Norristown line prospered. Red Arrow was acquired in 1970 by the Southeastern Pennsylvania Transportation Authority, which had already purchased the Philadelphia Transportation Company and would soon take over the commuter service of the Pennsylvania Railroad and the Reading, forming a fully integrated transit system for the Philadelphia region. The remarkable old bullet cars soldiered on, ultimately surviving for nearly six decades.

It has been half a century since the Philadelphia & Western ceased to exist as a corporate entity, before most of its current riders were even born. And yet hundreds of them still say they're commuting on "the P&W", even though many don't even know what the initials stand for.

And the older Main Line residents? They still refer to it, usually with a smile, as the "Pig & Whistle."

A previous volume, Red Arrow: The First Hundred Years, 1848-1948, covered the early history of Red Arrow Lines and its predecessor companies.

SERVICE PATTERNS, 1943-1953

Basic schedules remained unchanged during World War II, but a great many two-car trains were operated. Car miles jumped by 25 percent, restricted by the number of cars available.

South of Villanova the Norristown express trains stopped only at Ardmore Junction and Bryn Mawr. The running time to Norristown was 21 minutes northbound and 22 minutes southbound for regular express trains. Additional station stops were added to the "limited" trains so that more passengers could be carried, effectively ending the super-fast service. All rush hour trains were crowded with standees during the war. A few trains had to pass up passengers at some stations because of overcrowding, the first time in P&W's history that this had happened.

Norristown "limiteds" were reinstated in 1951 at the same time that a turnback track was built at Wynnewood Road for the operation of short-turn trains to that point. Wynnewood Road trains ran every 7 minutes during rush hours.

The frequency of trains to both Norristown and Strafford was increased to every 15 minutes on weekdays and Saturdays instead of every 20. In the rush hours, "limited" trains left 69th Street and Norristown one minute before the regular Norristown express trains. In a northbound direction the "limiteds" ran non-stop between 69th Street Terminal and Norristown in the mornings and stopped only at Bryn Mawr and Bridgeport in the evening peak periods. Southbound "limiteds" stopped only at Ardmore Junction in the mornings and either ran non-stop or stopped only at Villanova during the evenings. The "limiteds" required 16 minutes northbound

The Strafford branch began carrying fewer and fewer passengers, even though service levels were kept high. *Photo by Richard S. Short.*

THE TAKEOVER

and 17 minutes southbound; later an additional minute was added to the running times. The southbound operation meant that the regular express trains left Norristown when the preceding "limited" was only halfway across the Schuylkill River bridge and before receiving a green signal.

Implementation of the "limiteds" resulted in eight Norristown trains in each direction during the busiest one-hour periods, some of which were two-car trains.

Strafford trains during the peak periods ran express from 69th Street Terminal to Ardmore Junction and Bryn Mawr. They were followed a minute later by a Bryn Mawr train running non-stop to Wynnewood Road. Wynnewood Road trains left 69th Street Terminal one minute after each Norristown express and each Bryn Mawr express.

This ambitious schedule resulted in 23 trains in each direction during the busiest hour, or an average of one train every two and a half minutes. This was more trains than had ever been operated in P&W's history. With a combination of local and express trains, such a frequency required incredibly precise timing. But it worked, and P&W's reputation for on-time service grew even greater.

By the time the P&W was merged into Red Arrow nearly three years later, the number of peak trains was down to 21 per hour in each direction, still impressive.

Additional off-peak and Saturday service began on September 11, 1953. Norristown expresses ran every 10 minutes. Strafford local trains ran every 20 minutes, with Bryn Mawr locals every 20 minutes. So now off-peak midday service had trains leaving 69th Street Terminal every five minutes. This schedule produced the greatest number of daily trains ever operated by the P&W, no less than 408 one-way trains.

Lehigh Valley Transit's service after the war didn't fare so well. The hourly frequency to and from 69th Street Terminal was maintained until the end of the through Liberty Bell Limited service in 1949, but the half-hour service on weekends and holidays was eliminated. Local service north of Norristown continued to decline and by 1950 transferring between the P&W and LVT at Norristown had dropped so much that the LVT schedules didn't even bother to show P&W connecting train times.

RUNNING A LIBERTY BELL CAR

Operating a Lehigh Valley Transit 1000-series car was not as simple as running a P&W bullet car. While the actual control mechanisms were similar, a P&W motorman had a lot more to do when operating a Liberty Bell Limited. Howard L. E. Price, a P&W motorman and platform dispatcher from 1943 to 1975, remembers how it was.

P&W crews always handled LVT trains south of Norristown, recalled Price. The 1000-series cars ran almost as fast as the bullets. In its last few years of operation, the LVT departed from 69th Street Terminal at 22 minutes after the hour. Fares were collected before the cars left 69th Street Terminal. Stops were made at Bryn Mawr and Villanova only if there were passengers who wished to travel to points north of Norristown. In the declining years of the LVT there were few of these passengers, so Liberty Bell cars usually sped non-stop between 69th Street and Norristown.

Upon arriving at Norristown the P&W motorman put up the trolley pole, turned the power switch from third rail to overhead and called the LVT dispatcher for orders. The normal meeting point with the southbound car was at Marshall Siding on Markley Street, half a mile from the P&W terminal, but if the southbound Liberty Bell car was running late the P&W operator would be told to go two miles further onto private right-of-way to Brush Siding. After getting orders at Norristown from the LVT dispatcher, the motorman had to call the P&W dispatcher to tell him where the meet would occur. Then he inched down the ramp onto the street trackage and proceeded very slowly to the passing point. The meets of the cars were seldom simultaneous; one of the cars usually had to wait at least briefly for the other.

An Allentown-bound LVT 1000-series car approaches the Gulph Road underpass. Liberty Bell cars remained a part of the P&W until September 24, 1949. *Photo by Ronald DeGraw.*

After exchanging cars, the P&W motorman operated back to the Norristown Terminal, pulled the trolley pole and threw the car's third-rail switch. Then he called both LVT and P&W dispatchers. Late LVT cars could disrupt the P&W, which had an excellent reputation for on-time service. If late, the LVT car was not permitted to proceed south of Norristown until it could properly fit among P&W trains.

Southbound passengers paid as they left the car at 69th Street Terminal. The motorman then exited the car onto a small platform between the tracks, climbed down steps to the track level and threw the switch for the crossover at the unloading track. The single-end 1000-series cars had emergency backup controls in a cabinet at the rear of the car, but the operator had to kneel down to use them. He backed over the crossover and waited for a signal from the P&W dispatcher to proceed backwards to the turning wye opposite the P&W carbarn. Again he climbed out of the car to throw a switch, turned the car on the wye and once more had to wait for a signal from the dispatcher.

The car was then backed over the northbound rail against the flow of traffic to the separate loading track for the LVT at 69th Street Terminal.

No. 1008 slows for Villanova Station. With the silver-covered pilot and before all of the smoke damage to the sides, the cars were sleek and handsome. Photo by A. Gordon Thompson.

Most P&W trains usually carried heavy loads. The motorman here is G. Harry DeGraw. *Photo by Harre W. Demoro.*

In order to accomplish all of this and guarantee that northbound LVT cars would leave on time, the schedule allowed Liberty Bell cars a 62-minute layover at 69th Street Terminal. All this was cumbersome, time-consuming and very expensive. Two full-time P&W operators were required at all times—about 265 pay hours a week—to operate the Liberty Bell trains.

A PASSENGER'S PERSPECTIVE

P&W riders were very loyal. Many patronized the line for decades, and many preferred its frequent service, its on-time performance and its friendly train operators to the nearby electric service operated by the impersonal Pennsylvania Railroad.

The P&W, and later Red Arrow, received many letters from satisfied passengers. Many of them were kept in the company's files, including this one dated February 16, 1965, from William N. Tanner, Jr., who worked as a certified public accountant at Broad and Chestnut Streets in Philadelphia.

Dear Mr. Taylor:

For the past two months, I have been commuting on the old P&W. What a refreshing, nostalgic experience it is to be aboard one of these Red Arrows as it darts along the rails winding through these beautiful wooded hills.

Before one realizes it, he is returning the motorman's welcoming nod and chatting with the stranger seated next to him. Suddenly, it is a different world and one realizes it is men who keep this line alive while so many commuter roads have folded and sent their rails to the melting pot.

(These are) Men who are not just running a trolley. Men who like people. Men who grumble occasionally, but men who realize that they, with us, make the community. Men who with only one short labor strike in their history, sit down and solve their problems like men. Men who do not needlessly harm or inconvenience their customers, for they remember always that we, the people, have the same rights they have and respect our rights as we respect theirs.

Men like Bob the motorman on the morning Liberty Liner who opens his cab door every so often to peak back at the six retarded children to make sure they're all right, and who occasionally grumbles out, "Sit down, there," so quiet immediately descends upon them.

Or Big Harry, his conductor, whose towering football frame bends at the top to stay on the Liberty Liner platform. Big Harry, the gruff grizzly bear who barks through the train in a way which makes us friends.

Big Harry who, the morning I showed up without money or a ticket, replied to my queried, "Can I pay you tomorrow?", with a gruff "You'll have to!" When I left at Bridgeport, it was this same gruff bear who held the train as he reached in his pocket saying, "Here, Bud, take this. You're going to need some money to eat and get back to town." He had only seen me once or twice, but these are the men who make the Red Arrow a railroad that lives.

The men tell me that Big Harry is constantly wracked with pain. But it is Big Harry who waits around 69th Street on his off time to shepherd those retarded children as they come in the afternoon. Woe to the mother who isn't on time to meet her child. The taxi driver who comes late to pick up those kids never, never faces Big Harry late again.

It is a rare experience indeed to ride the P&W—swift Red Arrows darting through beautiful hills. Men and management who are human beings and who remember always that it is we, the public, who keep them in their jobs.

PIG & WHISTLE

Appendicies

STATIONS AND MILEAGE

Station	Miles	Established	Station	Miles	Established
69th Street Terminal (1)	0.00	1907	Wayne-St. Davids (6)	9.36	1907
Parkview	0.80	1953	Maplewood Road	9.69	1935
West Overbrook	1.48	1908	West Wayne (7)	9.98	1907
Penfield	1.94	1908	South Devon Avenue	10.24	1934
Beechwood-Brookline (2)	2.56	1907	Sugartown Road	10.58	1911
Wynnewood Road	3.15	1908	Strafford (original)	10.63	1907
Ardmore Junction	3.46	1907	Lancaster Avenue	10.80	1934
Ardmore Avenue	3.89	1907	Strafford	11.10	1911
Haverford College (3)	4.52	1908	Radnor (8)	7.85	1955
Haverford (existing)	4.65	1958	County Line	8.60	1929
Haverford (original)	4.72	1907	Conshohocken Road	9.21	1920
Bryn Mawr	5.36	1907	Gulph (original)	10.00	1912
Rosemont	5.81	1907	Gulph Mills (existing)	10.18	1954
Garrett Hill	6.32	1907	Hughes Park	11.01	1925
Stadium (4)	6.77	1933	King Manor (9)	12.34	1912
Villanova (5)	6.95	1907	Bridgeport (existing)	12.75	1958
Villanova Junction	7.28	—	Bridgeport (original)	12.84	1912
Willowburn	7.66	1938	Norristown Transportation Center	13.40	1989
Radnor	8.20	1907	Norristown (Main and Swede)	13.50	1931
Ithan	8.75	1907	Norristown (Penn and Swede)	13.60	1912

NOTES

(1) Called Union Terminal Station in P&W's first schedule in 1907
(2) Originally called Beechwood Park; name changed in 1923
(3) Abandoned 1958
(4) Originally open only for Villanova University sports events; opened full time in 1960
(5) Spelled Villa Nova until 1928
(6) Called St. Davids until 1928
(7) Called Wayne until 1928
(8) Originally called Radnor-Wyeth until the Strafford Branch was abandoned in 1956
(9) Originally called DeKalb Street, then King Road until 1926

Left: 69th Street, 1952. *Photo by Bob Foley.*

THE MAXIMUM SCHEDULE

The schedule that became effective on June 22, 1951, resulted in the greatest rush hour frequency ever operated on the P&W. Twenty-three local and express trains ran in each direction every hour during the busiest periods of the day, an average of a train every two and a half minutes.

This is what one hour of the northbound evening rush hour schedule looked like:

Leave 69th Street	Destination
4:59 P.M.	Norristown Limited
5:00 P.M.	Norristown Express
5:01 P.M.	Wynnewood Road Local
5:06 P.M.	Strafford Express
5:07 P.M.	Bryn Mawr Express
5:14 P.M.	Norristown Limited
5:15 P.M.	Norristown Express
5:16 P.M.	Wynnewood Road Local
5:21 P.M.	Strafford Express
5:22 P.M.	Bryn Mawr Express
5:23 P.M.	Wynnewood Road Local
5:29 P.M.	Norristown Limited
5:30 P.M.	Norristown Express
5:31 P.M.	Wynnewood Road Local
5:36 P.M.	Strafford Express
5:37 P.M.	Bryn Mawr Express
5:38 P.M.	Wynnewood Road Local
5:44 P.M.	Norristown Limited
5:45 P.M.	Norristown Express
5:46 P.M.	Wynnewood Road Local
5:51 P.M.	Strafford Express
5:52 P.M.	Bryn Mawr Express
5:53 P.M.	Wynnewood Road Local

NOTES

Northbound afternoon Norristown Limiteds stopped at Bryn Mawr and Bridgeport only. (A.M. northbound Limiteds ran non-stop; A.M. southbound Limiteds stopped at Ardmore Junction only; P.M. southbound Limiteds stopped at Villanova only or ran non-stop.)

Norristown Express trains stopped at Ardmore Junction, Bryn Mawr and Villanova, then made all stops to Norristown.

Strafford Express trains ran non-stop to Ardmore Junction, then Bryn Mawr, then made all stops to Strafford.

Bryn Mawr Express trains ran non-stop to Wynnewood Road, then local to Bryn Mawr.

PHILADELPHIA & WESTERN CORPORATE ORGANIZATION CHART

Philadelphia & Western Railroad Co. 1902-1907

Name changed to:
Philadelphia & Western Railway Co. 1907-1946

Name changed to:
Philadelphia & Western Railroad Co. 1946-1952

Name changed to:
Philadelphia & Western Street Railway Co. 1952-1953

Merged into:
Philadelphia Suburban Transportation Co. 1/1/1954

Acquired by:
Southeastern Pennsylvania Transportation Authority 1/29/1970

Subsidiary Companies

Southeastern Construction Co. 1905-1908

Beechwood Park Amusement Co. 1905-1910

Name changed to:
Homestead Real Estate Co. 1905-1911
Name changed to:
DeKalb Realty Co. 1911-1920

Name changed to:
Philadelphia. and Western Home Owners' Assn. 1920-1953

West Conshohocken Transit Co. 1910-circa 1920

Norristown Transit Co. (half ownership with Lehigh Valley Transit) 1910-1952

Millbourne Electric Light and Power Co.
Coopertown Electric Light and Power Co.
Gladwyne Electric Light and Power Co.
Ithan Electric Light and Power Co.
Gulph Electric Light and Power Co.
Interborough Electric Light and Power Co.
All formed in 1913

All merged into:
Interborough Electric Light and Power Co. 1913-1924

Main Line Transfer Co. 1922-1953

"Strafford" car 165 pauses at Bryn Mawr in 1964. Although signed for a regular run to 69th Street, this train was actually chartered by a rail enthusiasts' group. *Photo by Richard S. Short. Collection of Richard Lukin.*

ROSTER AND CAR PLANS

THE ORIGINAL ORDER

These are the cars that never arrived. When they were ready for delivery in the fall of 1905, P&W refused to accept them because the uncompleted railroad had no place to store them, was facing serious financial problems and was not nearly ready to open. The builder, St. Louis Car Company, eventually sold them to three other electric railway properties.

CAR NOS.:	1-22	LENGTH:	52' 1"	WEIGHT:	75,640
YEAR BUILT:	1905	WIDTH:	9' 0"	TRUCKS:	St. Louis
BUILDER:	St. Louis	HEIGHT:	13' 6"	WHEELS:	34"
COLOR:	Moss Green	SEATS:	56	MOTORS:	GE73

Nos. 1-12 were sold to United Railroads of San Francisco in 1906; they were scrapped in 1933 and 1935. Nos. 13-16 were sold in 1907 to the Sacramento Northern Railway; they were scrapped in 1941. Nos. 17-22 went to the Erie Railroad's Mt. Morris line in 1907 and operated until 1934. At least one survived as a work car into the 1940s.

Operation for United Railroads of SanFrancisco, car 6 was one of 22 cars ordered from the St. Louis Car Company in 1905. The car ordered was subsequently cancelled resulting in this car ending up in California. *Collection of Andrew W. Maginnis.*

The Erie Railiraod purchased six cars from the cancelled P&W order for useon its Mount Morris (NY) branch and numbered them in the 3100 series. **Top:** 3101 is on the heard end of a non-revenue train that was being used totest various types of springs in freight car trucks. *Collection of Malcom McCarter via Andrew W. Maginnis.* **Bottom:** Combine 3105 heads a passenger train at Avon, NY in 1907. *Collection of Malcom McCarter via Andrew W. Maginnis.*

APPENDICIES 197

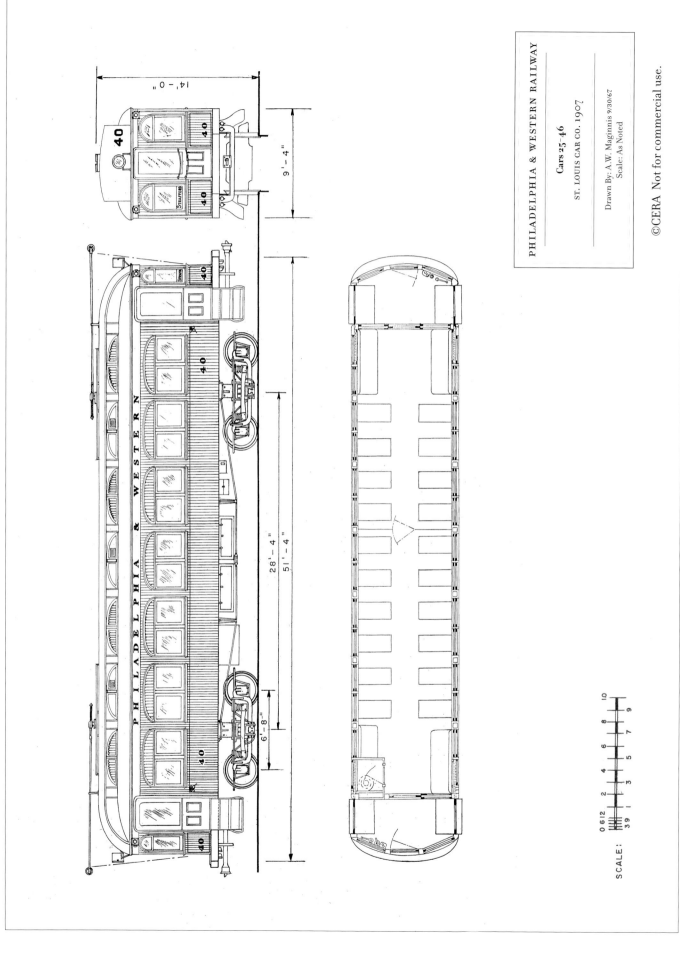

ST. LOUIS CARS

This was the first series of cars that actually operated on the P&W and were numbered 25-46. They were wooden and most had smoking compartments and restrooms. They were capable of only 45 miles an hour and required both a motorman and conductor. The arrival of the 50-series and 60-series cars in the 1920s permitted the retirement of half of the St. Louis cars. None of the St. Louis cars was needed after the bullet cars arrived in 1931.

All but one of the cars were scrapped during the 1930s. No. 46 was rebuilt into a work car in 1928 and renumbered No. 446.

CAR NOS.:	25-46	LENGTH:	52' 4"	WEIGHT:	82,000
YEAR BUILT:	1907	WIDTH:	—	TRUCKS:	St. Louis 60-1
BUILDER:	St. Louis	HEIGHT:	13' 8"	WHEELS:	34"
COLOR:	Moss Green	SEATS:	55	MOTORS:	GE73C

Nos. 32-46 had smoking compartments with 16 seats. Nos. 25-31 were straight coaches. No. 44 or No. 45 was scrapped in 1928; the scrapping date of the other car is not known. Nos. 34-43 were scrapped in 1933. Nos. 26, 29, 30 and 33 were scrapped in 1934. Nos. 25, 27, 28, 31 and 32 were scrapped in 1938. No. 46 was converted to emergency car No. 446 in 1928.

50-SERIES CARS

These cars were large and slow, and P&W was never pleased with them. The cars arrived in two different orders. They had a center vestibule and a smoking compartment, and were capable of only 45 miles an hour. They were never modernized or speeded up, and always required both a motorman and a conductor. They had no steps, so seldom operated to Norristown.

After the arrival of the bullet cars in 1931, the 50-series cars were placed in temporary storage. They went back into service for World War II, and operated until about 1953. Their last use was in Wynnewood Road short-turn service after the siding there was built in 1951. No. 50 retained its moss green paint until it was scrapped. Nos. 51-52 were repainted in bright red. All three remained on the roster in 1954, although they were not in service. All were scrapped the following year.

CAR NOS.:	50-52
YEAR BUILT:	1920, 1922
BUILDER:	Brill
COLOR:	Moss Green
LENGTH:	56' 0"
WIDTH:	10' 4"
HEIGHT:	12' 9"
SEATS:	56
WEIGHT:	78,480
TRUCKS:	Brill 27MCB-3X
WHEELS:	34"
MOTORS:	No. 50: GE263-A
	Nos. 51-52: GE73

Car 50, complete with trolley poles, looks quite handsome in this car builders' photo. *Collection of Bob Foley.*

Northbound at Mill Road (today's Victory Avenue) in 1944, car 52 still sported its green livery and center side door. The switch in the foreground leads to the P&W's 72nd St. shop facility. The Philadelphia Transportation Co. bus passing overhead was operating on Route E between 69th Street and Germantown. *Photo by Andrew W. Maginnis. Collection of Bob Foley.*

STRAFFORD CARS

The 60-series cars, also known as the Strafford cars, arrived in three different orders between 1924 and 1929. The cars originally had center vestibules and smoking compartments and required a motorman and a conductor. Top speed was only 45 miles an hour. When rebuilt during the 1930s into one-man cars, the top speed was increased to 70 miles an hour. At the same time, their livery was changed to the same dark red worn by the bullet cars. Throughout their life, the cars were referred to as "60 cars" by P&W employees.

Used principally for Strafford and Bryn Mawr service, all 11 cars were in service at the time of the merger with Philadelphia Suburban Transportation Company in 1954.

CAR NOS.:	60-70; later 160-170	LENGTH:	55' 2"	WEIGHT:	63,058
		WIDTH:	9' 0"	TRUCKS:	Brill 27MCB-2X
YEAR BUILT:	1924, 1929	HEIGHT:	12' 8"	WHEELS:	30",
BUILDER:	Brill	SEATS:	51, then 52 or 56	MOTORS:	WH535-B1; rebuilt to WH-537
COLOR:	Moss Green then Dark Red				

No. 60 was built in 1924 and originally contained Safety Car dead man controllers and folding Birney car doors, which were replaced with standard C-36 controllers and sliding doors within a few years. Nos. 61-65 were built in 1927 and Nos. 66-70 in 1929. No. 60 was rebuilt as No. 165 in 1931. Nos. 61-64 were rebuilt in 1931 as Nos. 161-164. No. 65 was rebuilt as No. 169 in 1935. Nos. 66-68 became Nos. 166-168 in 1931. No. 69 was rebuilt into No. 160 in 1935. No. 70 was converted to No. 170 in 1937. Nos. 168-170 were not speeded up until 1942. The cars were built with 60-horsepower motors and rebuilt with 100-horsepower motors.

Two 160-series cars pass at Radnor station on the Strafford branch in June, 1955. *Photo by Richard S. Short.*

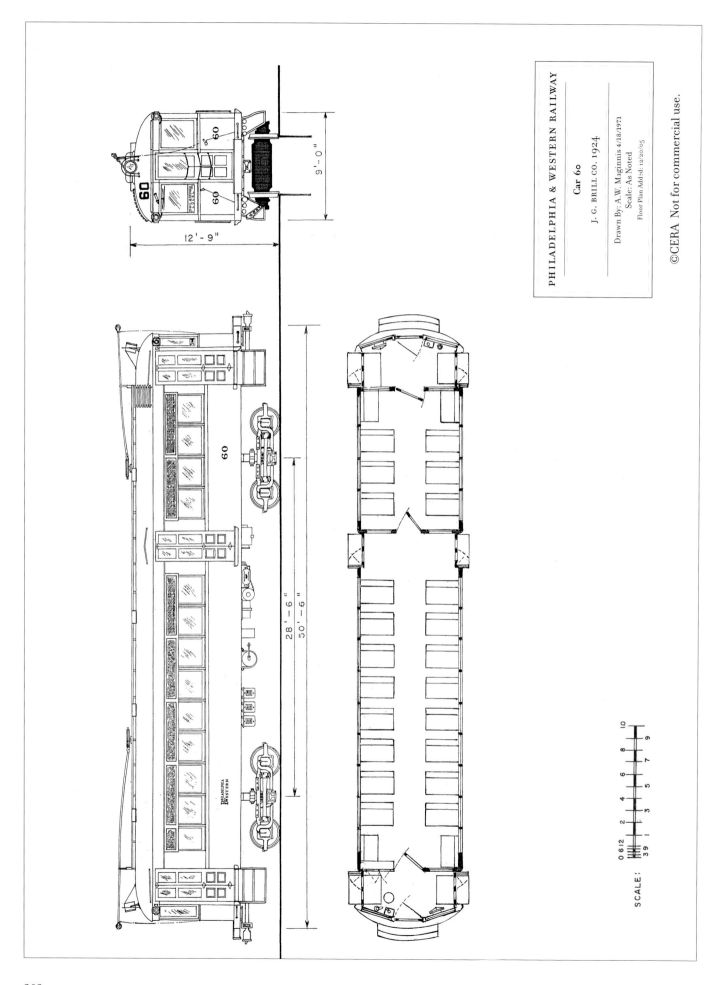

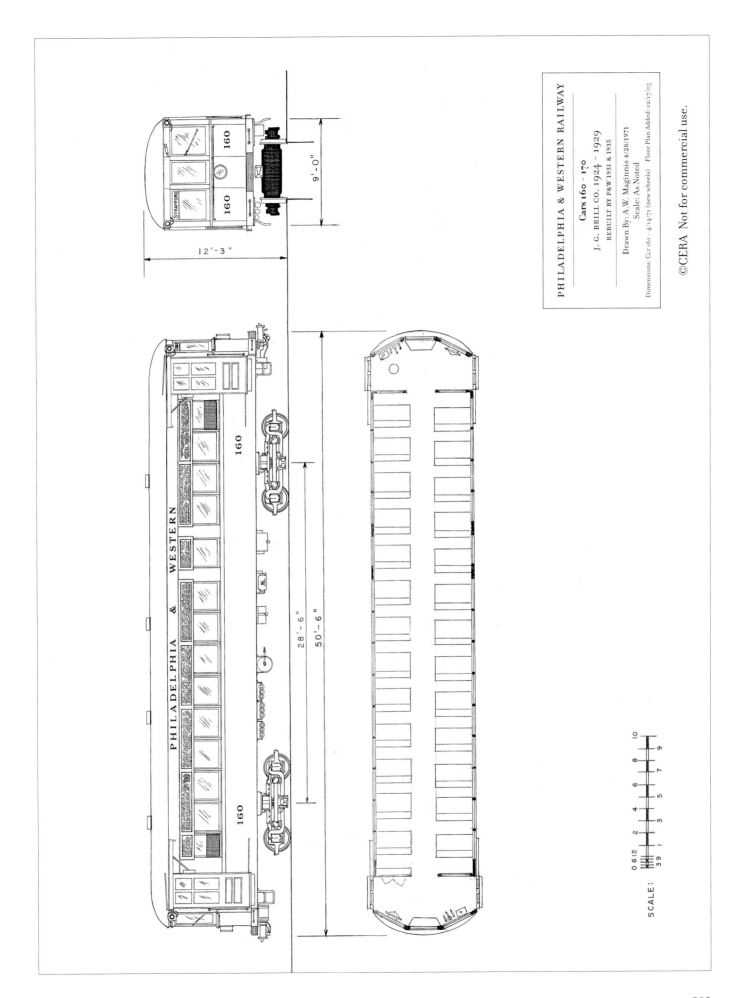

APPENDICIES

Car 164 heads a two-car rail enthusiasts' charter train at Wynnewood Road station in 1964. Aside for the company name change, little had changed since the P&W days. *Photo by Richard Lukin.*

The Strafford cars had rattan seats as seen in this view captured by the Brill Company's photographer. *Collection of Bob Foley.*

P&W successor Red Arrow Lines tried this variant of its familiar red and cream livery on car 167 in 1959. *Photo by Richard Lukin.*

In 1963, Red Arrow Lines purchased two articulated trainsets from the Chicago North Shore & Milwaukee Railway for use on the P&W. On November 17, 1963, the photographer recorded this photo showing one of the North Shore's former Electroliners at the 72nd Street shop. *Photo by Andrew W. Maginnis. Collection of Bob Foley.*

BULLET CARS

These revolutionary cars permitted running times to Norristown to be slashed by 33 percent and were the first lightweight, streamlined, high-speed railway cars in the world. They were also the first railroad cars to be built almost entirely of aluminum and the first whose design was the result of extensive wind tunnel testing. These sleek cars led the way for the production of streamliners for railroads throughout the world.

Each bullet car logged more than five million miles. The last of them ran for a remarkable 59 years, a fitting tribute to P&W President Thomas Conway, Jr., and to the once-great J. G. Brill Company. All 10 were still in service when the P&W was merged with Philadelphia Suburban Transportation Company in 1954. Throughout their life the cars were referred to by P&W employees as "200 cars".

CAR NOS.:	200-209	LENGTH:	55' 2"	WEIGHT:	52,290
YEAR BUILT:	1931	WIDTH:	9' 2"	TRUCKS:	Brill 89E2
BUILDER:	Brill	HEIGHT:	10' 6"	WHEELS:	28"
COLOR:	Dark Red	SEATS:	57, later 53	MOTORS:	GE706-B2

No. 203 was destroyed by fire on March 14, 1933. A replacement car arrived in April 1934. Originally capable of speeds of 90 miles an hour, their top speed was reduced to about 70 miles an hour after the removal of field taps and the reduction of line voltage. The removal of drop seats in the vestibules in the 1950s caused a small decrease in seating capacity.

The bullet cars were the very first lightweight, aerodynamically designed railroad cars ever built. This streamlined craze immediately spread to railroads around the world. *Collection of Ernest A. Mozer.*

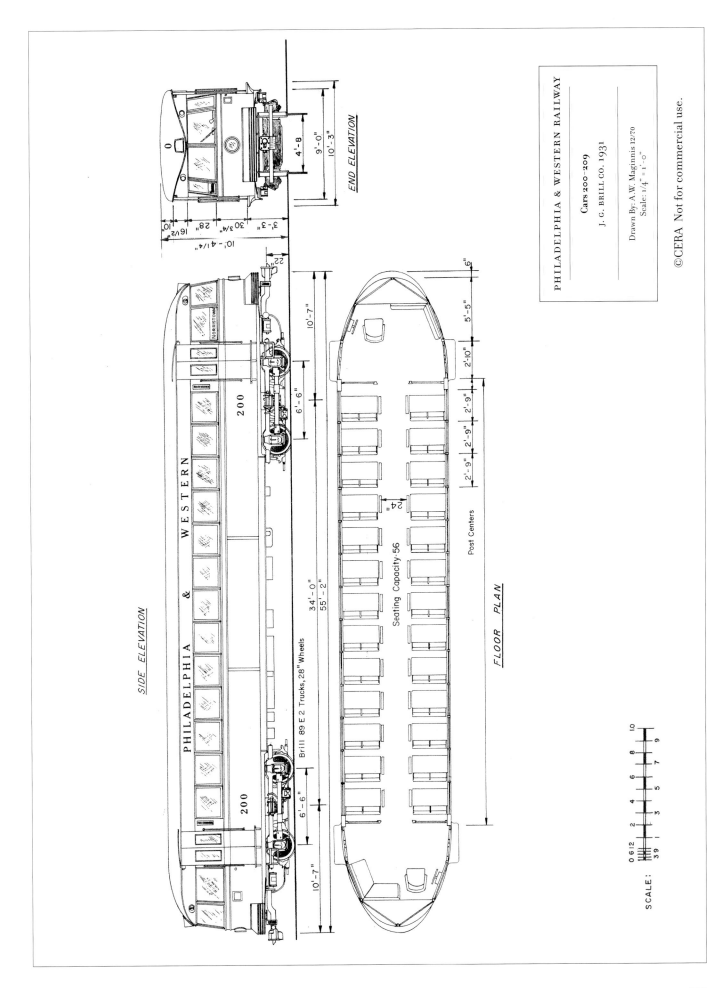

Work car 406 (2nd) had just entered service as the line's new "pickle car" when this photo was made on December 24, 1958. *Photo by Richard S. Short. Collection of Richard Lukin.*

Philadelphia Suburban Transportation Company #05 at Llanerch Car Yard. This was originally P&W #103 which was sold to PSA predecessor Philadelphia & West Chester Traction Company in about 1915. This car #103 was used in construction of the Norristown extension of the P&W. *Photo by Andrew W. Maginnis.*

WORK CARS

Number	Car Type	Acquired	Scrapped	Remarks
(two locos)+	0-4-0T Forney	1905	1920	Built 1881 by Baldwin; acquired from Manhattan Ry.
10+	Snow plow	1915	*	Built by Wason; trucks from No. 103
103+	Construction	1905	Sold	Double-cab flat car; sold to P&WCT as No. 05 about 1915
200-202	Flat cars	1908	?	Acquired from PRR; renumbered 201-203; rebuilt
203	Flat car	1911	?	Renumbered No. 204
300	Flat car	?	Sold	Sold to PST Co.
400+	Dump car	1938		Built by Differential; ex-Cincinnati & Lake Erie #700. Acquired by LVT and later transfered to P&W.
401+	Line car	1905	*	Built by St. Louis; originally No. 23, then 101, then 1
402 (1st)+	Freight motor	1905	1942	Built by St. Louis; originally No. 24, then 102, then 2; burned
402 (2nd)+	Freight motor	1943	*	Formerly Eastern Michigan Railways No. 2010. Built using frame of Cincinnati Hamilton & Dayton Ry. 847 (orig. Ohio Elec. Ry. 847) built by Cincinnati Car Company, 1914.
403	Flat car	?	?	Formerly "pickle" car, then oil tank car
404	Ballast car	1911	?	Steel; former No. 203; bought used from Beulah Coal Co.
405	Flat car	1907	1949	Steel
406 (1st)	"Pickle" car	1935	*	Sprayed calcium chloride on third-rail to prevent icing
406 (2nd)	"Pickle" car	1958	—	Was PTC W-48 dump car, built 1923; rebuilt to flat car in 1954
407	Crane car	1935	*	Steel flat car with American Ditcher crawler crane
408	Flat car	1944	*	Wood
409	Flat car	?	1938	Wood
410	Derrick car	1907	*	Wood; formerly No. 10
420	Flat car	1944	*	Steel
421	Flat car	1944	*	Steel
422	Hopper car	1946	*	Used; built by Mt. Vernon Car Co.; for ballast service
433	Flat car	1907	?	Wood, with oil tank
446+	Emergency car	1907	*	Formerly passenger car No. 46; converted in 1928

Notes:
? Data unknown
+ Indicates motorized car
* Indicates car still in service in 1954

Records on flat cars are inconclusive; several renumberings took place. In addition to those listed, six flat cars and six side dump cars were purchased for construction of the line in 1906. These were scrapped or sold shortly after the line opened.

P&W had two cars numbered 402. The first was destroyed by fire in 1942. It was eventually replaced by Eastern Michigan Railroad #2010 and numbered 402 as seen here. It is now at the Electric City Trolley Museum in Scranton, PA. *Photo by Steve Maguire. Collection of Andrew W. Maginnis.*

Originally assigned number 23, and later 101, 1, and finally 401, this work car was one of two identical units built by the St. Louis Car Co. in 1905. It was mostly used as a line car. *Collection of North Jersey Chapter, National Railway Historical Society.*

P&W's last surviving St. Louis car, #46, became "emergency" car #446 in 1928. *Photo by Aaron Fryer.*

APPENDICIES

A 1966 blizzard brought passenger service to a halt. Drifting snow kept plow #10 and its crew busy for quite some time. This view is at Bryn Mawr. *Photo by Andrew W. Maginnis. Collection of Bob Foley.*

Plow #10 at the 72nd Street yard. *Photo by Richard S. Short. Collection of Richard Lukin.*

P&W #407 consisted of an American Ditcher crane mounted on a flat car. Built by American Hoist & Derrick Co., the crane was purchased second-hand around 1930. The cab is homemade. *Collection of Fred W. Schneider.*

Car 446's attractive red livery had long since faced when this venerable car was photographed on track "O" along side the 72nd Street shop. This track had earlier been used by LVT freight runs. *Photo by Richard S. Short. Collection of Richard Lukin.*

APPENDICIES

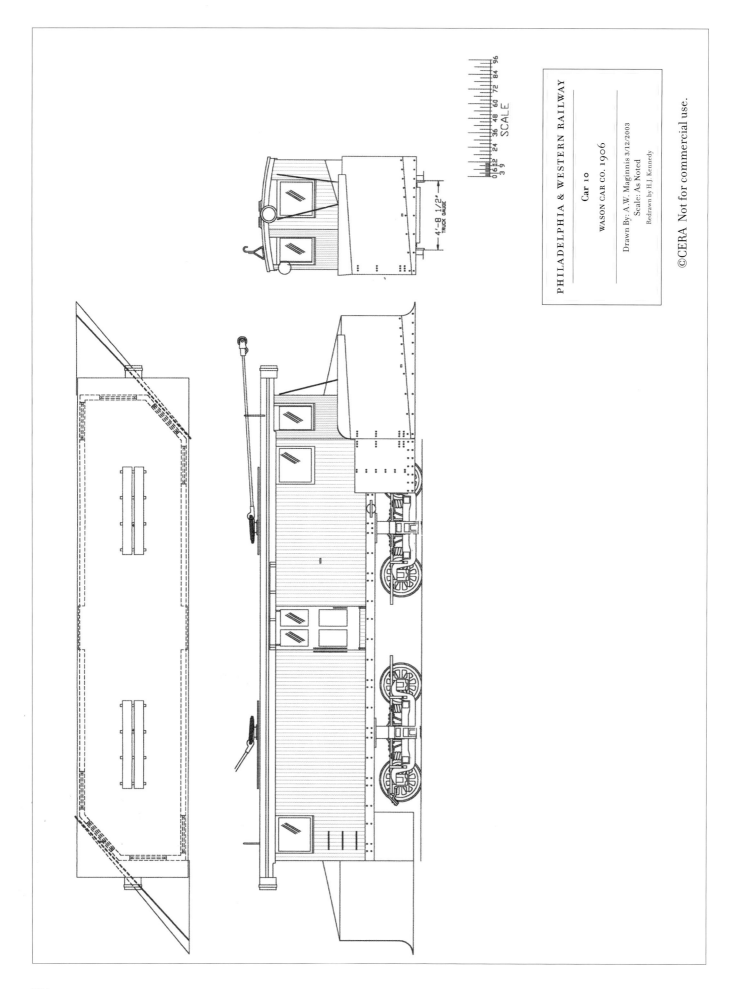

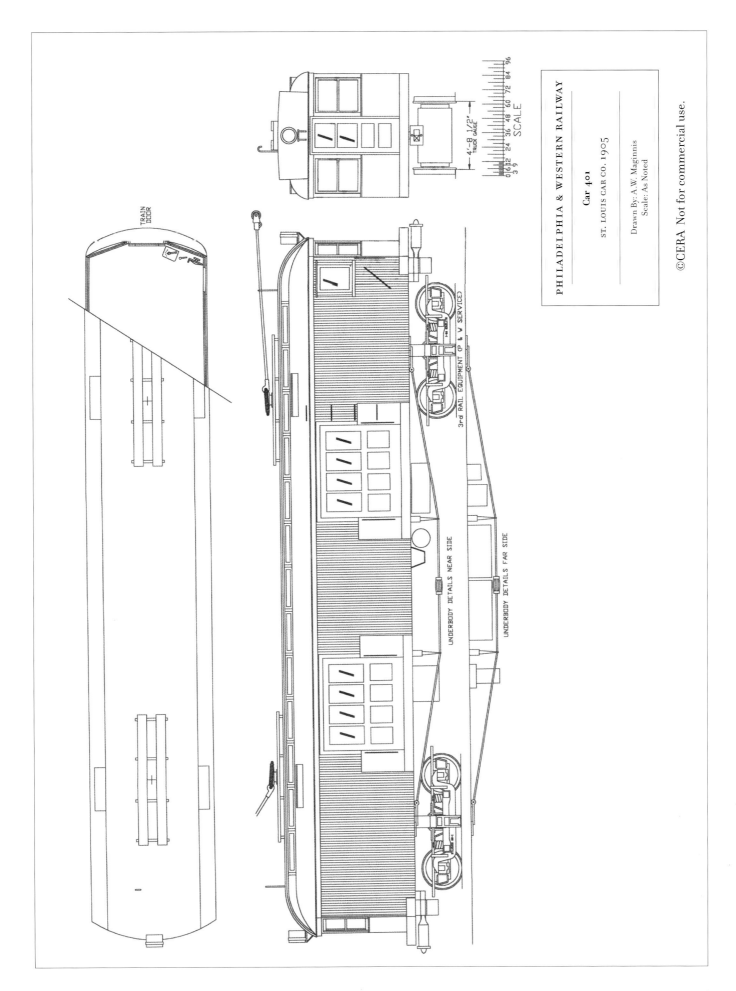

APPENDICIES

PIG & WHISTLE
Bibliography

BOOKS

Ackerman, Kenneth D. *The Gold Ring: Jim Fisk, Jay Gould & Black Friday*, 1869. New York: Harper & Row, 1988.

Allen, Charles Spencer, and Wesley Crook Wolfinger. *A Study and Description of the Liberty Bell Route of the Lehigh Valley Transit Co.* Easton, PA: Unpublished thesis, Lafayette College, 1919.

Barrett, Joseph. *The Sesquicentennial History of Saint Denis Parish*. Havertown, PA: Saint Denis Church, 1975.

Berner, Allan H., and Benson W. Rohrbeck. *Pennsylvania's Street Railways in Early Postcard Views*. West Chester, PA: Ben Rohrbeck Traction Publications, 1986.

Bezilla, Michael. *Electric Traction on the Pennsylvania Railroad, 1895-1968*. University Park, PA: Pennsylvania State University Press, 1980.

Blake, Henry W., and Walter Jackson. *Electric Railway Transportation*. New York: McGraw-Hill Book Co., 1917.

Bowman, Stanley F., Jr., and Harold E. Cox. *Trolleys of Chester County, Pennsylvania*. Forty Fort, PA: Harold E. Cox, 1975.

Bryant, Keith L., Jr., editor. *Railroads in the Age of Regulation, 1900-1980*. New York: Facts On File, 1988.

Burgess, George H., and Miles C. Kennedy. *Centennial History of the Pennsylvania Railroad Company*. Philadelphia: The Pennsylvania Railroad, 1949.

Carlson, Stephen P., and Fred W. Schneider, III. *PCC: The Car That Fought Back*. Glendale, CA: Interurban Press, 1980.

Cory, Lee. *Stories of the Pittsburg, Shawmut & Northern Railroad*. Angelica, NY: Pittsburg, Shawmut & Northern Railroad Co. Historical Society, no date.

Cox, Harold E. *The Road From Upper Darby*. New York: Electric Railroaders' Association, 1967.

Cudahy, Brian J. *Cash, Tokens and Transfers*. New York: Fordham University Press, 1990.

Cupper, Dan. *The Pennsylvania Turnpike: A History*. Lebanon, PA: Applied Arts Publishers, 1990.

Davis, Patricia J. *End of the Line*. New York: Neale Watson Academic Publications, 1978.

DeGraw, Ronald. *The Red Arrow*. Haverford, PA: The Haverford Press, 1972.

DeGraw, Ronald. *Red Arrow: The First Hundred Years, 1848-1948*. Glendale, CA: Interurban Press, 1985.

DiFilippo, Thomas J. *The History and Development of Upper Darby Township, 1609-1987*. Privately published, no date.

Drury, George H. *New York Central in the Hudson Valley*. Waukesha, WI: Kalmbach Books, 1995.

Faris, John T. *Old Roads Out of Philadelphia*. Philadelphia: J. B. Lippincott Co., 1917.

Left: Work motors 401 and 402 pass the long-shuttered Villanova tower. *Photo by Bob Foley.*

Foesig, Harry, and Harold E. Cox. *Trolleys of Montgomery County*. Forty Fort, PA: Harold E. Cox, 1968.

Garforth, Harry J. *Rails Through Manayunk*. Telford, PA: Silver Brook Junction Publishing Co., 1999.

Heimburger, Donald J. *Wabash*. River Forest, IL: Heimburger House, 1984.

Hendy, Anne-Marie. *American Railroad Stock Certificates*. London: Stanley Gibbons Publications, 1980.

Hilton, George W., and John F. Due. *The Electric Interurban Railways in America*. Stanford, CA: Stanford University Press, 1960.

Hungerford, Edward. *Men of Erie*. New York: Random House, 1946.

Jodard, Paul. *Raymond Loewy*. New York: Taplinger Publishing, 1992.

Jones, William C., and Charles Albi, editors. *More Rail Classics*. Denver, CO: Intermountain Chapter, National Railway Historical Society, 1976.

Keenan, Jack. *Cincinnati & Lake Erie Railroad*. San Marino, CA: Golden West Books, 1974.

Klein, Maury. *The Life and Legend of Jay Gould*. Baltimore: The Johns Hopkins University Press, 1986.

Klein, Maury. *Unfinished Business: The Railroad in American Life*. Hanover, NH: University Press of New England, 1994.

Kriebel, H. W. *A Brief History of Montgomery County, Pennsylvania*. Norristown, PA: The School Directors' Association, 1923.

Kulp, Randolph L., editor. *History of Lehigh Valley Transit Company*. Allentown, PA: Lehigh Valley Chapter, National Railway Historical Society, 1966.

Kulp, Randolph L., editor. *The Lehigh Valley Transit Company's St. Louis Cars*. Allentown, PA: Lehigh Valley Chapter, National Railway Historical Society, 1961.

Kulp, Randolph L., editor. *The Liberty Bell Route's Heavy Interurban Cars*. Allentown, PA: Lehigh Valley Chapter, National Railway Historical Society, 1969.

Kulp, Randolph L., editor. *The Liberty Bell Route's 700 Series Interurbans*. Allentown, PA: Lehigh Valley Chapter, National Railway Historical Society, 1955.

Kulp, Randolph L., editor. *The Liberty Bell Route's 800 Series Interurbans*. Allentown, PA: Lehigh Valley Chapter, National Railway Historical Society, 1958.

Lichtenstein, Claude, and Franz Engler, editors. *Streamlined: A Metaphor for Progress*. Zurich, Switzerland: Lars Muller Publishers, n.d.

Lind, Alan R. *From Horsecars to Streamliners*. Park Forest, IL: Transport History Press, 1978.

Maier, Phyllis C., and Mary Mendenhall Wood. *Lower Merion—A History*. Ardmore, PA: Lower Merion Historical Society, 1988.

McKelvey, William J., Jr. *Liberty Bell Route: A Photographic History*. Berkeley Heights, NJ: Canal Captain's Press, 1989.

Messer, David W. *Triumph II: Philadelphia to Harrisburg, 1828-1998*. Baltimore: Barnard, Roberts and Co., 1999.

Middleton, William D. Traction Classics. *The Interurbans: The Great Wood and Steel Cars, Volume One*. San Marino, CA: Golden West Books, 1983.

Middleton, William D. Traction Classics. *The Interurbans: Extra Fast and Extra Fare, Volume Two*. San Marino, CA: Golden West Books, 1985.

O'Connor, Richard. *Gould's Millions*. Garden City, NY: Doubleday, 1962.

Plachno, Larry. *Sunset Lines: The Story of the Chicago, Aurora & Elgin Railroad, 2—History*. Polo, IL: Transportation Trails, 1989.

Reed, Robert C. *The Streamline Era*. San Marino, CA: Golden West Books, 1975.

Riegel, Robert Edgar. *The Story of the Western Railroads*. Lincoln, NE: University of Nebraska Press, 1964 (originally published 1926).

Rinker, Harry L. *The Schuylkill Navigation: A Photographic History*. Berkeley Heights, NJ: Canal Captain's Press, 1991.

Robertson, Archie. *Slow Train to Yesterday*. Boston: Houghton Mifflin, 1945.

Rohrbeck, Benson W. *Trolleys to the Delaware Water Gap*. West Chester, PA: Ben Rohrbeck Traction Publications, 1989.

Shank, William H. *The Amazing Pennsylvania Canals*. York, PA: American Canal and Transportation Center, 1991.

Shank, William H. *Indian Trails to Super Highways*. York, PA: American Canal and Transportation Center, 1988.

Shank, William H. *Pennsylvania Transportation History. A Supplement*. York, PA: American Canal and Transportation Center, 1990.

Smallwood, Charles A. *The White Front Cars of San Francisco*. South Gate, CA: Interurbans, 1970.

Stover, John F. *History of the Baltimore and Ohio Railroad*. West Lafayette, IN: Purdue University Press, 1987.

Swett, Ira L. *Interurbans of Utah*. Cerritos, CA: Interurbans, 1974.

Taylor, Frank H. *Valley Forge: A Chronicle of American Heroism*. Philadelphia: James W. Nagle, 1905.

Whitman, Frederic Bennett. *Western Pacific, Its First Forty Years: A Brief History*. New York: Newcomen Society in North America, 1950.

Wilson, William Hasell. *The Columbia-Philadelphia Railroad and Its Successor*. York, PA: American Canal and Transportation Center, 1985 (reprint of 1896 edition).

Combined Atlases of Montgomery County, Pennsylvania, 1871, 1877, 1893. Norristown, PA: Historical Society of Montgomery County, 1986.

The Way is Clear. Rochester, NY: General Railway Signal Co., Bulletin 124, 1912.

MAGAZINE ARTICLES

Blossom, Edward H. "Liberty Bell Route," *Trains*, January 1951, pp. 44-48.

Conway, Thomas, Jr. "Rapid Transit Must be Improved to Alleviate Traffic Congestion," *Traffic Quarterly*, January 1962, pp. 103-118.

Conway, Thomas, Jr. "Some Necessary Steps to Capitalize the Possibilities Inherent in the New Car Developments," reprinted in *Headlights*, October-December 1985, pp. 11-13.

Cox, Harold E. "The Philadelphia & Western Story," *Traction & Models*, October 1967, pp. 6-10.

Crawford, David E. "The Philadelphia & Western Story," *Headlights*, March 1962, pp. 4-14.

Dewees, Donald N. "The Decline of the American Street Railways," *Traffic Quarterly*, October 1970, pp. 563-581.

Edwards, E. Everett. "Ten Years Ago," *The Bulletin*, National Railway Historical Society, Vol. 26, No. 4, 1961, pp. 26-41.

Elsner, Henry, Jr. "EMT-P&W Box Motor," *Traction & Models*, February, 1976, pp. 22-25.

Goshorn, Robert. "The Electrification of the Paoli Line," *The Bulletin of Radnor Historical Society*, 1994, pp. 12-19.

Goshorn, Robert. "The Philadelphia and Columbia Rail Road," *Tredyffrin-Easttown History Club Quarterly*, Vol. XXIII, No. 2, 1985, pp. 63-79.

Goshorn, Robert. "The Philadelphia and Lancaster Turnpike Road Company," *Tredyffrin-Easttown History Club Quarterly*, Vol. XXIII, No. 1, 1985, pp. 25-36.

Goshorn, Robert. "When the Trolley Ran to Strafford," *Tredyffrin-Easttown History Club Quarterly*, Vol. XVII, No. 3, 1979, pp. 59-66.

Guido, Francis A. "San Mateo Suburban Line: The Big Subs," *Western Railroader and Western Railfan*, August 1975, pp. 1-8.

Hansen, Zenon. "New Haven's Nova: The Comet," *Passenger Train Journal*, July 1989, pp. 22-27.

Hilton, George W. "The Wrong Track," *Invention and Technology*, Spring 1993, pp. 46-54.

Kaplan, Donald R. "Brills in the Hills, Part One," *Railfan & Railroad*, September 1989, pp. 42-52.

Kaplan, Donald R. "Brills in the Hills, Part Two," *Railfan & Railroad*, October, 1989, pp. 59-65.

Lynch, James J. D., Jr. "The Darby Creek Low Grade Line," *The High Line*, Volume 17, August 1999, pp. 31-43.

Maginnis, Andrew W. "Early Classic Interurbans of 69th Street Terminal, Part I," *Trolley Talk*, December 1967, pp. 2-5.

Maginnis, Andrew W. "Early Classic Interurbans of 69th Street Terminal, Part III," *Trolley Talk*, June, 1968, pp. 2-5.

Maginnis, Andrew W. "Early Classic Interurbans of 69th Street Terminal, Part IV," *Trolley Talk*, 1968, pp. 2-8.

Maginnis, Andrew W. "Interurban Cars of Lehigh Valley Transit Co., Part I," *Trolley Talk*, December 1968, pp. 1-6.

Maginnis, Andrew W. "Interurban Cars of Lehigh Valley Transit Co., Part II," *Trolley Talk*, April 1969, pp. 1-9.

Maginnis, Andrew W. "Lehigh Valley Transit Co. Club Car #1030," *Trolley Talk*, December 1990, pp. 1-4.

Maginnis, Andrew W. "Lehigh Valley Transit Co. Liberty Bell Route 700 Class 'DeLuxe' Cars," *Trolley Talk*, December 1990, pp. 1-5.

Maginnis, Andrew W. "New Faces of the Red Devils," *Trolley Talk*, December, 1991, pp. 1-5.

Maginnis, Andrew W. "Philadelphia & Western Railroad's First Cars, Nos. 1-22, Part 1," *Trolley Talk*, March/April 1997, pp. 2-5.

Maginnis, Andrew W. "Philadelphia & Western Railroad's First Cars, No. 1-22, Part II," *Trolley Talk*, May/June 1997, pp. 2-4.

Maginnis, Andrew W. "Red Arrow's Other Car Barn—72nd Street," *Trolley Talk*, August 1973, pp. 1-5.

Maginnis, Andrew W. "Trolley Freight Service on the Lehigh Valley Transit Co.," *Trolley Talk*, July-August 1999, pp. 2-9.

Middleton, William D. "Arch Windows and Walkover Seats," *Trains*, September 1969, pp. 37-39.

Middleton, William D. "The Brill Bullet," *Trains*, July 1966, pp. 26-29.

Middleton, William D. "Goodbye to the Interurban," *American Heritage*, April 1966, pp. 22-41, 66-71.

Middleton, William D. "Modelers' Notes on the LVT,' *Model Railroader*, June, 1961 pp. 38-42.

Mierzejewski, Alfred C. "High-Speed Motor Trains of the German National Railway, 1920-1945," *Railroad History*, Autumn 1996, pp. 57-67.

Olsen, Walter R. "Philadelphia & Western System," *Model Railroader*, August 1972, pp. 48-52.

Plachno, Larry. "Conway, Butler and Modern Electric Rail Cars," *Scale Model Traction and Trolleys Quarterly*, Winter-Spring 1992, pp. 15-21.

Polleys, W. V. "The Norristown Branch of the Philadelphia & Western Railroad," *Public Service Journal of Stone & Webster*, 1911, pp. 402-407.

Reutter, Mark. "Streamliners: The Dazzle of the New," *Vintage Rails*, Spring 1996, pp. 28-37, 66-71.

Shannon, Joel, and Ken Snyder. "Schuylkill Valley Lines," *Motor Coach Age*, October 1980, pp. 4-16.

Smatlak, John. "Brill's Other Bullets," *Railfan & Railroad*, January,1992, pp. 59-66.

Smatlak, John. "Comparing the Bullets," *Railfan & Railroad*, February,1992, pp. 42-47.

White, John H., Jr. "Spunky Little Devils: Locomotives of the New York Elevated," *Railroad History*, Spring 1990, pp. 21-71.

Xaras, Theodore A. "The Cardington Branch," *The High Line*, Vol. 8, No. 1, Autumn 1987, pp. 1-14.

Young, Andrew D. "The Interurban, Part II," *Locomotive and Railway Preservation*, January/February 1988, pp. 32-41.

Zimmerman, Karl. "The Western Maryland: A Brief History," *Locomotive and Railway Preservation*, January-February 1990, p. 41.

"Imagination Rebuilds a Transit System," *Transit Journal*, May 1939 (reprint).

"Improvements on the Philadelphia & Western Ry.," *Electric Traction Weekly*, July 15, 1911, pp. 795-797.

NEWSPAPERS

Ardmore Chronicle
Bryn Mawr Herald
Daily Local News, West Chester
The Evening Bulletin, Philadelphia
King of Prussia Courier
The Main Line Times, Ardmore
The Morning Call, Allentown
The New York Times
Norristown Herald
Norristown Register
The Norristown Times
The North American, Philadelphia
The Philadelphia Inquirer
Philadelphia Press
The Philadelphia Record
Philadelphia Telegraph
Public Ledger, Philadelphia
The Suburban and Wayne Times, Wayne
The Times Herald, Norristown
The Village Record, West Chester

ARCHIVAL MATERIALS

Chester County Historical Society, West Chester, PA
  Extensive file of early newspaper clippings; photographs.

Free Library of Philadelphia, Philadelphia, PA Copies of *Street Railway Journal* and *Electric Railway Journal*; early newspaper files.

Hagley Museum and Library, Greenville, DE
  Red Arrow Lines Collection.
  Corporate files, minute books and photographs of Philadelphia Suburban Transportation Company and its predecessor companies, including Philadelphia & Western Railway Company.

Historical Society of Montgomery County, Norristown, PA Historical information; photographs

RECOMMENDED READING

There are dozens of fine books available for those who may wish to delve further into the fascinating era of the electric interurban railway. The interurban was surely one of America's least successful, and one of its shortest-lived, industries. But at its peak, around World War I, it thrived mightily, reaching a total of 17,000 miles of line and affecting the daily lives of millions of Americans.

Many interesting books on the subject are listed in the bibliography. Publication data is included here for those books not shown in the bibliography. Unfortunately, some of the books are out of print.

The Electric Interurban Railways in America, by George W. Hilton and John F. Due, remains the classic overview of the interurban industry. It includes a listing of interurbans by state as well as route maps.

William D. Middleton is unquestionably the dean of interurban history and has published many fine books on the subject. *The Interurban Era* (Milwaukee, WI: Kalmbach Publications, 1961) is the best general overview. Middleton has written a splendid trilogy on the most important of the interurban cars (two are shown in the bibliography; the other is *Traction Classics. The Interurbans: Interurban Freight, Volume Three*). These books include chapters on the P&W bullets, the LVT 800-series cars, the FJ&G/Bamberger bullets, the C&LE "Red Devils" and the LVT 1000-series.

Middleton has also done books on two of the three large and interesting Chicago area interurbans, the Chicago, North Shore & Milwaukee Railroad (*North Shore, America's Fastest Interurban*, San Marino, CA: Golden West Books, 1964) and the Chicago, South Shore & South Bend Railroad (*South Shore: The Last Interurban*, Bloomington, IN; Indiana University Press, revised second edition, 1999). Another fine book on the South Shore is Donald R. Kaplan's *Duneland Electric: South Shore Line in Transition* (Homewood, IL: PTJ Publishing, 1984).

The history of the third big interurban in the Chicago area, the Chicago, Aurora & Elgin Railroad, has been superbly covered in two volumes by Larry Plachno, including the key role played by Thomas Conway. The three Chicago interurbans were among the biggest, fastest and most successful in the country. The South Shore and the P&W are the only remaining electric railways in North America that were built as interurbans.

Jack Keenan's very enjoyable history of the Cincinnati & Lake Erie, a Conway creation, is highly recommended.

All of Randolph Kulp's wonderful little books on the Lehigh Valley Transit Company provide substantial information about one of the few successful interurbans in the East.

Interurbans thrived particularly in the Midwest, and the Central Electric Railfans' Association (Box 503, Chicago, IL 60690) has published many fine books on this amazingly comprehensive transportation network. The biggest interurban system, the 1000-mile Pacific Electric Railway centered on Los Angeles, has been the subject of dozens of books.

A new way to view—literally—the old interurbans is through videos, and there are now hundreds available on the old trolley and interurban routes. Probably the best overview and the most professionally done is Carl R. Schultz's *Trolleys: The Cars That Built Our Cities* (Transit Gloria Mundi, 1991). The same company has done a splendid paean to the P&W bullet cars, simply entitled *Bullet* (1989).

Several videos also exist on the Lehigh Valley Transit Company, and include scenes of LVT on the P&W. *Liberty Bell Limited* is produced by Traction Video. *Liberty Bell Route*, by Rail Tape Productions, features the 1950 film of LVT historian Charles W. Houser. Herron Rail Video has produced *Cincinnati & Lake Erie*, which includes footage of the "Red Devils" that later ran on the Liberty Bell Route and their famous race with a biplane.

The Conshohocken Road station certainly looked well-worn in this 1964 view. *Photo by Richard Lukin.*

BIBLIOGRAPHY

Bullet #6 (206) was parked at 69th Street late one night in January 1964. *Photo by Richard Lukin.*